LIBERTY OF CONSCIENCE:
ROGER WILLIAMS IN AMERICA

LIBRARY OF RELIGIOUS BIOGRAPHY

Liberty of Conscience

Roger Williams in America

Edwin S. Gaustad

WILLIAM B. EERDMANS PUBLISHING COMPANY
GRAND RAPIDS, MICHIGAN

Library of Congress Cataloging-in-Publication Data

Gaustad, Edwin Scott.
    Liberty of conscience : Roger Williams in America / by Edwin S. Gaustad
      p.   cm.   — (Library of religious biography series)
    Includes bibliographical references and index.
    ISBN 0-8028-0153-6
    1. Williams, Roger, 1604?-1683. 2. Baptists—Rhode Island—Biography.
  3. Separatists—Massachusetts—Biography. 4. Separatists—England—
Biography. 5. Freedom of religion—History—17th century.
I. Title. II. Series.
BX6495.W55G38 1991
286'.1'092—dc20
  [B]   90-20017
                                               CIP

"We Agree, As formerly hath been the libertyes of the Town: so Still to hold forth Libertye of Conscience."

—Providence Agreement, 1640

84328

For Liliana Marie & Samuel Scott

Contents

Foreword

The name of Roger Williams, like that of John Winthrop or Captain John Smith, remains alive in American historical memory. All were founders of colonies that became part of the original thirteen United States. Americans identify Roger Williams as the founder of Rhode Island and as a resolute defender of religious liberty. We might even recall that it was Roger Williams rather than Thomas Jefferson who first used the image of a hedge or wall of separation between church and state.

Yet Roger Williams remains a far more distant and elusive figure than the founders of Massachusetts Bay and Virginia. Partly this is because he was such a quarrelsome dissenter (John Quincy Adams, loyal son of Massachusetts, referred to him as "a polemical porcupine"). Few followed Williams or admired his Rhode Island experiment in his own day. A century and a half later, even those like Jefferson and Madison who arrived at similar conclusions owed little to Williams's defense of religious liberty.

Roger Williams also remains elusive because he was a

complicated individual living in complex times. He graduated from Cambridge in 1627 on the eve of the Puritan migration to the New World and the English Civil War. He gladly followed John Winthrop to Massachusetts Bay but quickly denounced the "city on a hill" as a flawed experiment. He was a dissenter extraordinaire, more successful in decrying the inadequacy of other systems than in building his own. Yet in his writings, many of which were published in London, Williams wrestled with the same momentous issues that confronted John Milton, Oliver Cromwell, and William Penn.

This study of Roger Williams is biography at its best. In crystal-clear prose, Edwin Gaustad invites the reader into the world of Roger Williams—a man committed to liberty of conscience out of deep religious conviction, not out of indifference. This study makes accessible the significance of Williams in his own day, the essential force of his ideas, and his legacy in subsequent American history. *Liberty of Conscience* also serves as an outstanding primer on the subject of religious liberty in America. Nothing could be more timely given the complicated issues of church and state that embroil American society at the close of the twentieth century.

Nathan O. Hatch

Preface

In 1991 Americans celebrate the bicentennial of the first ten amendments to the United States Constitution, these being popularly and even proudly known as the Bill of Rights. While Roger Williams had no hand in writing the First Amendment, we may well suppose that he would have taken great pleasure in its guarantees. He would have approved of both of the religion clauses—"the Establishment clause" telling government that when it tried to help religion, it only hurt; and "the Free Exercise clause" telling government to keep its clumsy hands as far as possible from the religious conscience.

Roger Williams had much to say about these subjects, as well as about several others. He did not always speak his piece with economy or grace, but he unfailingly spoke it with courage and passion. So that his voice may be more clearly heard, in the pages that follow seventeenth-century spelling has been changed to conform to modern usage, and Williams' haphazard and excessive use of italics has been abandoned. Titles and passages of poetry, however, have been reproduced without change. No modern vocabulary has been introduced; where insertions have been necessary to make his meaning clear, these appear in square brackets.

It is always a pleasure to express appreciation to those who have made the path of scholarship less rocky, sometimes more scenic. Albert T. Klyberg, director of the Rhode Island Historical Society, extended every courtesy, as did Richard K. Showman, editor of the Nathaniel Greene papers for the Society. In the John Carter Brown Library, Norman Fiering made a month-long summer fellowship possible and provided other kinds of "fellowship" in the Brown University community. Mark Noll, general editor of the series in which this volume appears, gave the manuscript an extraordinarily perceptive and critical reading. The Research Committee of the University of California, Riverside, Academic Senate has generously supported this research, and the library staff of that institution has provided ready and cheerful assistance. Once again, my perceptive wife has applied her skilled touch in ways too numerous to list.

When Americans have finished celebrating the major anniversary of their Bill of Rights, they will then rush on toward a brand new millennium. On that subject Roger Williams also had much to say, along with his peers in England and in the New World. We now stumble over words like "eschatology" and "apocalypticism" and even "millennialism." But in facing the twenty-first century, we may stumble less over words like "civility" and "conscience" and even "spiritual health." These simpler words of Williams may somehow help us find our way through the next thousand years—more or less.

Homecoming

House Bill Number 488, passed by the Commonwealth of Massachusetts in 1936, formally expunged from the laws of that state the sentence of exile imposed upon Roger Williams over three hundred years before. It took fewer than thirty words to unravel that one tangled knot of so much intervening history. "Resolved," the Bill declared, "That the sentence of expulsion passed against Roger Williams by the General Court of Massachusetts Bay Colony in the year sixteen hundred and thirty-five be and hereby is revoked."

Three years later in the state of Rhode Island and Providence Plantations, on a high hill overlooking Roger Williams' own town, citizens gathered to unveil a monument to the man of whom neither portrait nor ancestral home has survived. At three o'clock on a June afternoon, the 103rd Field Artillery Band played the national anthem, the resident Roman Catholic bishop delivered the invocation, and, much later, the resident rabbi of Temple Emanu-El offered the benediction, this symbolic pluralism stirring—if anything could—the long buried, long neglected ashes of Roger Williams. The assembled audience also joined together in singing an eighteenth-century hymn:

> O God, our help in ages past,
> Our hope for years to come,
> Our shelter from the stormy blast,
> And our eternal home.

In a ceremony commemorating Roger Williams, the phrase "stormy blast" may have struck some in attendance as particularly apt.

Then in 1984 the United States of America set aside a four-and-one-half acre "Roger Williams National Memorial" on a site not far from Williams' dwelling, altogether obliterated by the centuries. On an October afternoon the National Park Service dedicated its only facility in the state of Rhode Island with, once again, music, prayers, and words of remembrance. Small though this park was, the struggle for it had been large and long. The legislative labors, begun over a quarter of a century earlier by Senator Theodore Francis Green and concluded by Senator Claiborne Pell, typified the difficulties that both Rhode Island and Roger Williams repeatedly encountered.

Senator Pell, delivering the main address on October 8, noted that in 1636 thirteen families had banded together to create "the first genuine democracy—also the first church-divorced and conscience-free community—in modern history." Williams never gave up, the senator pointed out, nor did "those of us who wanted a national memorial to Roger Williams." This memorial, Pell concluded, should always remind us that the freedoms for which Williams fought, like the park itself, "did not come easily." As the Kentish Guards of the state militia's fife and drum corps played and as the colonial flags of New England swayed in that autumn afternoon, this lesson deserved to be remembered: freedom does not come easily. But the man who lived that lesson to the fullest also deserved to be, and was in fact being, remembered.

In the course of his long and troubled life, often cast down and often cast out, Roger Williams had at last come home.

1 Exile from England

The sixteenth-century Reformation jolted and fractured the Western world with such force as to scar all the land forever. To mention the names of only Martin Luther (1483-1546), Ignatius Loyola (1491-1556), and John Calvin (1509-1564) is to suggest a dimension of the jolting that, in the long view, shook up institutions and alignments as much as the earlier voyages of Columbus managed to do. By the time Roger Williams was born, early in the seventeenth century, the religious map of Europe bore little resemblance to one drawn a mere hundred years before.

Luther's Ninety-five Theses of 1517, followed by more radical treatises in the 1520s, plunged all of Germany into bitter religious and political struggles. When a generation or so later the dust began to settle, northern Germany had become largely Lutheran along with Denmark, Norway, Sweden, and portions of northeastern Europe. Lutheran preachers had, with less effect, also proclaimed their version of the Christian message in the Netherlands, in England, in Austria and Bohemia. The Peace of Augsburg in 1555 acknowledged the reality of religious division in Germany, though few at that time anticipated its permanency.

Roman Catholicism, the prevailing religion for all of Europe prior to Luther, strongly resisted this novel and deeply disturbing destabilization of both the church universal and the Holy Roman Empire (under Charles V from 1519 to 1556). Among the Catholic nations, Spain took the lead in countering the sudden and surprising Protestant surge, with Loyola and his Society of Jesus (Jesuits) conspicuous in their obedience and service to the papacy. Not only Spain and Portugal remained unflinchingly Catholic, but Italy and Ireland as well. France also retained its Catholic allegiance, though with some difficulty and division along with much bloodshed. Portions of Switzerland preserved the Catholic heritage, and for a time the Netherlands as well. By the middle of the sixteenth century, however, options were no longer limited to Lutheran on the one hand and Catholic on the other.

A native of France but later leading citizen of Geneva, Calvin offered another form of Protestantism often designated by the name Reformed. While parts of Switzerland did become Calvinist, even more significant conquests were made in England, Scotland, and ultimately the Netherlands. Appearing on the turbulent scene later than either Luther or Loyola, Calvin presented a more systematic theological version of what, from his point of view, the Protestant Reformation was all about— what was being rejected as "papist" and mere tradition, what was being embraced as biblical and historically authentic. Calvin gave theologians far beyond the confines of Geneva much grist for their doctrinal mills, and those mills ground on for centuries to come.

In the turmoil of schism and war, of disputation and defense, sixteenth-century Europe also saw many minor movements that, finding no political patronage, generally remained obscure and often short-lived. Radical reformers, the left wing of the Reformation, came in many forms: some mystics, some evangelicals, some rationalists, some revolutionaries and apocalypticists. Their followers were few, their enemies multitudinous. Lutherans, Calvinists, and Catholics all found these radicals worthy only of condemnation and persecution. Protestants saw them as an embarrassment to their new and unproven cause; Catholics saw them as the inevitable consequence of a shattered ecclesiastical unity. Most were pacifists, most rejected political alliances (not that any were offered), most came from the ranks of the powerless and disinherited. Those called Anabaptists (or re-baptizers) emphasized the necessity of personal, voluntary, strenuous commitment to the religious calling and to the small, withdrawn-from-the-world community of faithful believers. When one group of Anabaptists took over the town of Münster in western Germany in 1534, they attempted by bloody force and polygamous revolution to turn Münster into a New Jerusalem. Instead, they turned it into an epithet and a curse: the very name was enough to damn all Anabaptists and, for that matter, virtually all of the radical Reformation. Over the entire European continent the sixteenth century was a seething time.

Across the water in England, life was equally turbulent and political stability equally elusive. Henry VIII (1509-1547), once called Defender of the Faith by a grateful pope, began in 1529 to push Parliament toward a series of actions that resulted just five years later in a complete separation of the English church from the papal authority in Rome. Accomplished at the highest political levels, this separation altered behavior and belief in the average parish very little indeed. Henry attracted the attention of most citizens when he dissolved the monasteries, redistributing the land and weakening the social and economic position of Catholicism throughout the kingdom. But did Henry move toward Calvinism or Lutheranism or his own brand of Catholicism? The truth is that Henry moved toward Henry, declaring himself the "Supreme Head in earth of the Church of England," gathering to himself "all honours, dignities, preeminences, jurisdictions, privileges, authorities, im-

3

munities, profits, and commodities." Henry became the principal reformer and enforcer and, if need be, theologian for the newly separated institution, whose precise path was yet to be determined.

The next two reigns, both brief, proved to be extraordinarily difficult for many, as the nation veered first sharply toward a more rigorous Protestantism, then just as sharply back toward a restored Catholicism. During the five years of Edward VI (1547-1553), only child of Henry and his third wife, Jane Seymour, England was called to a uniformity and conformity in religious worship according to the Book of Common Prayer and Administration of the Sacraments, first composed in 1549. Severe penalties were set down for any deviation from the prescribed forms as well as for speaking "anything in derogation or depraving of the said book, or anything therein contained." A straight and clear path for all to follow seemed to have been set, but Edward, a sickly lad, died of consumption when only fifteen years of age.

In the next five-year reign (1553-1558), Mary Tudor, daughter of Henry and his first wife, the Spanish Catholic Catherine of Aragon, drew the nation back to the ancient religion of Rome and of Spain. Whereas Catholics had been vigorously persecuted under Edward, now Protestants felt the sword under Mary, who deplored the fact that England had "swerved from the obedience of the See Apostolic, and declined from the unity of Christ's Church." The Parliamentary Acts that Henry had promoted twenty years earlier were repealed as Mary in 1554 invited the pope's representative in England "to call us home again into the right way from whence we have all this long while wandered." Persecutions under this Tudor queen gave her the unhappy appellation of "Bloody Mary" even as it gave England its most widely read book apart from the Bible: John Foxe's passion-inflaming *Book of Martyrs*.

Mary died late in 1558, however, and was succeeded by yet another daughter of Henry VIII, this one born not to the Catholic Catherine but to the woman for whom Henry put

Catherine away—Anne Boleyn. Elizabeth I, by heritage, by necessities of state, and perhaps by disposition, turned toward Protestantism. But she used religion, as she did her eligibility for marriage, as a tool in the complexities of both foreign and domestic affairs. Her virtues were many, among them being a longevity that kept her on the throne for nearly half a century. During the years from 1558 to 1603, England began to moderate the wild swings in political loyalties and religious sentiments. England also during that time began to assert itself more forcefully upon the Western world scene, notably so after the defeat of the Spanish Armada in 1588. Elizabeth even took tentative (and unsuccessful) steps toward establishing an English presence in the New World comparable to that already achieved by Portugal and Spain. Her death in 1603 brought no end to those adventures, though it did mark the end of the Tudor sovereigns and the beginning of the Stuart line with James I. It also marked, in all probability, the year in which Roger Williams was born.

Born of middle-class parents in London, the third of James and Alice Pemberton Williams' four children, Roger grew to manhood during the reign of James I, from 1603 to 1625. In the first two decades of his life, the young Williams grew up in the national Church of England (St. Sepulchre's Church was the local parish), acquired enough fundamentals of education to equip himself for admission in 1621 to the Charterhouse Grammar School (the grammar being Greek and Latin, with facility and correctness in English being wholly assumed). Enjoying the patronage and employment of the famous jurist Sir Edward Coke, Williams was rescued from a middling life of trade and potential obscurity. Following his preparatory education, and probably still with Coke's advice and assistance, Williams in 1624 entered Pembroke College of Cambridge University. Filling in that bare outline is more a matter of conjecture than of historical record. Williams himself left behind no detailed account of his youthful days, and his boyhood contemporaries did little to shore up the many gaps.

5

Williams could hardly have been immune to excitement about England's more successful ventures in the New World, the first permanent English settlement, Jamestown, being named in honor of the reigning monarch, and the country of which it was a part, Virginia, so called in tribute to Elizabeth, the Virgin Queen. Captain John Smith (1580-1631), colonial adventurer and early governor of Virginia, was in fact a member of that same St. Sepulchre's parish in London. But in addition to the excitement about worlds beyond the ocean sea, of pirates gaining gold and taking lives, of courageous voyages of exploration (and "Principall Navigations," to quote England's great propagandist and promoter Richard Hakluyt the Younger), the air bristled with the crackling excitement of religion.

Of religion? Excitement? Generations and centuries after Williams, one must be reminded that it was religion, not romantic love, for which one fought and died. It was religion, not mayhem and murder, that sent men and women to the Tower of London or to capital punishment in less prestigious quarters. It was religion, not bulldozers or bombs, that moved mountains and nations and shaped worlds, dividing the whole earth (as in the papal line of demarcation) with the stroke of a pen, or uniting much of that earth (as in the Catholic Reformation) in a holy crusade. And it was religion, above all else, that moved and shaped Roger Williams.

In one of his rare comments on his youth, Williams as an old man testified that he had been religious from an early age. More than sixty years ago, he wrote in 1673, "the Father of Lights and Mercies touched my Soul with a love to himself." Williams was not trying to be secretive or cryptic, for most of his contemporaries would understand this single sentence as opening up the deep truths of Puritan conversion. Sometime in his early teens Williams moved from innocence or self-indulgence into guilt, and then moved once more into a glorious sense of having been accepted by, redeemed by, none other than the Creator of the universe. A single human life—frail, fallible, broken, blemished—had, through no merit or power of its own, been made

6

strong and whole. All blemishes, or in theological terms, all sins, had been washed away. One had become a new creature: rejuvenated, revitalized, reborn. How could such a stupendous transformation take place?

Not through striving, or fasting, or praying, or bribing or by any other ordinary human means. Salvation had come, miracle of miracles, as a gift: free, undeserved, no strings attached. If it could be explained at all, one turned (in Williams' seventeenth-century England) to the Bible for familiar language that helped make sense out of a wonder. "For by grace are ye saved through faith, and that not of yourselves: it is the gift of God" (Eph. 2:8). No boasting, no reliance upon one's works, "for all have sinned, and come short of the glory of God." On the other hand, one depended wholly upon "being justified freely by [God's] grace, through the redemption that is in Christ Jesus" (Rom. 3:23-24). To biblical language, one might well add the language of sermons heard week after week, explaining the sordid corruption of human nature, the bright promise of divine love. In the Puritan world, conversion changed everything, here and hereafter.

Sociologically, the person chosen or elected by God now identified with a holy community, a church, a gathered fellowship of the redeemed. This person also participated in a historical community, the "cloud of witnesses" to Christian truths from the first century to the present time. However impoverished or lowly born, one now belonged to a sanctified elite, a belonging made certain and secure because the choice was God's, not man's. Psychologically, the new saint now found assurance, "blessed assurance," in being no longer weak and despised but strong and caressed. As Jesus had healed the sick, made the deaf to hear, and given sight to the blind, so now a heavenly Savior granted light and truth to those who, without the gift of grace, had been listless, lost, empty, and confused. Theologically (and that dimension of the conversion experience cannot be ignored), one had moved from Satan's dominion to God's; one had escaped the terrors of hell to dwell on the delights of heaven. One had put on the whole armor of God, to wage his wars and win victories in his name.

This fundamental reversal and renewal of life brought Roger Williams immediately into an active connection with the local Christian church (where he recorded many of the sermons in shorthand) and into an exacting, lifelong study of the Scriptures. As for other Puritans, so for Williams, conversion was not the end of a process but the beginning of a lifelong growth in grace. Religion was, moreover, no Sunday avocation, but a momentous option that determined how one should live, where one should live, and indeed if one should live at all. When Williams was in his teens, the Thirty Years War broke out on the Continent, with religion in the early years as the crucial factor. In England and, indeed, in Williams' own parish, burning men and women at the stake had not been forsaken. Heresy could be more fearful than treason, and theological precision far more necessary than either science or sanitation.

Certainly by the time he was in college, if not well before, Williams came to see Christianity as more than a commitment of faith, though it had to be that above all else. It was also, however, a religion of wondrous complexity and some contradiction. Differences abounded, not only among his Dutch and French playmates in commercial London, but among his fellow countrymen and women as well. Edward VI and Mary I had represented sharp and mutually exclusive options, but in the days of Elizabeth I and James I the differences grew more subtle, more elusive, more tantalizing, and, within the local parishes, unmistakably more contentious. The Elizabethan "settlement" had settled much, but surely not all, especially in that bloody gladiatorial arena called religion.

The Church of England, Henry's *Anglicana Ecclesia*, was of course the most obvious option, the virtually inescapable option, when Roger Williams was growing up. All over England, it was the legally established church, the official church, the national church. To hold any office under the government, one had to be a member of the Church of England; to be admitted into either Oxford or Cambridge, one had to be a member of the Church of England; to aspire to any social standing whatsoever, to be within the bounty of the king or the blessings of the law, one had to be a member of the Church of England. Other options were hard to conceive, even more difficult to embrace.

Roman Catholics, of course, did not all disappear from the island with a mere wave of the royal scepter. Disenfranchised, forbidden to worship in public, suspected, mistreated, and on occasion executed, the Catholic minority continued to exercise, privately, its ancient option, even as it continued to hope for another of those great reversals of fortune and sentiment such as Mary Tudor had briefly brought forth. Indeed, during Elizabeth's long reign, plots and rumors of plots regarding a restoration of Roman Catholicism (with France or Spain hovering in the background) kept religious anxieties and animosities running high. So many of these rumors centered around Mary Stuart ("Queen of Scots"), who had been raised in France as a Catholic, that Elizabeth at long last consented to her beheading early in 1587.

In the two decades before James' ascension to the throne, over one hundred Catholic priests had been put to death, sometimes along with the lay men or women accused of assisting or hiding them. Nonetheless, by 1603 more than eight thousand Catholics could still be found in England, most of them in the Cheshire and Lancashire regions. Nor did the raging anti-Catholicism moderate significantly during Roger Williams' boyhood days. In fact, the so-called Gunpowder Plot in 1605, an attempt to blow up the Houses of Parliament and the king as he met with them, revealed Catholic conspiratorial intentions behind that thwarted and ill-advised scheme. The resulting hostility against Catholicism, foreign and domestic, led to a celebration every November 5, Guy Fawkes Day, in which the pope was hanged in effigy. This festivity, though it commemorated the deliverance of the nation from the hands of its enemies, could not be separated from inflammatory rhetoric against Catholics in general, against Jesuits in particular, and against the

9

papacy over all. Guy Fawkes Day was celebrated with as much vigor in colonial New England as it was in Old.

The issue of Roman Catholicism was, to be sure, more than a matter of religious options, more than a purely domestic concern. The nation's very survival was deemed to be at stake, with both France and Spain seen as ready to seize any opportune moment to direct assassinations, encourage rebellion, incite the Irish, undermine the economy, or, if all else failed, invade the island. The Church of England could count on strong national support in the costly contest between Anglicanism on the one hand and Catholicism on the other. Anti-Catholicism filled the very air that one breathed in England, as "papist" tarred any proposal or person so labeled, as "jesuitical" became a synonym for the deceitful, cunning, and totally untrustworthy. In building fortress-like walls against Roman Catholicism, the national church had lots of help in keeping that particular enemy outside the gate.

Enemies within, however, presented another set of problems. For the Church of England still left many unsatisfied as to its true character, its exact theology, its precise stance with respect to that Reformation that had rocked the Western world. The national church was clearly no longer *Roman* Catholic, but was it in some sense still "Catholic"? The national church was clearly neither Lutheran nor Anabaptist, but in just what sense or to just what degree was it "Protestant"? Many responded that the Church of England was a genus all its own, neither Roman Catholic nor Continental Protestant but a middle way between the two. Others responded that the Church of England had only a political or cosmetic face-lift in the sixteenth century, that substantial changes in piety or liturgy or doctrinal understanding had never taken place. Those who wanted the Church of England to take the Reformation more seriously, to follow its implications more consistently, came to be known as Puritans.

Puritanism, drawing upon a medieval strain of personal piety and expounding a covenant theology that highlighted God's promises to humankind and the latter's appropriate response to those gracious promises, developed as a faction or wing or pressure group with the national church. When James rode from Scotland down to London in 1603, a large number of Puritans presented him with a list of reforms (the Millenary Petition) that they wished to see instituted as quickly as possible. Looking at this list tells us something of the Puritan program around the time that Roger Williams was born.

The Puritan "humble suit" to James begged that services of worship themselves be so reformed as to eliminate such lingering Catholic practices as bowing at the name of Jesus, making the sign of the cross at baptism, and reading from the Apocrypha in church; furthermore, the Puritans argued, "no popish opinion [should be] . . . any more taught or defended." With respect to the clergy, the Puritans urged the king to remove all unqualified and unfit ministers from office, specifically those unable to preach a sermon at least every Sunday. Nor should any clergyman hold more than one pastoral office or receive income from any parish in which he did not reside. Clergy, moreover, should be allowed to marry, with all laws enforcing or encouraging celibacy stricken from the books. Excommunication should no longer be employed as a political weapon, and it should never be imposed without the approval of the local pastor. The petitioners concluded with the hope that God had "appointed your highness our physician to heal these diseases; and we say with Mordecai to Esther, 'Who knoweth whether you are come to the kingdom for such a time.' "

James proved not to be the healing physician the Puritans had been hoping for. The king did meet with some Puritans at Hampton Court the following year, but he responded to few of their concerns. By his grace and favor he permitted a new translation of the Bible into English, the famous and enduring King James Version appearing in 1611. But he strongly supported the office of a powerful, monarchical bishop ("no bishop, no king," James reputedly remarked) and then offended Puritans more in 1618 by issuing his Book of Sports, which made Sunday more a holiday than a holy day—at least from the

Puritan point of view. James had little sympathy for the view "that no honest mirth or recreation is lawful or tolerable in our religion," and even less sympathy for the Puritan tendency to treat obedience to the Book of Common Prayer as a casual or voluntary matter. Puritans would obey that old book as well as James' new book, and bishops were directed to enforce conformity strictly or, failing that, to drive dissenters from the kingdom.

This hard line aggravated the situation of the Puritan party within the Church of England. Should they, against their conscience, give outward conformity to the law, all the while working diligently to purge the Church of its errors? Or should they, in obedience to their conscience, refuse to conform and suffer the consequences: fines, imprisonments, expulsions, or executions? Those who chose the latter course during the reigns of Elizabeth and James came to be known as Separatists, though many other names were also applied. In Elizabeth's time, men such as Robert Browne and Henry Barrow found the heavy hand of the state so oppressive that they felt obliged to withdraw altogether from the established church and its polluting political partnership. Browne in 1582 produced a tract whose title said it all: *A Treatise of Reformation without Tarrying for Anie, and of the Wickednesse of Those Preachers which will not Reforme till the Magistrate Commande or Compell Them.* Language inside was even stronger as Browne condemned the whole corrupting coziness between the bishops and the princes, calling on all faithful Christians to avoid "the Popish disorders, and ungodly communion of all false christians and especially of wicked Preachers and hirelings." Having spoken his mind so freely, Browne found it necessary to flee to Holland, taking a small congregation with him. He later returned to England and submitted himself to the authority of the national church.

Henry Barrow, also in the 1580s, assumed leadership by virtue of his strong advocacy of separation and his unrelenting attack upon the compromising, moderating stance of the Church of England. For Barrow, the national church was worse than just a temporizing institution not yet fully reformed: it was hopelessly stained, altogether unfaithful, more anti-Christian than Christian in its character. Though often protesting that he was misunderstood, Barrow could only be offensive, if not threatening, to all authority, civil and ecclesiastical. When he and a companion set up a Separatist congregation in London itself in 1592, his impudence could no longer be endured. Barrow and two others were arrested the following year and hanged for denying the authority of the queen in all matters pertaining to the church. That none should fail to get the point, Parliament passed a law in 1593 providing severest penalties for all persons who dared to "impugn her majesty's power and authority in causes ecclesiastical, united and annexed to the imperial crown of this realm." The law warned those who failed to attend church or who persuaded others to absent themselves or who failed "to receive communion according to her majesty's laws and statutes" that prison awaited them—as it did any who were so reckless as to gather "at any unlawful assemblies, conventicles, or meetings, under color or pretense of any exercise of religion, contrary to her majesty's said laws and statutes."

Separatism fared no better in the time of King James (and Roger Williams). The most famous Separatist congregation, from an American perspective, gathered in the town of Scrooby in Nottinghamshire, meeting always in secret, fearful for the lives and property of its individual members, and always keeping one eye out for the sheriff, who might at any time be coming down the road. Around 1607 the congregation, meeting in an inn operated by William Brewster, decided that they, like others before them, must flee to Holland. There they could worship openly and honestly in a manner pleasing to God and agreeable to their own consciences. Leaving England was not easy, however, for one emigrated only with official approval. The congregation, having no reason to suppose that such approval might ever come, determined to leave secretly, hiring a ship privately, and crossing the English Channel—they hoped—both quickly and quietly. In fact, a severe storm blew them off course, way north to the coast of Norway, so that it took these Separatists an incredible fourteen days to complete their journey to Amsterdam.

After some years in that large commercial city, the church agreed that Leyden would offer less temptation to their youth, more opportunity to maintain their English lives until (until!) king and Parliament and church came to their collective senses. They therefore removed the church from Amsterdam to Leyden, where they waited. And waited. When after ten years or so in Holland, it became apparent that no great Reformation was in the offing back home, despair descended upon the homesick congregation.

If they stayed on in Holland, they lost their identity as English men and women. If they returned to England, they lost their integrity as Christian men and women. True to their country or true to their God—which should it be? And who on earth should be forced to make such a cruel choice? These separating Puritans, now about to assume the more familiar name of Pilgrims, were saved from that cruel choice by the possibility of sailing not for England but for English soil some three thousand miles away. There, far from sheriffs and bishops and fines and jails, they could perhaps worship as they chose, raise their children as English (not Dutch) boys and girls, and prosper in their own land, initially in the employ of the Virginia Company. Negotiation for this major migration, too large an enterprise to be carried on in secret, too great a distance to be traversed without some support, was complex and difficult. But after two or three years of conversation and mutual concession, these hardy souls set out from Leyden for Plymouth in England. Then in September of 1620 they sailed on the Mayflower for Virginia, but made landfall far to the north, near Cape Cod, and decided to settle there in a place that they promptly named Plymouth. In the following decade, these Pilgrims and Roger Williams would come to know each other well.

Other Separatists back in England followed still different theological or ecclesiastical paths. Under the leadership of John

Smyth, former fellow of Christ's College, Cambridge, another small congregation also gathered in Nottinghamshire, also feared the sheriff and other authorities of the state, and also determined in 1607 that flight to Amsterdam was the only possible course for men and women whose religious consciousness had been singularly raised. Having been influenced by both Robert Browne and Henry Barrow, John Smyth in Amsterdam fell under the additional influence of Dutch Mennonites, sober survivors of the Anabaptist enthusiasm of the previous century. Smyth, already convinced of the corrupt nature of the Church of England and of the need for a congregation of the fully committed, now concluded that a corrupt church could never have administered a correct baptism. He decided around 1609 to baptize himself and several others, thereby setting up a baptism of believers in a pure church over against a baptism of infants in a polluted church. In so doing, John Smyth created the first English Baptist church.

The following year Smyth composed (in Latin) twenty articles that outlined the distinctive positions of his exiled congregation. Article Twelve declared that "The church is a company of the faithful, baptized after confession of sin and of faith." "Company of the faithful" meant that a church did not consist automatically of everyone living within the bounds of a geographically defined parish: the church was not part of the world but was drawn out of and away from the world. Only the "faithful" could belong. And because all faithful were on the same spiritual plane, the congregation itself would choose its own officers: overseers (bishops) or elders "to whom the power is given of dispensing both the word and the sacraments," as well as deacons, "men and widows, who attend to the affairs of the poor and sick brethren." Baptism, of course, followed one's voluntary confession of sin and declaration of faith; no valid baptism could ever precede such confession and declaration. Baptism had no saving power within itself; rather, it was "the external sign of the remission of sins, of dying and being made alive, and therefore does not belong to infants."

Smyth died just two years after the words quoted above were written, and thus he had no opportunity to lead his congregation either back to England or to English soil far away. Thomas Helwys, a close associate of Smyth's, shared the latter's sentiments but did not approve of his efforts to establish a formal link with the Mennonites. Unlike Smyth, Helwys did lead his followers back to England, deciding that if they were to preserve honor, they would have to face persecution. His major work, *The Mistery of Iniquity* (London, 1612), guaranteed that persecution would come. Despite an effort to present the book to King James personally, Helwys was neither received nor believed by royalty. Contenting himself with penning a note to the king, Helwys informed His Royal Highness that he was a mere mortal, not God, and that he therefore had no power over the immortal souls of his subjects, nor any power to "set spiritual Lords over them." This was not popular doctrine in 1612, nor for many years thereafter. Helwys, as a consequence, spent the last two or three years of his life in Newgate Prison, dying there in 1615 or 1616.

After Helwys' death, Baptist leadership fell upon the shoulders of John Murton, who shared the conviction that civil officers should keep their noses and their hands out of ecclesiastical affairs. "Earthly authority belongeth to earthly kings," Murton wrote in 1615, "but spiritual authority belongeth to that one spiritual King who is KING OF KINGS." It is the foulest of crimes, Murton also argued, to force people's "bodies to a worship whereunto they cannot bring their spirits." These early Baptists all promised civil obedience to the state; they argued vigorously, however, against spiritual obedience to any other than God. Convincing few, they endured sustained persecution, suffering "many years in filthy prisons," Murton wrote, "in hunger, cold, idleness, divided from wife, family, calling, left in continual miseries and temptations, so as death would be to many less persecution." Like Helwys, Murton spoke from personal experience, experience of which Roger Williams was clearly aware and to which he later made explicit reference.

16

Smyth, Helwys, and Murton were General Baptists—that is, unlike the Calvinists, they believed that Christ died not just for the Elect but for all mankind. His work of atonement was "general," not restricted or "particular." Shortly after Williams left England for the New World, however, Calvinist or Particular Baptists also appeared on the English scene, sharing even more of the Puritan theology and acquiring even more of a standing in the religious community of seventeenth-century England. Beginning in London around 1633, the Particular Baptists agreed that baptism must be limited to believers, not administered willy-nilly to infants. Within a few years they also agreed that this baptism must be by immersion or "plunging," this being a more appropriate symbol of the "dying and being made alive" of which Smyth had spoken.

Within a single decade, one congregation of Particular Baptists had become seven, this sharp increase leading to the first group Confession of Faith among the Baptists. In 1644 the group voiced its conviction that the church must be a "company of visible saints, called and separated from the world." The congregation, moreover, was to be its own authority and subject to the wishes of no other body, ecclesiastical or civil. And the magistrate's chief duty with respect to religion was "to tender the liberty of men's consciences." Without that liberty, these Baptists declared, no other liberty was worth mentioning.

All of this Baptist history, on the other hand, is very much worth mentioning for at least two reasons: first, Roger Williams saw himself in some respects and at some junctures of his life as spiritually if not formally identified with that tradition; and second, the enemies of Roger Williams labored mightily to place him in the Baptist (or better yet, the Anabaptist) camp, the better to discredit his views and unify the opposition against him. The title of the 1644 statement indicates that English Baptists knew what they were up against so far as public opinion was concerned: *The Confession of Faith, Of Those Church Which are Commonly (Though Falsely) Called Anabaptists.* Their point was that London was not Münster, nor was Boston or Salem or Providence or Newport. It was a point that those opposed to the Baptists doggedly refused to accept.

Long before the 1644 Confession was published, Roger Williams had completed his education at Pembroke College (he received his Bachelor of Arts degree in 1627). He continued at Cambridge in further study for another year and one-half, accepted employment in the Church of England in 1629, and assumed the post of private chaplain on the estate of Sir William Masham at Otes in the county of Essex. Here Williams moved in a higher level of society than had been his custom (though the chaplain ate with the servants), and he was near neighbor to many of the Puritan party who were eager to pursue further reform in the Church of England. It was also here that Roger Williams, in his mid-twenties, considered the serious matter of marriage.

Little correspondence has survived from Williams' early days in England, but in one letter written in the spring of 1629 the ardent youth wrote of rumors floating about concerning a young woman and his own "unworthy self." The young woman in question was Joan Whalley, of distinguished ancestry and of a social standing considerably above that of Roger Williams. Apparently others agreed that Williams' confessions of utmost humility were totally appropriate: he was unworthy. In a letter to Joan's aunt, Williams freely admitted that his financial resources were few, that there was even some "Indecorum" in asking the possible bride "to condescend to my low ebb." But, Williams rather desperately explained, he was not without other matrimonial prospects, nor was he without prospects of more remunerative and dignified positions either in England or elsewhere. Therefore, to the aunt, he dared to be "bold to open to your Ladyship the whole Anatomy of the business." Candor did not conquer, however, nor did love, despite its enduring reputation to the contrary. Williams, failing to receive permission to request the young lady's hand in marriage, turned elsewhere for approval and solace.

In December of 1629 he married Mary Barnard, daughter of a Nottinghamshire clergyman and companion or sometime maid in the household where Roger served as chaplain. The two were married in the parish church not far from the Masham estate, a church later to receive more renown as the burial place for John Locke, an Englishman also caught up in revolution and in concern about civil and religious freedoms. Mary and Roger continued to live on the large estate of Sir William Masham, Puritan leader and helpful friend to Roger Williams not only in his youth but in later years as well. The young couple, Roger about twenty-six and Mary twenty, had less than a year together before their lives took a critical turn.

For in 1629 much else besides affairs of the heart was afoot in the Puritan community. James I had been succeeded in 1625 by his son, Charles I, who ruled with little respect for either Parliament or the Puritans. Elevating William Laud to the office of bishop of London in 1628 (and later making him Archbishop of Canterbury), Charles signaled to all dissenters and nonconformists and agitators that the heavy hand of both state and church would be turned unrelentingly against them. Persecution intensified as absolutism grew ever stronger. Puritans who had heretofore not fled to Holland, who had not taken the dread step of separating themselves from the national church, now found their way hard as stone and their future fearfully dark. For loyal church men and women, still believing it vital to nudge, inch by painful inch, the whole ecclesiastical establishment somewhat further along in the direction of a true Reformation, Separatism (after the manner of Browne or Barrow, Brewster or Helwys) was unthinkable. Total conformity was equally unthinkable, and persisting dissent was rapidly ceasing to be an option. No way out was in sight.

Just out of sight, however, an exit might be found. The government, encouraging colonization abroad, allowed joint-stock companies to solicit investors, raise money, and sponsor expeditions or "adventures" to land that England claimed in North America. Claims would mean little if the English did not actually settle, as the French, Dutch, and Spanish had proceeded to do. As early as 1620 the king had granted New England lands to an entity known as the Council for New England. Then in 1628 a charter was extended to a group of Puritan merchants under the title of the New England Company; soon after, in March of 1629, this grant received royal confirmation with a change of name to the Governor and Company of the Massachusetts Bay in New England—more simply known in history as the Massachusetts Bay Company. Under the aegis of this company and its first governor, lawyer John Winthrop, the future of New England—and of Roger Williams—began to take shape.

While the evidence is not conclusive, it appears that Williams and Winthrop became acquainted in 1629 as a great many Puritans weighed their chances for carrying out any significant religious reform in England, or more immediately their chances for staying out of prison. The odds looked good for neither. Charles had dismissed Parliament in order to rule with an iron hand. William Laud had made strict conformity to the Book of Common Prayer his highest priority. Roman Catholicism was growing in England, not withering away. The national church continued to support unlearned clergy, "Dombe Ministers," who were incapable of preaching a sermon, then punished any who journeyed from such a parish to another where learned and judicious preaching could be heard. That established church also punished godly ministers who did not conform in minor details of ceremony, details not essential to solemn worship "but things indifferent." Such ministers were often abruptly removed from a parish with no provision made for baptisms, burials, or marriages in a locality suddenly deprived of all ministry whatsoever. Indeed, the church did not seem to be moving toward Reformation but further and further away from it.

And yet, should Puritans leave England in large numbers at the very time that their voice was so greatly needed? Was it not the duty of earnest Christians to accept persecution and tribulation rather than flee from it? Was colonization abroad not filled with great risk of failure, perhaps scandalously so, thus bringing discredit to the Puritan cause altogether? What of friends and loved ones left behind? Would they not be wronged, as well as church and country, by an abandonment at such a time as this?

The objections were weighty and real, and the answers to them were generally arrived at only after much searching of heart and soul. "This Land grows weary of her Inhabitants," Winthrop reluctantly concluded in 1629; it placed less value on human life than on that of horses or sheep. Moreover, "the Fountains of Learning and Religion are so corrupted," Winthrop noted, that our children have no proper examples set before them. Men in high places worry about fashion, not faith; they strain at gnats and swallow camels. A venture to the New World, if only the private gamble of a few, would be difficult to justify in the eyes of God, but now—in 1629—"it appears to be a work of God for the good of his Church in that he hath disposed the hearts of so many of his wise and faithful servants, both ministers and others, not only to approve of the enterprise but to interest themselves in it." The clinching argument for Winthrop, as for so many others besides, was this: "It will be a service to the Church of great consequence to carry the Gospel into those parts of the world."

So by the spring of 1630 large numbers of Puritans prepared to leave Old England for New, to leave a corrupted church for a reformed and reforming one. They were not Separatists, however; they were churchmen who could, three thousand miles away from Charles and Laud, do what they were not permitted to do at home—namely, create a true Church of England. Such a church, cleansed of all remaining taints of popery, concerned more about piety than politics or preferment, inspired by a common commitment and an uncommon zeal, could demonstrate to all who might look and listen that the Protestant Reformation had at last appeared in its proper English manifestation. The *Arbella*, carrying Winthrop and his party, left England April 7, 1630, arriving two months later in

Salem harbor. Within a decade, some fifteen to twenty thousand emigrants followed, leaving behind the land that had grown weary of its inhabitants.

Eight months after Winthrop's ship sailed from Southampton, Roger and Mary Williams boarded in Bristol a ship bound for waters near Boston. It was hardly the most obvious thing to do, for news trickling back from Salem, Charlestown, and Boston was not encouraging. If the Williamses had delayed another six months, the news reaching them would have been even more disheartening, for that first winter in and around Boston was bitterly grim. Death and disease stalked the settlers huddled against a cold more severe than that of England. The barest necessities of food, clothing, and shelter came with the greatest difficulty if they came at all. No one spoke of profits for the Massachusetts Bay Company, only of survival. Yet, men, women, and children continued to come, bringing new blood, new hope, new foodstuffs, new skills to strengthen those who had first braved the furious ocean.

One had, after all, to count the cost of staying behind as well as the cost of going, like Abraham, to a land he knew not of. One had to weigh dangers known against those unknown. One had to consider exile, voluntarily chosen or not, in terms of livelihood, civil loyalty, and Christian responsibility. One had, in the midst of England's dark gloom, to think on how best to light a candle, then how to keep that sputtering flame from being snuffed out. At length, Mary and Roger Williams, along with twenty other passengers, boarded the *Lyon* and set out across treacherous seas under the able command of Master William Peirce.

If, as the Chinese say, a journey of a thousand miles begins with a single step, here in Bristol a single step led to a journey of thousands of miles. Captain Peirce knew his way, insofar as any could know his way across an ocean notoriously unpredictable in winter time. For John Winthrop had sent the *Lyon* back to Bristol to gather more provisions, more lemon juice (to prevent scurvy), more settlers to replace those dying or discouraged. Peirce did well on all fronts, including navigation, and brought his ship safely into harbor in less than two months—a good crossing in cold and unforgiving waters. We have no record of the inevitable hardships of this particular voyage, no record of sermons preached at departure (if there were such) or compacts made upon arrival (if there were such). We know only that when the *Lyon* dropped anchor off Nantasket on February 5, 1631, John Winthrop and his underfed, underclothed company received ship, crew, and passengers with great joy. Winthrop also noted in his journal that "Mr. Williams, a godly minister," had along with his young wife now come into the new land.

A few months before Winthrop and his fellow passengers had debarked in Massachusetts, the governor had set forth ideals and hopes for the inhabitants of this Christian commonwealth: to "seek out a place of Cohabitation and Consortship under a due form of Government both civil and ecclesiastical," to assure that public interest would "oversway" all private interests, and to covenant with God and each other "to serve the Lord and work out our Salvation under the power and purity of his holy Ordinances." Winthrop called this sermon "A Modell of Christian Charity." Christian charity would soon be put to its severest test.

2 Exile from Massachusetts

For the Puritan exiles in and around Salem, the winter of 1631 had been cruel. Two hundred new settlers had died, and many resolved to return home. Those who remained faced starvation, lived in crude cellars clawed from the earth, and tried to fend off freezing temperatures more severe than anything they had known in England. Shortly after Mary and Roger Williams stepped ashore in Massachusetts in February, the wintry gales subsided markedly—perhaps the only promising omen in connection with these newest colonists. By the time the *Lyon* arrived, the Winthrop party had surveyed land south of Salem, gradually settling on a large peninsula jutting out in a body of water soon to be known as Boston Bay. That area offered more land than Salem, some protection from ocean winds and enemy ships, and land whose narrow neck could be defended against Indians. When spring arrived, corn was planted, supplies were laid in against the next winter, a modest fur trade was launched, and some ship building was begun. The village of Boston (named after the town in Old England where John Cotton served as pastor) grew slowly, augmentation coming chiefly from newly arriving ships.

Soon after their arrival in the New World, Roger and Mary Williams made their way to Boston, where they, like all hardy souls, found welcome. Roger was even invited to serve as the parish minister, an invitation that—in light of later events—is profoundly ironic. The offer was extended because Williams was a man of good education and good reputation, but more than that, simply because he was there. Other clerical leaders (John Cotton, for example) had yet to leave England. However pleased Williams may have been by this tempting invitation, he found it necessary to turn it down. It was evident from the outset that Williams would travel his own path, and he would often travel it alone.

His conviction gradually formed that separation from the Church of England had to be complete and without hesitation or ambiguity. Regarding the Boston church in particular, Williams later wrote, "I durst not officiate to an unseparated people, as upon examination and conference I found them to be." The Winthrop party, though subject to persecution back in England, still wished to remain bound to their nation and its church. Only in this way, these Puritans believed, could they purify that national church and redeem that beloved land. Their idealism was high, their motivation clear, their method—for Williams—suspect. It was not possible, or if possible, not honorable, he argued, to pledge loyalty to an institution that one intended to remake. One could not be both in the Church of England and at the same time busily engaged in its undoing. Such a position, such a "middle walking," lacked both logical consistency and spiritual integrity.

"My conscience was persuaded," Williams wrote—and how often that conscience would be persuaded by his own convictions, how often it would refuse to be persuaded by the convictions or arguments of others—"against the national church and ceremonies." Williams had not brought a wife across three thousand miles of turbulent seas to stifle a conscience that had been threatened and cramped in England. He would keep his "Soul undefiled" and he would not "act with a doubting Conscience." All of which meant, at this juncture in April of 1631, that he would not accept the honor of being Boston's chief minister: he would return to Salem, a coastal town with its own earlier and independent tradition.

Salem (its name was chosen from the Bible) had been founded in 1628, its first church being gathered the following year, with the separatist principles of the Plymouth Pilgrims providing the model. Williams might well find more room for his conscience in crowded Salem than in nearly empty Boston. In 1629 the Salem church adopted a single sentence covenant for its members, a pledge so charitable and simple as to cause Williams no difficulty at all: "We Covenant with the Lord and one with another, and do bind ourselves in the presence of God, to walk together in all his ways, according as he is pleased to reveal himself unto us in his Blessed word of truth." Williams could and did agree to associate himself with this church; the church, on its part, agreed to ask Williams to assume a pastoral responsibility, assisting the chief minister, Samuel Skelton, another Cambridge University man. When it was evident that Williams was interested, Salem was pleased. Boston, however, was not.

The Bostonians were aggrieved not so much by Williams' preference for Salem's offer over their own as by the grounds for his refusing their church. Not only did he object that they had not cut themselves cleanly from England's church, but he even questioned the right of magistrates to enforce purely religious demands. These laws of the First Table, as they were called (i.e., the first stony tablet of commandments presented to Moses on Mt. Sinai), were not regulations of a civil society or a political order: they belonged to the realm of religion, not of politics. The requirement to love God, to eschew idolatry, to keep the Sabbath, to avoid blasphemy—these were matters for the individual conscience, not for the sheriff, whether in Old England or New. So argued Williams. Boston disagreed.

Winthrop and company maintained that this was precisely the kind of argument that would destroy the enterprise in which they were engaged. Magistrates and clergy needed to work together to achieve common ends; in a hostile wilderness, government, both civil and ecclesiastical, must rely upon a firm partnership to make Massachusetts work. In the midst of anxieties regarding even survival, steady hands and sure authority offered the only possibility of success. Williams would challenge that authority and unsteady those hands. And if that were true in Boston, it was no less true in Salem. Though theoretically wholly independent of authorities in Boston, the Salem church soon received strong advice and urging from Boston concerning Roger Williams. Boston "marveled" that Salem would proceed in so precipitous a manner, acting without the counsel of sister churches, being ready to receive a man who had been all too ready to reject Boston. When advised of Boston's concerns and of Williams' contentiousness, Salem withdrew its offer.

Separatism, or the sectarian principle of church purity, had brought Williams from England to America, then moved him from Boston to Salem, and now moved him once more. If the Massachusetts Bay Company refused to see things his way, perhaps the Plymouth Company (about forty miles south of Salem, by water) would be more sympathetic. The Pilgrims had separated from the Church of England, after all, and had made some of the very same arguments that Williams found himself now making. So by August of 1631, Roger and Mary moved once again, hoping to find at last the solace and comfort of a like-minded community of saints.

For about two years, the young couple resided in the Plymouth Colony, and there Mary gave birth to their first child in August of 1633. Roger served as assistant to the pastor, Ralph Smith, began a long and sensitive engagement with the neighboring Indians, and continued to reflect on what separation really required. The colony's governor, William Bradford, described Williams as "a man godly and zealous, having many precious parts." On occasion, however, the zeal outmatched the godliness, or so it seemed to Williams' neighbors nearly everywhere, including Plymouth. Williams worried that Plymouth's separation was not as clear-cut as he had thought, or as he now wished. When members of the Plymouth church visited England, they joined in services of the national church and then were received back in Plymouth without any complaint or grievance being lodged against them. That worried Williams— who promptly worried others.

Toward the end of 1633, he fell "into some strange opinions," Governor Bradford reported, "which caused some controversy between the church and him." Both the church on its part and Williams on his grew increasingly discontent, with the result that with some abruptness Williams decided that it was time to move again—back to Salem and the jurisdiction of Massachusetts Bay. In less than two years in New England, Williams had already managed to achieve a reputation for irascibility; that reputation was destined to enlarge mightily and swiftly. But he had in those brief years also managed to establish a rapport with and understanding of the native Americans unmatched by any of his countrymen in the New World.

Roger Williams' first published book dealt not so much with theology as with anthropology and linguistics. Though he was unable to get it published until years after, he made the first notes for it in those early Plymouth days. So soon did Williams reveal himself to be a keen and sympathetic observer of the Indians, an apt pupil of their language (chiefly the Narraganset dialect), a critic of the intruding European civilization, and something of a poet. Williams labored to understand the unfamiliar and strange, convinced that "Nature knows no difference between Europeans and Americans in blood, birth, bodies, &c., God having of one blood made all mankind."

The book, *A Key into the Language of America*, was, as its full title page indicated, part dictionary, part cultural anthropology, and part "Spirituall Observations, Generall and Particular." The "observations" were designed to instruct the English, not the Indian, instruction of the latter being left (for Williams) to God's good time, "in his own most holy season." It was the English, both in the New World and the Old, who most needed the *Key*, for without it, they tended to think only in terms of the Indians' barbarity and their own superiority. What folly! The "wild Americans," Williams noted, were more courteous and civil in their dealings with each other, and even with strangers, than the English usually managed to be. Or, in his versification,

> If Natures Sons both wild and tame,
> Humane and Courteous be:
> How ill becomes it Sonnes of God
> To want Humanity?

Williams, who many times benefited from hospitable Indians (especially when repulsed by inhospitable English), noted that he had often seen them leave their own dwellings so that a stranger might sleep therein. Jews and Christians, on the other hand, "have sent Christ Jesus to the Manger." Indians also had a great appreciation of nature, perhaps too great, but how much better to have too much than to have little or no sensitivity at all.

> They have no helpe of Clock or Watch,
> And Sunne they overprize.
> Having those artificiall helps, the Sun
> We unthankfully despise.

The English, moreover, justified their grabbing of Indian land by claiming that these simple folk did not really believe in property rights. On the contrary, Williams observed, "the Natives are very exact and punctual in the bounds of their Lands, belonging to this or that Prince or People," even bargaining among themselves for a small piece of ground. Williams' broad advice to the English found its poetic summary:

> Boast not proud English, of thy birth & blood,
> Thy brother Indian is by birth a Good.
> Of one blood God made Him, and Thee, & All,
> As wise, as fair, as strong, as personall.

In his preface to the *Key*, Williams wrote that beyond his

chapter on the Indians' religion, "I shall further present you with a brief Additional discourse concerning this Great Point." That brief discourse, long lost from the published canon and discovered some two centuries after its author's death, reveals a rare respect for the spiritual integrity of the native American. In *Christenings Make Not Christians,* Roger Williams explained why he declined to be a missionary pressing conversion upon the Indian, why it was better to wait upon God and "his own holy season." Forced conversion was no conversion at all, Williams pointed out, any more than was required conformity "to some external submission to God's Ordinances." To have dominant cultures or powerful nations determine the religion of a powerless people was to learn absolutely nothing from the history of the ancient or the European world.

Williams felt strongly about "monstrous and most inhumane conversions" forced upon native populations in both North and South America—"yea, ten thousands of poor Natives, sometimes by wiles and subtle devices, sometimes by force compelling them to submit to that which they understood not." Williams wanted no part of that kind of "conversion," even though "I know it would have been easy for myself, long ere this, to have brought many thousands of these Natives" to what he called an "Antichristian conversion." He could have required some observance of one day in seven, could have baptized or christened in the rivers, could have "maintained priests and forms of prayers." And why had he not done so? "I answer, woe be to me, if I call light darkness or darkness light. . . . Woe be to me if I call that conversion unto God, which is indeed subversion of the souls of Millions in Christendom, from one false worship to another." "Christendom"—that is, a polluting mixture of politics with religion—was not merely unacceptable to Roger Williams, it was abhorrent. To fail to distinguish between a voluntary and comprehending acceptance of the gospel and a compulsory and purely formal kind of worship was to repeat the tragic mistakes of days gone by. Or in the stronger and more vivid language of Williams, "The not discerning of this truth hath let out the blood of thousands in civil combustions in all ages; and made the whore drunk, & the Earth drunk with the blood of the Saints and witnesses of Jesus." Native Americans deserved better than persecution disguised as evangelism.

BATTLING WITH MASSACHUSETTS BAY

English Americans deserved better too. Whether in Boston or Salem or Plymouth, religion must be kept free of politics, and conversion free of armies and courts. Conscience must be undefiled. Williams felt so strongly about separation from the Church of England not simply because he saw its ceremonies and clergy as insufficiently Protestant but because a national church was by definition a political church. England, like all of Europe, was an instance of *Christendom,* not of Christianity—a distinction that Williams would spend most of the remainder of his life trying to make unmistakably clear. He wanted Boston and New England to be not another trite example of Christendom but a sparkling new manifestation of genuine Christianity: thirsting only after righteousness, not after political patronage and power. To be sure, history overflowed with examples of compulsion in religion, "but so did never the Lord Jesus bring any unto his most pure worship." Demanding that men believe was, said Williams, like requiring "an unwilling Spouse . . . to enter into a forced bed." Even the Indians, he noted, abhor that.

Plymouth provided Williams with ample opportunity to know and appreciate those Indians, even as it gave him further opportunity to be confounded by his own countrymen. Did they not understand how politics and the interests of state perverted the medieval church? Did they not learn from England's bloody turmoil during the reigns of Henry, Edward, Mary, Elizabeth, James, and Charles? Did they not flee from the brutal hand of Archbishop Laud in order to escape and avoid all such brutal hands, now and forever? Was not Plymouth more perceptive than all others in this matter of genuine religion? To that last

31

question, Williams reluctantly concluded in the negative, and so in the fall of 1633 he resolved to return to Salem.

While in Plymouth, Williams wrote another book that, unfortunately, has not survived. Because it was so severely refuted, however, we know that in it Williams questioned the very right of the English to occupy land that properly belonged to the Indians. What was it about Christendom, Williams wondered, that empowered Christian kings to give away land that wasn't even theirs? English colonization was nothing more than "a sin of unjust usurpation upon others' possessions." Indians owned the land before Europeans arrived; they would continue to own the land until appropriate purchases or agreements had been made. John Winthrop responded that land which "lies common, and hath never been replenished or subdued is free to any that possess or improve it." With respect to the Indians, Winthrop added, "if we leave them sufficient for their use, we may lawfully take the rest, there being more than enough for them and us." Or as John Cotton later noted, "We did not conceive that it is a just title to so vast a continent, to make no other improvement of millions of acres in it, but only to burn it up for pastime." Winthrop, already aware that Williams bore watching, would now be even more on guard against this man who insisted on challenging nearly everyone and everything.

By the end of December 1633 the Massachusetts authorities took official notice of Williams' unsettling opinions, especially this matter of land and the right of King Charles to grant a patent or exclusive title to "all that part of America" from 40 to 48 degrees northern latitude, "from sea to sea," together with "all the firm lands, soils, grounds, havens, ports, rivers, waters, fishing, mines and minerals." All this and more the king granted to the Massachusetts Bay Company for their "sole and proper use" and to "their successors and assigns forever." No word about the Indians. The Company's charter, as firm a foundation as Massachusetts could hope to build on, was manifestly legal. But was it right?

The General Court, that amalgam of the governor and his

assistants that functioned as a legislative, judicial, and executive body all in one, found that Williams not only threatened their charter but insulted their king. Williams was called upon to pledge that Charles I was his king too, and that no disloyalty was intended. Williams offering this and other satisfactions, the Court took no punitive action but sought out leading clergy for further advice. John Wilson and John Cotton, now together leading the Boston church that Roger Williams had turned down nearly three years before, concluded that the latter's language was somewhat ambiguous or obscure and that varied interpretations were possible. His retraction or explanation should therefore be allowed to stand. For the moment the General Court was mollified, but this was only Round I.

Hardly waiting to catch his breath or to give his adversaries a chance to catch theirs, Williams proceeded to voice other opinions that were sure to agitate and infuriate. The next issue that surfaced, in March 1634, strikes the modern reader as less than momentous: veils. More specifically, the question was whether women should wear veils in church, or as the biblical query went, "Is it comely that a woman pray unto God uncovered?" (1 Cor. 11:13). Williams, for once, did not originate the controversy. The Boston church had vigorously debated the question, with John Cotton answering in the affirmative (it *was* comely) and John Endecott (sometime governor of the colony) answering in the negative. In Salem, the principal pastor, Samuel Skelton, had taken a strong stand in favor of veils as early as 1630. It was Williams' lot to inherit the fight, but of course he never ran from a fight. So he joined in, full voice, to argue that indeed female members of the Salem congregation should wear veils in church, and not only there but in any "public assemblies." After Samuel Skelton died in August 1634, Williams, who continued to agitate for veils, exercised even more influence in the Salem church.

The next controversy that fall was somewhat more momentous: flags. At least it had the virtue of returning to a major Williams theme—keeping politics and religion, the civil and the ecclesiastical, as far apart as humanly possible. On November 5 some Salem residents desecrated the English flag by cutting out the cross that symbolized, for Williams and others, the alliance that deserved the name of Christendom but hardly that of Christianity. Besides, that particular red cross in England's flag had been bestowed by the pope, making it a symbol of things even more obnoxious than politics. Actually it was John Endecott who led the campaign to remove the cross, but Williams was assumed to be behind this as behind every other novelty or noise that came from Salem. In this episode, however, a point was conceded. Even John Cotton questioned the propriety of a papist cross in an English flag. Eventually, Endecott was formally rebuked for acting in so rash and disrespectful a manner, but over the next half-century the cross was quietly dropped from New England's official flag.

The General Court continued, nevertheless, to be deeply concerned about Roger Williams. Members of the Court could quickly pass over veils and flags, but they could not get themselves unstuck on that matter of legal title to the very land on which the Court sat and on which their homes were built. Again, despite his earlier recantation, Williams was accused of "teaching publicly against the king's patent, and our great sin in claiming right thereby to this country, etc." The "etc." evoked his earlier complaints about the magistrate's right to enforce laws of the First Table and about the churches' failure to attain a pure form of worship. In March of 1635 the Court restrained itself once more from taking any definitive action against this noisiest of Puritans, their anxieties allayed in part by John Cotton, who argued that Williams was not a traitor: he merely questioned, on theological grounds, the moral right of the king to donate land that wasn't his. If Williams erred in this matter, perhaps it was more a matter for the censure of the church than the condemnation of the Court. Round II ended in another draw.

If only Roger Williams would be quiet and content, read his Bible and pray with his fellows, and lead a godly and sober

Christian life—if only. The Court had met in March; by April, Williams was at it again, and this time more was at stake than just veils and flags. All male inhabitants sixteen years of age and above were required to take an oath of loyalty to the governor and all other duly elected or appointed officials, the oath concluding (in the fashion of the day) with the words "so help me God." Fine for church members to take such an oath, said Williams, but for the unbeliever to be required to repeat such words was a sacrilege. "A magistrate," Williams declared, "ought not to tender an oath to an unregenerate man," for that would be to cause him "to take the name of God in vain." Well, I never thought about that, might have been the reply of a John Winthrop or a John Endecott or a thousand magistrates in England. Well, think about it then, Williams might have replied, for you are toying with the human conscience as with a frivolous plaything.

But was not Williams treating the civil order as a mere convenience, or even a superfluity? Without the solemn commitment of every male resident to obey the laws and officers of the General Court, what security did government have? God must be invoked as the witness to all agreements and contracts, to all testimonies and treaties, and whether the parties to such agreements were regenerate or unregenerate was wholly beside the point. Or was it? Only if consciences were beside the point. Only if form and ceremonies counted for more than faith and the devout heart. Only if one had difficulty discerning a difference between the world and the church. Many had just such difficulty, Williams concluded, as people prayed with Christians and non-Christians alike and took communion with whomever they would. (Winthrop even asserted that Williams carried his penchant for purity so far as to refuse to take communion with any but his own wife.) Let the magistrate deal with citizens as members of a civil society only, Williams pleaded, and let the church keep itself unspotted from the world.

Tensions mounted as Boston feared that Salem would be turned into a seedbed of Separatism—or worse. Fears were aggravated when the Salem church appointed Williams its official Teaching Elder in the summer of 1635. Now the nature of ecclesiastical government no less than civil government was threatened in New England. Public opinion in and around Boston, and even to a degree in Salem, was turning against Williams, who, whenever he won a compromise on one point, immediately pressed for surrender on several more. So he was summoned once again, on July 8, to the General Court. There, confronted by both clergy and magistrates, Williams was told that his opinions were "erroneous and very dangerous," and that he should be removed from his church office. The Court had no authority to remove him from that office, but the authority they did have was even better. The town of Salem had petitioned the Court for a grant of land on Marblehead Neck. Under the circumstances—*all* the circumstances—the Court found it expedient to deny the request until the church, so ill-advised as to elevate Williams to high office, came to its senses. Round III, while not decisive, suggested that the Court was getting ready for a showdown.

The Court's high-handedness was most egregious, argued Williams and several of his fellow members as well, not allowing for even a token recognition of the congregational autonomy of the Salem church. The congregation protested to the other churches in the colony against this violation of their liberty, but the elders of those churches responded by refusing to read the Salem letter to their own membership. The Court, for its part, resolved not even to seat the deputies from Salem at its next meeting. At least for the moment, Williams had his church with him as he, on their behalf, wrote in late July to protest such totally arbitrary and autocratic behavior.

Congregations owed each other, at the very least, mutual respect, if not Christian love, Williams observed. Any local church may rightly decide when it is most convenient to present a letter from others "dear and well beloved in Christ," "but wholly to conceal or suppress the letters of the church we yet see not" as within their prerogative. The early Christian church heard letters from the apostles and from other communities

(Acts 15:30) and so, said the Salem church, the church in Boston should deal with us. The "multitude," as the Bible says, deserve to be informed, not just the magistrates or the clergy. Gathered together as the body of Christ, the church "shall find a wisdom greater than theirs in the midst among them, even Jesus Christ who is himself made their wisdom." But by not even presenting our letters, you have cut yourself off from that possibility, Williams and the Salem church declared. Furthermore, you find us guilty without a hearing: "we must needs profess our exceeding grief that a church of Christ shall undergo a punishment before [assembled], be punished (if there were due cause) before exhorted to repentance in a rule to Christ." The Salem congregation did not expect the Boston church to act like the General Court; they sought compassion and understanding, but instead of bread, they received a stone.

On both sides, positions hardened in August and September. Williams fell ill, but was thereby neither softened nor silenced. He urged the Salem congregation to separate itself entirely from all other churches in the Bay Colony, an action so extreme, so drastic, that few were prepared to go along with him. And if Williams did not hesitate to issue ultimatums, neither did the General Court. Weary of sparring and temporizing, the Court by October prepared for a knockout blow. The tough-minded decision was made easier by the realization that Roger Williams had few remaining defenders—no longer any support from the Plymouth Colony, no longer the backing of a united fellowship in Salem, no more interventions now by John Cotton trying to explain away or mitigate the radical's intemperate outbursts. On October 8 Roger Williams stood once more before the bar of Massachusetts justice, and he stood alone.

The authorities never lacked for evidence. Williams kept speaking, kept writing letters against the magistrates and against the churches, kept inventing new ways to challenge and unnerve. The young colony, a mere five years old, was still on trial in its own mind, and even more in the mind of authorities back home. One could hardly expect that it would once again deal gently with a man who had cast doubt on nearly everything that Massachusetts held dear: its charter, its General Court, its churches, its land, and most of all its promise. Williams would be given the opportunity to recant, the further opportunity to be persuaded by the arguments of the learned Thomas Hooker (founder of Connecticut), and a last night for final reflection and searching of soul. From the perspective of the magistrate, every leniency was shown. From the perspective of the Separatist, conscience could not be defiled.

When the Court reconvened the next morning to take care of many matters involved in running a colony, the magistrates learned that Williams had not been moved, either by their leniency or by Hooker's fluency. No room for maneuver remained. Williams must be cut off from the civil order that he seemed determined to weaken or destroy; he must be cast out from their midst. "Whereas Mr. Roger Williams, one of the elders of the church at Salem, hath broached & divulged diverse new & dangerous opinions," the Court began, and whereas he had questioned and defamed both magisterial and clerical authority, and whereas he maintained his objectionable opinions without hint of repentance or retraction, "it is therefore ordered, that the said Mr. Williams shall depart out of this jurisdiction within six weeks." If he failed to leave within that allotted time, the Court would forcefully eject him, prohibiting him from ever returning to Massachusetts Bay without their specific permission. Round IV belonged to the Court.

BATTLING WITH JOHN COTTON—AND WITH HISTORY

It all seemed quite clear. The fact is, however, that few episodes in colonial American history have been more vigorously debated, more passionately defended or decried. The major protagonists, John Cotton and Roger Williams, continued to fan the flames of public controversy until Cotton's death in 1652, and they did not argue alone. Massachusetts historians came to

Cotton's defense along with political conservatives and Puritan apologists everywhere. Rhode Island historians came to Williams' defense along with political radicals and Baptist apologists everywhere. One judicial action on one October morning reverberated from Boston to London and back again, echoed from the seventeenth century to the twentieth, and will most probably continue to echo well beyond. The fundamentals of the dispute had moved far beyond veils and flags.

Soon after the Court's sentence was handed down, Cotton and Williams exchanged several letters. Most of this correspondence has unfortunately been lost, but one long letter of Cotton's (written early in 1636) has survived, along with Williams' well-considered and even more lengthy reply. Each man claimed respect for the person of the other, though disagreeing sharply with the other's view. Each man appealed to the Bible for support of his position, and each understood himself to grasp the fullest expression of the Protestant Reformation and the Puritan exodus from England. Each man also blamed the other for the climactic events of October 9.

The two adversaries did agree, however, on the principal charges brought against Williams. First, said Cotton, "that we have not our Land by Patent from the King, but that the Natives are the true owners of it, and that we ought to repent of such a receiving it by Patent." The second charge related to Williams' stubborn insistence that "a wicked person" should not be called upon to take an oath or to join in a prayer since these were "actions of God's Worship." Third, that Puritans in New England should not participate in the services of worship of the national church in Old England. And fourth, Cotton concluded, "that the Civil Magistrate's power extends only to the Bodies and Goods, and outward state of men." That was a pretty good summary, Williams acknowledged, regretting only that Cotton and his peers could not see the full implications of each of these four points.

Holding such views, Williams had only himself to blame for the banishment, Cotton declared. "You overheated yourself

39

in reasoning and disputing against the light" of God's truth, finding fault everywhere except where it ought to have been found: in yourself. In short, the General Court did not banish you, Mr. Williams; you banished yourself. Well, in some sense you may be right, Williams conceded. If "Mr. Cotton mean my own voluntary withdrawing from those Churches resolved to continue in those evils, and persecuting the witnesses of the Lord presenting light unto them," then, yes, it was my own decision. Indeed, added Williams, may "the act of the Lord Jesus sounding forth in me (a poor Ram's horn) the blast" manage at length to "cast down the strength and confidence of those" who substitute the inventions of men for the true ordinances of God.

If, on the other hand, John Cotton meant that the civil banishment "from their common earth and air" was self-inflicted, then, said Williams, "I . . . observe with grief the language of the Dragon in a lamb's lips." This was the same sort of drivel used against all the martyrs of all the ages: "it is your schism, heresy, obstinacy" that is responsible, and "the Devil hath deceived thee." Besides all this, Cotton spoke of the civil banishment as though it were the equivalent of an expulsion from the church. How strange he should talk this way, "except he silently confess that the frame or constitution of their Churches is but implicitly National." You've made my point, Mr. Cotton, and I thank you: politics and religion have become one in Massachusetts, as Christendom takes the place of Christianity. Otherwise, Williams might have been excommunicated from the Salem church but still have been permitted to live in Massachusetts Bay. But no: "the Commonweal and Church is yet but one, and he that is banished from the one, must necessarily be banished from the other also."

To make his case that Roger Williams had deluded himself and had permitted the Devil to deceive him, John Cotton noted that "it is no new thing with Satan to transform himself into an Angel of light, and to cheer the soul with false peace, and with flashes of counterfeit consolation." Consider, for example, said Cotton, the case of John Smyth, founder of the English Baptists,

40

who on his deathbed spoke of the great consolations of Jesus ministering to him. Yet, this must have been Satan, not Christ, for one has only to look at "the gross and damnable Armini- anism and Enthusiasm delivered in the confession of his faith." Well, Williams responded, "although I knew him not," many have testified that "he was a man fearing God, and I am sure Mr. Cotton hath made some use of those principles and arguments on which Mr. Smyth and others" built their case against the national church. In fact, Williams added, even Satan himself would be forced to admit that "multitudes of God's Witnesses (reproached under the name of Brownists and Anabaptists) have kept themselves from the errors of the wicked, and grow in grace and knowledge of the Lord Jesus." But, Williams gra- ciously allowed, "I will not make odious and envious compari- sons."

Williams' great problem, Cotton contended, was that fa- miliar "holier than thou" complex: Williams would be purer than anyone else, his church more separate than any other church, his principles more faithfully adhered to than by any since the days of the apostles. Cotton's great problem, Williams contended, was that having begun a process of separation from the Church of England, he stopped halfway; he preferred a path of moderation, a "middle walking," to a path of perfect faithful- ness. On both sides, the language turned even stronger.

John Cotton seized the gauntlet thrown down. "Instead of halting between Christ and Antichrist," as Williams had charged, "we conceive the Lord hath guided us to walk with an even foot between two extremes." On the one hand, "we neither defile ourselves with the remnant of pollutions in other Churches," nor do we on the other hand condemn all other churches that have not rid themselves of every remaining taint of false worship. "This moderation," said Cotton, "we see no cause to repent of." But Roger Williams, Cotton scornfully ob- served, thinks that radical surgery, or better yet, butchery, is the only cure for every problem. He would "heal every sore in a member with no other medicine but abscission from the body."

Only the most brutal physician would so treat the body of Christ, his church.

Only the most compromising churchman, Williams shot back, would claim that he could walk with an even foot between two extremes. John Cotton's "practice in gathering of Churches seems to say he must separate; and yet he professeth there are but some remnants of pollution amongst them [from] which he dares not separate." Can one have his cake and eat it too? As for the charge of surgery or butchery, Williams said he did not advocate separation for "every sore of infirmity or ignorance." But when one sees "an Ulcer or Gangrene of Obstinacy" that is about to destroy the health of the whole, then indeed one may, one must separate from that church. "Conscientiously and peaceably to separate from a spiritual communion of a Church" hardly deserves the name of butchery, but if one wants to use that word, it may be more aptly applied to what happened on October 9 in Boston—"to cut off persons, them and theirs, branch and root, from any civil being in their territories." And to do so for what reason? Only "because their consciences dare not bow down to any worship, but what they believe the Lord Jesus appointed."

And now one arrives at "the sum of my Controversy with Mr. Cotton": whether or not "that false Worshiping of the true God be not only a spiritual guilt liable to God's sentence and plagues, but also an habit, frequently compared in the Prophets and Revelation 17 to a spirit and disposition of spiritual drunkenness and whoredom, a soul sleep and a soul sickness." From that sound spiritual sleep Williams would awaken Cotton and all others. Those very grounds upon which the Puritans opposed the rule of bishops, the required conformity to the Book of Common Prayer, and the "prostitution of the Ordinances of Christ to the ungodly"—those same principles require a continued, consistent separation "of holy from unholy, penitent from impenitent, godly from ungodly." To act in any other way, said Williams, would be to attempt "to raise the form of a square house upon the Keel of a Ship." Whatever strange structure would result from this clumsy carpentry, of one thing we can be sure: it "will never prove a soul saving Ark or Church of Christ Jesus, according to the Pattern."

Mr. Cotton, would he only recognize it, already walks in the way of separation, Williams noted. "Of what matter do they profess to constitute their Churches, but of true godly persons? In what form do they cast this matter, but by a voluntary uniting, or adding of such godly persons whom they carefully examine, and cause to make a public confession of sin, and profession of their knowledge and grace in Christ?" And so it should be. But this is not the way that England's national church operates, as Cotton recognizes, since immigrants who attempt to establish an Anglican church in Massachusetts are systematically suppressed. Separation has already occurred, Mr. Cotton; therefore, admit it, glory in it, pursue it. Rising to rhetorical heights, Williams proclaimed that the essential difference between the church and the world must never be confounded or muddled. When God's people open "a gap in the hedge or wall of Separation between the Garden of the Church and the Wilderness of the world, God hath ever broke down the wall itself . . . and made his Garden a Wilderness, as at this day." The only way to set things right is carefully, earnestly to clean out that garden and rebuild that wall. If God is ever pleased "to restore his Garden and Paradise again, it must of necessity be walled in peculiarly unto himself from the world." And that, Mr. Cotton, is the sum of the controversy between us: you have allowed the world to invade and corrupt the church.

While all these words may sound like a heavy cannonade, they were merely the opening salvo. Others, especially contemporary Massachusetts historians, quickly joined in the battle. Nathaniel Ward (the "simple cobbler") defended his colony against the charge that it denied religious liberty. Not so, said Ward: "all Familists, Antinomians, Anabaptists, and other Enthusiasts shall have free Liberty to keep away from us." The Devil, if he had his "free option," would wish nothing more than the "liberty to enfranchise all false Religions." "Polypiety,"

43

Ward added, "is the greatest impiety in the World." Does one wish to speak of liberty of conscience? Ward would inform his readers of what such consisted: it was the liberty "to contend earnestly for the Truth; to preserve unity of Spirit, Faith, ordinances, to be all like minded, of one accord." Any commonwealth that dared to offer a full liberty in matters of religion would then be obliged to offer a full liberty in morality, "else the Fiddle will be out of tune, and some of the strings crack."

William Hubbard, a pastor in Ipswich and author of *A General History of New England,* reported that "the more judicious sort of Christians," both in Old England and New, regarded Williams "as a man of a very self-conceited, unquiet, turbulent, and uncharitable spirit." Some even called him "divinely mad." Noting "the heady unruliness of his Spirit, and the incorrigibleness thereof," Hubbard likened Roger Williams to "a vessel that carries too high a sail" and is therefore "apt to overset in the stream, and ruin those that are embarked with him." Another historian, Nathaniel Morton of Plymouth, author of *New Englands Memoriall,* found Hubbard's views so congenial that he quoted them at great length in order that history might serve up its clear moral. "This much was thought to be inserted," Morton wrote, "concerning the great and lamentable Apostacy of Mr. Williams that it may be a Warning to take heed of a gradual declining from, and forsaking the Churches of Christ and Ordinances of God in them." Williams had become a byword and a sign, warning the unsuspecting traveler of the path that led to sure destruction. His was a *Pilgrim's Progress* in reverse, ending up not in the Celestial City but mired forever in a Slough of Despond. Which was another way of saying that Williams founded Rhode Island.

A WINTER'S WILDERNESS

When in ͨ ᵕ ᵕ of 1635 the Court passed its sentence of banishment against Roger Williams, officialdom granted him six weeks in which to put his affairs in order and prepare himself and his family (child number two was born that very month) for the required departure. The Court's indulgence contained a stern proviso: that during this period of time, Williams was not to go about drawing others to his dangerous opinions. Apparently, Williams kept his silence so far as public preaching was concerned, but those calling at his home heard opinions as strong as before. A vow of silence would never have come easily for Williams, even if voluntarily offered; imposed from the outside, it was sure to be broken.

Within a month Boston heard that the Salem separatist still talked, still entertained "company in his house," still maintained even "such points as he had been censured for." The Court summoned the voluble preacher to appear before it, but Williams begged off on the grounds of illness. Very well, we will come to you, said the Court, or we will see that, under escort, you are brought to us. In January the Court determined that Williams must be sent back to England forthwith. Every additional day that he remained in the Bay Colony was a day of increased danger and disturbance to the civil order. Or, as Cotton later noted, the magistrates decided that a winter voyage out of the country was better than "a winter's spiritual plague in the Country." The Court dispatched a sea captain to Salem to bring Roger Williams back immediately so that he might be placed on "a ship then ready to depart" for England.

In Salem friends and neighbors learned of the plan in time to alert Williams. Also, more surprisingly, John Winthrop, out of friendship and that Christian charity noted aboard the *Arbella*, quietly advised him to leave the colony as expeditiously as possible. When the Court's emissaries arrived at the family home, "they found he had been gone three days before; but whither they could not learn." They could not learn "whither," for Williams himself hardly knew. All he knew was that he did not want once again to fall into the hands of the Bay authorities, nor did he want to be sent back to England to fall beneath the blows of Archbishop Laud. One other thing he knew: the way

45

things were going, he stood a better chance with the Indians than with his own countrymen.

And so in January 1636, in bitter winter, "exposed to the mercy of an howling Wilderness in Frost and Snow, &c.," Williams on foot painfully made his way out of Massachusetts, throwing himself on the mercy of the "savages"; for fourteen weeks, he reported, he knew not what bread or bed did mean. But even in the midst of such suffering, spiritual lessons could be learned.

> God makes a Path, provides a Guide,
> And feeds in Wildernesse!
> His glorious Name while breath remaines,
> O that I may confesse.
>
> Lost many a time, I have had no Guide,
> No House, but Hollow Tree!
> In stormy Winter night no Fire,
> No Food, no Company:
>
> In him I have found a House, a Bed,
> A Table, Company:
> No Cup so bitter, but's made sweet,
> When God shall Sweet'ning be.

At length Williams made his way southward, beyond the borders of the Bay Colony and of Plymouth Colony as well. When he arrived at the headwaters of Narragansett Bay, he decided to stop. Here he would occupy land only by agreement with the Indians (no patent from King Charles); here he would bring family and send for friends and neighbors; here he would name his village Providence, "in a Sense of God's merciful Providence to me in my distress." Here, most of all, he would try to erect that wall between the garden of the church and the wilderness of the world.

Actually, Williams and a few neighbors from Salem first attempted to settle on the east side of the Seekonk River, far away—they thought—from any prior English claim. But after building crude shelters and sowing seed in the springtime,

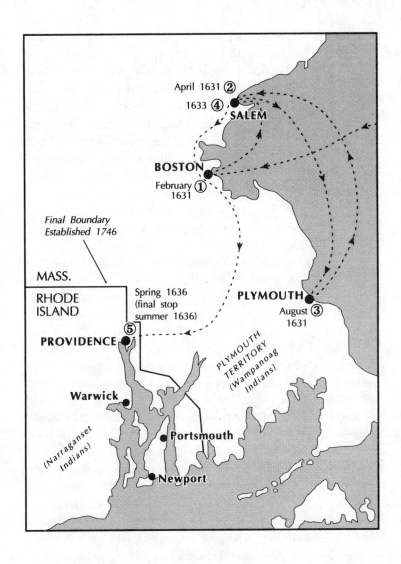

April 1631 ②
1633 ④ SALEM

BOSTON
February ①
1631

*Final Boundary
Established 1746*

MASS.

RHODE
ISLAND

Spring 1636
(final stop
summer 1636)

PROVIDENCE ⑤

Warwick

*PLYMOUTH
TERRITORY
(Wampanoag
Indians)*

PLYMOUTH
August ③
1631

*(Narraganset
Indians)*

Portsmouth

Newport

The Migrations of Roger Williams in New England

Williams heard from his "ancient friend" Edward Winslow, governor of the Plymouth Colony at this time. Winslow "lovingly advised me (since I was fallen into the edge of their bounds, and they were loath to displease the Bay) to remove but to the other side of the water." Then, Winslow added, Roger Williams would have the whole country free before him, and they all could "be loving neighbors together." Plymouth, of course, had not formally exiled Williams, though now, said Williams, he was "as good as banished" by that colony as well. Yet, when a Pokanoket Indian (Massasoit) later complained to Plymouth that he held title to land across the Seekonk where Williams had settled, the colony declared that they would not allow Williams to be uprooted once more. "I should not be molested and tossed up and down again," Williams reported, "while they had Breath in their Bodies."

So Williams and his friends found rest across the river and around a bend, coming up to the very top of Narragansett Bay. Here, near a "sweet spring," Williams would build his own house, lay out lots for his fellow colonists, and encourage the planting once more of crops before winter set in. The hardness of that first year was mitigated chiefly by the valuable contacts that Williams had already established with the Indians. He had traded with them, lived with them, respected them, and earned their trust. Now they came to his aid.

Narraganset sachems Canonicus and Miantonomo first deeded the land to Williams, then along with other Narragansets and Wampanoags assisted the early settlers by offering seed and sometimes food as well. For hoes and axes and other necessities, Williams found it necessary to mortgage his house in Salem; he also began building a house just up from that sweet spring along the steep hillside extending to the east, hoping that by the following spring his wife and small children could join him, along with still more friends from Salem or Dorchester. At least eight householders were present in 1637, and within the next couple of years two dozen more arrived.

By 1638 it seemed advisable to incorporate the township,

48

the agreement carefully noting that the laws of the town extended to "civil things" only. By 1640, urbanization had proceeded to a point where not every issue could be decided by a
general town meeting. Thirty-seven "masters of families" determined that four arbitrators should be chosen to act in their
behalf in routine matters. Twelve articles of agreement were
drawn up, the second one reading (in part), "We agree, As
formerly hath been the liberties of the Town, so Still to hold forth
Liberty of Conscience." Roger Williams, whose signature was
appended to the twelve articles, must have taken some small
satisfaction in so simple, so forthright, so costly a declaration.

Even though John Winthrop had participated in that crucial vote against Roger Williams, the two men maintained a
friendship and a correspondence for a decade following the
exile. They inquired after the health of each other's families, they
joined in a cattle-raising enterprise on Prudence Island (in Narragansett Bay), and they addressed each other in terms of genuine respect. Williams looked to Winthrop for assistance in
maintaining some contact with the larger Puritan world, both in
England and in Massachusetts. Winthrop looked to Williams for
assistance in dealing with the Indians and in keeping him informed about tribal movements or intentions.

Soon after the founding of Providence, Williams wrote to
the governor of Massachusetts inquiring, in effect, How does
one run a colony anyway? It was a pressing question, since no
joint-stock company arranged for this settlement, no charter laid
down its bounds or authority, no sermon aboard the *Arbella*
gave it a star to steer by. "Much honored Sir," Williams wrote
to Winthrop in the summer of 1636, "the Condition of myself
and those few families here planting with me, you know full
well. We have no patent," nor at this stage of our development
does it seem proper to have governors or magistrates to rule
over us. At the moment, therefore, "the masters of Families have
ordinarily met once a fortnight and consulted about our common peace, watch, and planting." For the time being, mutual
consent and neighborly love seemed to work, but Williams

knew this would not last indefinitely. Some more formal arrangements or agreements would need to be made, and in that connection "I shall humbly crave your help." Precisely what advice Winthrop offered is not known, since his answer has not survived. What is known, however, is that Williams did proceed, on terms of equality among the householders, to arrive at the agreements noted above.

INDIANS AND ANTINOMIANS

If Williams craved the help of Winthrop, the latter needed Williams' assistance against the powerful Pequots, the very name in Algonquian meaning "destroyer." These Indians, not native to New England, moved in the sixteenth century from the upper Hudson River area into the lower Connecticut River Valley. The migration was more that of a conquering army whose brutality alienated other Indian groups, just as the Pequots in the 1630s alienated both the Dutch and the English. By 1636 tensions between the Pequots and the English mounted as stories of atrocities aggravated the fear of settlers, especially those moving into the Connecticut Valley. Massachusetts Bay prepared for attack, even as the Pequots (Williams reported to Winthrop) "hear of your preparations" and began arming themselves with guns as well as planning to use a "witch" that would "sink the pinnaces by diving under water and making holes."

English fears multiplied many times over when rumors spread that the Pequots were trying to form an alliance with the Narragansets, thus uniting the two most powerful tribes against colonization in New England. Such an alliance must, at all cost, be prevented. Swallowing its pride, the General Court hurriedly wrote to Williams, beseeching him "to use my utmost and Speediest Endeavors to break and hinder the League labored for by the Pequots." In October 1636 Williams, alone in a canoe, rowed "30 miles in great Seas, every minute in hazard of Life," to meet with the Narraganset sachems, who were also consulting with Pequot emissaries at that time. Williams, admittedly ill at ease in the presence of the Pequots, "whose Hands and Arms (me thought) reeked with the blood of my Countrymen murdered and massacred by them," nonetheless persisted in his own negotiations for three days and nights. His victory was total. He not only persuaded the Narragansets not to join in with the Pequots, but on the contrary to ally themselves with the English. Williams also interceded with lesser tribes, volunteering to march farther into the interior. He was persuaded, however, that he could be of more use back in Providence, "as an Agent between the Bay and the Army" and also as an "Interpreter and Intelligencer."

Williams' service in these critical negotiations was so valuable that Massachusetts even debated, Williams later reported, "whether or no I had not Merited not only to be recalled from Banishment, but also to be honored with some Remark of Favor." But while Williams had friends in the Bay Colony, he also had enemies, and the General Court took no action in this regard. On other matters, however, the General Court, assisted by Plymouth and Connecticut (founded in 1635), took strong action—against the Pequots. In 1637 full-scale war broke out, New England's first serious engagement against the Indians. A devastating attack on a Pequot fort near the Mystic River in late May broke the back of Pequot military might. Some of their leaders escaped, and Williams urged Winthrop to see that "Pursuit be continued" without delay. Other battles followed in July and August, with the Pequots suffering successive defeats. By the time the Pequot War formally ended in September 1638, the Pequots had been utterly destroyed as a tribal entity. English military superiority had been clearly established, and colonization—even in the Connecticut River valley—was set to proceed apace. Other tribal leaders could not but wonder if the fate of the Pequots was an ominous warning of what might await them all.

While carrying on its military struggle against the Pequots, Massachusetts Bay found itself deeply enmeshed in another, more familiar kind of struggle—once more against religious dissent. This time the dissent bore a burdensome label: antinomianism. The word, literally meaning "against the law," pointed to a pivotal issue in Puritan understanding of conversion. All Puritans agreed that salvation was a *gift* of God: unearned, unmerited, no recognition of or reward for righteousness in any respect. Good works had absolutely nothing to do with bringing salvation about. Once one was saved, however, "the fruits of the Spirit" or righteous living might well be the best external sign of one's being a new creature in Christ. Or, to put it another way, morality did not lead to salvation, but salvation did result in morality. On that solid theological foundation a stable and orderly society could be built. To question this intimate connection between religion and morality was to risk being branded with the dreaded name of "antinomian." Being an antinomian in New England was bad; being an antinomian in John Cotton's congregation was worse; being an antinomian female preacher was worst of all.

  Anne Hutchinson, who, with her family, had followed John Cotton from old Boston to new, praised her pastor as one who emphasized the all-powerful, all-sufficient grace of God, never hesitating to drive home the point that salvation was God's choice, not man's. What could a person do to ensure his salvation or even make it more probable? Nothing, Cotton replied. Trust in no outward ceremony or deed, Cotton warned, for all these are but "dross and dung." Everything concerning one's spiritual state originated with and was sustained by God, Cotton preached. In those gatherings of friends who came to her home to have the sermon further unfolded, Anne Hutchinson warmly endorsed and expanded upon those sentiments. Other ministers in Massachusetts might place too much emphasis on works, but not her beloved Elder Cotton. For him, as for her, grace was all; works, as the Bible said, were only "filthy rags." Since works did not bring salvation, one might well go on to argue that works had absolutely nothing to do with salvation, either before or after the spiritual new birth. The bond between religion and morality was accidental, not essential. But in going that far, one earned the unhappy label of antinomian.

Apparently Anne Hutchinson went that far. Apparently she thought her pastor had gone that far as well. As John Cotton scrambled to dissociate himself from this faithful and perhaps overly zealous member, other ministers, smarting under the charge that they preached a "covenant of works," prepared to bring formal charges against her. In May 1637 Cotton managed to substitute an informal consultation for a judicial proceeding. Anne Hutchinson spoke freely at what she thought was a friendly and private meeting. What she said was sufficiently shocking, however, that some who were present urged that she be brought to trial. In November the trial took place, with Governor John Winthrop presiding.

In addressing the court and the spectators crowded into the Cambridge meetinghouse, Winthrop listed the charges against the defendant. Like Roger Williams, she had "troubled the peace of the commonwealth and the churches," but more specifically she had said things "very prejudicial to the honor of the churches and the ministers thereof" and had persisted in holding private meetings in her home. All these things were neither "comely in the sight of God nor fitting for your sex," Winthrop added. And again, like Williams, she persisted in speaking her opinions long after having been warned against doing so. In its early phases the trial got nowhere, chiefly because the defendant was sharper than her accusers and could match Scripture with Scripture to justify what she had done and said.

At one juncture, however, Anne Hutchinson was maneuvered into declaring that she held her negative view of several ministers not on biblical grounds but on the grounds of an immediate revelation made to her. Now the issue was not simply grace versus works; Hutchinson had suddenly acquired yet another label: she had shown herself to be an "enthusiast." This terrifying tag meant not that she was overwrought or emotional but that she had the presumption to claim that God

53

spoke directly to her. Like Joan of Arc, she had heard "voices"; like Christian fanatics through the ages, she would be bound not by Bible or clergy or creed but only by her private revelation. Against this horror, the court almost as one shrank, and against this latest troubler, the court would quickly act. "The revelation she brings forth is delusion," Winthrop declared, and "the danger of her course among us . . . is not to be suffered." Therefore (and Roger Williams, tried in similar circumstances just two years before, could no doubt have predicted what was coming), "she shall be banished out of our liberties and imprisoned till she be sent away." Four months later, she was also excommunicated from her church in Boston.

Banished, but to what place of refuge? One year before, Roger Williams had indicated that his new settlement would be open to the destitute, especially with respect to conscience. Those who lacked the power or the wealth to maintain their spiritual independence would be welcomed in Providence, or some nearby place out of Massachusetts' bounds. Like Williams, Anne Hutchinson had followers—indeed, even more than he. In March 1638 over eighty householders, still in Boston, signed a civil compact "solemnly in the presence of Jehovah [incorporating] ourselves into a Body Politic, & as he shall help will submit our persons, lives, and estates unto our Lord Jesus Christ, the King of Kings." That accomplished, the group began its search for their place of refuge. With Roger Williams' help, they fixed on the largest island in Narragansett Bay, called Aquidneck or sometimes simply Rhode Island. On the northern end of the island, the Hutchinsonians founded a town later called Portsmouth, while at the southern end the even more significant town of Newport was created the following year. By 1639 Williams' colony had three towns: Providence, Portsmouth, and Newport, and soon would have a fourth, Warwick. Religious dissent played a significant part there as well.

Samuel Gorton, like Williams, settled for a time in Plymouth soon after his 1636 arrival in New England. There he, too, was found to be a man of singular opinions, a danger to the peace and stability of that colony. Ordered out of that long-suffering Pilgrim colony in 1638, Gorton determined to throw his lot in with the Hutchinsonians who were settling at Portsmouth. Even there, however, his contempt for all authority (ecclesiastical and civil) and his emphasis upon the indwelling of the Holy Spirit in all believers (a point that Quakers just a few years later would stress even more strongly) made him a difficult member of any community. Emphasizing the full equality of the sexes, the full equality of family members, the equal right of all to govern, and the equal right of all to refuse to be governed, Gorton threw his weight against first this faction, then another, soon finding himself rejected by all. When officials tried to contain him, he responded by calling them "asses." Eventually, he was ordered to jail, whipped, and at last banished from the entire island, from Portsmouth to Newport.

By early 1641 he was in Providence, where surely he would be welcomed as a sincere searcher after truth. Williams' letter to Winthrop in March of that year suggests how warm the welcome was. "Master Gorton, having foully abused high and low at Aquidneck," Williams wrote, "is now bewitching and bemadding poor Providence." Gorton rejected all external ordinances of the church, questioned every exercise of civil authority (such as that of the four Providence arbitrators appointed in 1640), and plunged into the midst of bitter land disputes that already had the Providence settlers arrayed against each other. Williams strongly implied that if Gorton stayed, he would leave—taking up residence perhaps on one of the small empty islands in the bay where no one else was around to fight or fuss.

It was Gorton, however, who left. Together with his followers (when he wasn't on the attack, he could be quite personable), he occupied a large tract of land south of Providence to which the name Warwick was later given. His troubles were far from over, however. Gorton had to fight off Indian claims to the land, then Massachusetts claims, and finally a force of forty men from the Bay Colony who carried him and others to Massachusetts for trial on the grounds of resisting arrest, condemning the magistrates, and perpetrating blasphemy. No doubt more charges could have been added, for Gorton, like Williams, kept his enemies well supplied with evidence to be used against him. In 1643 Gorton and several others narrowly escaped a death sentence in Boston (it failed by only two votes); instead, each man was forced to wear "a great iron chain bolted fast to his leg, and in this condition to get his living by his labor, or starve." Massachusetts citizens were strictly forbidden to extend any charity to the Gortonites. Nor did the story of Samuel Gorton end there. Yet he recognized, as did Roger Williams and many others, that whatever else might be done or said or believed in Rhode Island, no one was secure until land titles rested on some better guarantee than had yet been found.

When Gorton first appeared in Providence, Roger Williams had already joined with twenty other men and women in establishing in 1638 the first church in America of the Baptist (or as the Bay Colony much preferred to say, Anabaptist) persuasion. The distinguishing feature of such a church was that it rejected infant baptism and embraced adult or "believer's baptism." Having come to the conclusion that baptism made sense only when preceded by a voluntary declaration of faith, Williams appointed one of the twenty to baptize him, and then he proceeded to baptize that member and the remainder of the group. After all, he had long been charged with being sympathetic to "Anabaptists" who rejected all civil interference in church affairs and who insisted on a total voluntarism in matters of religion. He had also sprung to the defense of English Baptists and would for years ahead come to the defense of the struggling knots of Baptists in Rhode Island and elsewhere. So for him personally to participate in the formation of a Baptist church in his own town of Providence made perfect sense—at least for a time.

On the island of Aquidneck, meanwhile, one of the men who helped to found the town of Newport in 1639, John Clarke, had already won Williams' attention and admiration. Clarke, who had emigrated to Massachusetts in November 1637, the very month of Anne Hutchinson's trial, reported that he "was no sooner on shore, but there appeared to me differences among them touching the covenants." Some, he noted, pressed hard for the "Covenant of works," while others argued passionately for the "Covenant of grace that was established upon better promises." Tipping his hand as to where his own sympathies lay, Clarke, after conferring with Williams and with elders in Plymouth, decided to join the Hutchinsonians in their ambitious settlement on that large island. A clergyman and physician, Clarke gathered a church in Newport about the time that Williams gathered his church in Providence. By 1644, Clarke's church was clearly a Baptist (that is, a baptizing) church, assuming for a time an even more central role in the life of that infant denomination. In the 1640s and far beyond, Clarke and Williams shared in significant undertakings on behalf of Rhode Island and on behalf of liberty of conscience.

Though Williams was constantly occupied (and harassed) by the innumerable details of governance in Providence, he found time to establish a trading post, perhaps as early as 1637, among the Narragansets well to the south of Providence (near the present town of Wickford, Rhode Island). Here he worked to recoup some of his losses in moving and being moved about; here he also kept up his observations of Indian life, mixed with Dutch as well as English traders (he had learned Dutch as a youth in London), resisted the financial temptation to sell either liquor or guns to the Indians (as the Dutch did), and found some measure of quietness and peace away from the quarrels in town. Some of his family occasionally stayed with him there as well, a family that continued to grow as Mary Williams gave birth to a son in 1638, a daughter in 1640, and more sons in 1642 and late 1643. That raised the total to six children—four sons and two daughters.

By 1643 Williams also felt that he could no longer postpone yet another move, although this one would be temporary. He was compelled to go to London in order to secure, first, a royal charter for his much-besieged colony and, second, a printer willing to give voice to his much-misunderstood positions. Boston not only refused to print any of Williams' writings, but it would not even suspend the banishment long enough to allow him to traverse Massachusetts in order to board a ship for London. So in March he traveled to New Amsterdam (later New York City), where he was free to take passage to England. As his ship pulled away from the dock, he witnessed dramatic evidence of the warfare then being waged between the Dutch and the Mohawks. "Mine eyes saw their flames at the Town's end," he later reported, "and the Flights and Hurries of Men, Women, and Children," many of whom were seeking passage back to Holland. Unhappily, among the victims of the Mohawk attack on Long Island were Anne Hutchinson and several of her children, recently removed from Aquidneck Island.

3 Exile in London

Roger Williams left a country embroiled over religion to arrive at one in even greater turmoil. King Charles had fled London, Archbishop Laud had been thrown into the Tower, and the whole country had been plunged into civil war. When Williams appeared on the scene in the summer of 1643, the forces of a Puritan Parliament (the Roundheads) had been at war with the forces of a beleaguered king (the Cavaliers or Royalists) for almost a year. Initial indecisive battles only stiffened the resolve of both sides, a majority of Parliament in June 1643 deciding that it no longer owed any loyalty whatsoever to the king. On July 1 the Westminster Assembly held the first of its nearly twelve hundred meetings aimed at reforming religion in England; deputies from Scotland, twenty members of the House of Commons, and 121 clergymen spent five and one-half years trying to fashion some new and agreeable form of church government. Nothing stable, nothing certain, nothing beyond question or challenge—Roger Williams' very own element.

A CHARTER FOR RHODE ISLAND

From one point of view, the moment was not propitious for seeking favors, such as a patent or charter for a minor colony (if it really was a colony) far away. Far more pressing matters—such as saving the kingdom—commanded the attention of Royalist and Roundhead alike. The king had his army; Parliament, which had to raise one, selected Oliver Cromwell, who, as a Puritan reformer, dedicated his army to rigid discipline and serious religion. Cromwell had a countryside to win over (and eventually a king to capture); Parliament had a government to run (and eventually a nation to heal). Affairs of state crowded the agenda—momentous and demanding affairs. What might be happening in or around Narragansett Bay would simply have to wait. Williams, though an impulsive man, did on occasion know how to wait. In this instance, his restless energies were put to use in helping provide wood for chilled Londoners suffering from a coal strike at Newcastle.

From another perspective, however, Williams had come at a good time to press the case of Rhode Island. England's religious confusion offered openings that would not have existed when Charles and Laud ruled all. The air was filled with talk of religious toleration, and Cromwell's army was filled with examples of religious diversity. Suddenly those who had been the powerful insiders—Anglicans and monarchists—were on the outside, while those more accustomed to looking on from afar—Presbyterians and Independents—were running the show. And in addition to receiving the benefits of that major upheaval, Roger Williams was able to call on special friends who, now in 1643-1644, held key positions that had been denied them just a year or two before. And even those who did not hold major offices had a new capacity to shape the opinions of the power brokers and of the public at large.

Among the sturdiest of those friends was Henry Vane, his friendship with Williams sealed not only by similar religious opinions but also by the happy coincidence that he, too, had been exiled from Massachusetts. Vane had gone to Massachusetts in 1635 and in less than a year had been elected governor, when he was still only twenty-three years old. But what might have seemed the beginning of a great career in the Bay Colony was cut short when the following year he was voted out of office, and within a few months (August 1637) returned to England. His fall from favor resulted from his association with the Antinomian Party, the Winthrop forces—as we have seen—moving against all so afflicted in 1637. Williams first met Vane soon after he arrived in Massachusetts, just weeks before the Court banished him in October 1635. From Rhode Island Williams maintained contact with the young Englishman, especially during Vane's governorship and his own involvement with the Pequots.

So here they were in London, old friends (Vane now all of thirty years of age), nursing old wounds, and preparing to strike blows for free religion that they had been prevented from striking heretofore. Soon after arriving in London, Williams heard Vane deliver a "heavenly speech" to Parliament urging that all the labors of godly and sober persons—all who "profess to seek God" and "desire to see light"—be allowed to flourish. Similar words had been heard in Rhode Island and would often be heard again. As the fortunes of Vane (actually Sir Henry Vane) continued to rise in the 1640s and fifties, those of Williams rose correspondingly.

But there were other friends as well: Sir William Masham, for example, who had befriended Williams before he left for the New World; Sir Thomas Barrington, who would soon die, but not before assisting Williams; and Sir Robert Rich, Earl of Warwick, who in November 1643 was placed in charge of colonial affairs. All of these political allies would be critical for Williams (against the representatives of Massachusetts and Connecticut), who hoped to obtain clear title to land that the Puritan colonies wanted for their own. And Williams also had a literary friend— John Milton. Known chiefly for his sustained poetic masterpieces, Milton in the 1640s had plunged into the same turbulent

61

waters surrounding Williams. And he had plunged in on behalf of the right side—namely, civil and religious liberty. Williams and Milton grew up in London not far from each other, attended parish churches near each other, and studied at Cambridge during the same years; yet the surviving evidence suggests that their personal contacts were few. Milton did recommend his printer to Williams, and Williams did later instruct Milton in Dutch as Milton refreshed Williams' knowledge of Greek, Hebrew, and Latin. And in 1644 both men published their major treatises dedicated to liberty: for Milton, freedom of the press, and for Williams, freedom of conscience.

With such friends, Williams in early 1644 dared to press forward with his petition for a charter. He cultivated other members of Parliament, he wooed the eighteen commissioners who had the actual power of decision, he attended sessions of the Westminster Assembly to determine what was uppermost on people's minds, and—most difficult of all—he held his peace on other issues burning in his breast. To his surprise, he found in many of his contacts that his name was known, not as the Massachusetts exile or Providence patriarch, but as the author of a fascinating little book on Indians. Having spent the months at sea in 1643 preparing his manuscript for the printer, he had been ready to deliver *A Key into the Language of America* into the hands of the man Milton had recommended, Gregory Dexter. By September the book was out, and Londoners were intrigued. Everything about the American Indian fascinated them, certainly in the days since Pocahontas had been received by royalty nearly thirty years before. Williams' book told them much more than they had previously known, and he managed to convey his information in a way that transcended political and religious differences. Had Williams planned to assure himself an entrée into the polite circles of society, he could have done no better than to have this as his first published book. This *Key* opened more doors than he knew.

By March of 1644 the commissioners were prepared to vote on the humble application on behalf of Providence Plantations.

Williams still had opponents, if not enemies, but their number proved insufficient to block his cause. With a margin of two votes, Williams won this critical victory. He now had, duly signed and sealed, his "Free Charter of Civil Incorporation and Government for the Providence Plantations in the Narragansett Bay in New England." The name Rhode Island did not appear, for only as Williams was pursuing his cause in England were the citizens on Aquidneck deciding on that as the official name for their large piece of land. Thus, the nation's smallest state came to have the longest name: the State of Rhode Island and Providence Plantations. In 1644 Williams was content with the shorter name and the stronger claim, content with an official document that would slow—though it did not stop—the predatory efforts of Massachusetts and Connecticut to carve up Rhode Island between them. Williams was also pleased that he could now unburden himself of those other matters that England needed to hear about, though the hearing might not be as favorable as that which had been given to his book on Indians.

"ERRONEOUS OPINIONS, RUINATING SCHISMS, DAMNABLE HERESIES"

With the charter safely tucked away, Williams could turn to that which in heart and mind he had never left: the question of what power properly belongs to a civil government, what power ought properly to be exercised by a church government, what liberty should be granted to the individual conscience and sincere seeker after truth, or, in Williams words, "what Precept or Pattern hath the Lord Jesus left you in his last Will and Testament?" Much of England wrestled with these and similar questions in 1644. Perhaps one recently returned from New England could be of some help. Perhaps not. When John Cotton, back in Boston, learned what Williams was up to, he expressed his astonishment at the latter's presumption. "As if New England were but an handful," Cotton observed, Williams now wanted to take on all of England and Scotland and the "choicest ornaments of [those] two populous nations." Not content to stop there, however, Williams would instruct the entire Westminster Assembly and even "the High and Honourable Court of Parliament." Such audacity was enough to take one's breath away.

Everyone had an opinion in 1644, however, no matter how ill-founded or fleeting it might be. So simply to be in fashion, if nothing more, Williams had a right to express his also. But, of course, much more than fashion was on his mind; he sought to mold what opinions he could in so unsettled and unsettling a time. When one looked at religion, the contention could not be described solely in terms of Roundheads versus Cavaliers, or even Puritans versus Anglicans. That was little more than a place to begin. For Puritans found themselves divided between Presbyterians (who dominated the Westminster Assembly) and Independents (who provided the congregational polity of New England), and both groups soon found themselves besieged by a fusillade of sectarian groups and charismatic prophesiers. The Presbyterians and the Independents were divided only on the issue of the proper nature of church government; theologically they stood together in the Calvinist tradition. Presbyterians believed in a close connection among individual churches and some authority (in the form of a synod or assembly) over those churches. Independents, on the other hand, stressed the autonomy of each congregation and worried about connections that grew too close and too "helpful." Both groups rejected bishops, but many feared that Presbyterians would, in Milton's words, create a "second tyranny," stifling freedom in preaching and printing until "Bishops and Presbyters are the same to us, both name and thing." Would the Westminster Assembly reject one kind of ecclesiastical tyranny only to substitute a somewhat more subtle form of its own?

Independents in the Assembly, though a small minority, shared Milton's concern about Presbyterian tyranny. Under the leadership of such men as Henry Vane and Oliver Cromwell, the Independents argued for a measure of toleration—though they, too, feared an uncontrolled and rampant sectarianism. Early in 1644 a group of Independents—the Five Dissenting Brethren, as they were often called—felt compelled to publish *An Apologeticall Narration* in an effort to make their position clear. These men had fled to Holland during Archbishop Laud's heavy-handed rule but maintained a keen interest in the reform of England's Church, of which they saw themselves as still a part. The point of their "Apology" was to find some middle path between Presbyterian rigidity on the one hand and sectarian madness on the other. In their argument they took hesitant steps toward religious liberty but did not embrace it.

That hesitancy deeply troubled Roger Williams. Consequently, he responded to the apology issued by the Independents with pointed interrogations, or *Queries of Highest Consideration,* presenting them "in all Humble Reverence" to the five dissenters and beyond them to the Westminster Assembly and Parliament as well. John Cotton was right: for Roger Williams New England was hardly a large enough battlefield upon which to engage the omnipresent enemy—it was but "a handful."

Williams had genuine respect for Parliament. He questioned neither the patriotism nor the sincerity of the members' religious convictions. He did question their right to control the convictions of others, however, just as Milton in his famous *Areopagetica* (also published in 1644) questioned the right of Parliament to determine what men and women should read, think, or say. Books had to be licensed before they could be printed, and if printed without a license, they could be burned— along with their authors. "Who can pass," Williams asked in a preface to Parliament, "the many Locks and Bars of any [of] the several Licensers appointed by you?" Still, Williams did get by the bars and locks, though he chose to publish his pamphlet anonymously, knowing that people in power are seldom willing to "hear any other Music but what is Known to please them."

The main section of the work consists of twelve questions, largely rhetorical, addressed to the "Five Dissenting Brethren" together with the commissioners from Scotland appointed to the

Westminster Assembly. Williams began by asking, none too gently, what biblical warrant for the Westminster Assembly could be found in the New Testament. He himself found there nothing called "Assembly of Divines"; rather, he found only the church, only the gathering of the saints, who exercised no civil power whatsoever. Nor did he find in the New Testament any office of the pope or any office that would justify Henry VIII's setting himself down "in the Pope's Chair in England as since his Successors have done."

To emphasize that most awkward point, Williams explained that he simply did not understand what biblical pattern was being followed when Parliament erected a "Spiritual Court"—namely, the Westminster Assembly. To create such a court was to elevate the temporary wisdom of 1644 into some sort of eternal truth, to subject the "heavenly Jerusalem" to the "vain uncertain and changeable Mutations of this present evil world." Should any be of such short memory as not to know what "changeable Mutations" Williams had in mind, he quickly reviewed English history from Henry to Edward, Edward to Mary, Mary to Elizabeth, then James I, Charles I, and now Parliament. And in every one of these reigns, absolute religious conformity had been required: conform first this way, then quickly the opposite way. Enforcing such conformity to one kind of worship was, said Williams, "spiritual rape." He pled that Parliament now would "never commit that rape, in forcing the consciences of all men to one Worship, which a stronger army and Sword" might in the future, as it had in the past, suddenly alter.

Plenty of precedent might be found in the Old Testament for creating laws, religious laws for a whole nation—namely, Israel. But, asked Williams, are you followers of Moses or of Christ? And if of the latter, then the obligation of Parliament or of the Assembly is to find in the New Testament "one footstep, Print or Pattern" for a "National holy Covenant, and consequently . . . a National Church." Of course, Williams' argument was assisted by the fact that the New Testament church was a persecuted church; no connection between the civil state and the outlawed church was even conceivable. Persecution was, of course, an evil, but it had the advantage of keeping the church pure. Nero, said Williams, was less the enemy of Christianity than Constantine. So he could ask legislators and divines to search the New Testament through and through, confident they would find not the least "footstep" leading to a national church. But reason no less than Scripture tells us that coercing one religion upon all is like making one suit of clothes for everyone to wear, one size shoe to fit every foot. With regard to national religion, "it seems not possible to fit it to every conscience."

Though Williams was a careful student of the Bible, studying it in both the original Hebrew and Greek, and though he relied heavily on biblical authority or precedent for many of his own sometimes eccentric views, he nonetheless recognized that the ancient book was filled with ambiguities and what he called mysteries. Once one enters upon the business of prescribing precisely what is orthodox, then one has to "solve" all these mysteries and provide the only "correct," the only state-approved interpretation. And this, of course, was impossible. "Can you clear up," Williams asked, "the mysteries of Daniel's 2300 days (Daniel 8), Daniel's 7 weeks and threescore and 2 weeks, his one week, and his half week (Daniel 9)?" No, the Westminster Assembly, attended by who cares how many divines, could not clear this up, much less could Parliament. That being the case, "we query," Williams wrote, "whether the blood of so many hundred thousand Protestants, mingled with the blood of so many hundred thousand papists" spilled since the Reformation "be not a warning to us their offspring?" Doctrinal definitions, backed by the power of the state, produce only one result: oceans and oceans of blood.

In their *Apologeticall Narration*, the five Independents had indicated that they expected more light on some of the hard questions of Christian faith. That, in Williams' opinion, was an honorable and reasonable expectation. But what was neither honorable nor reasonable was their willingness "to Persecute all others as Schismatics, Hereticks, &c., that believe they see a further Light." And again, what pattern does one find in "Christ's Book" for such persecution? It is in the nature of wolves to attack the lambs, but not in the nature of the lambs of God to attack the wolves.

Williams concluded his *Queries* not with questions but with a series of hard-hitting assertions. Writing in an almost staccato style, he in swift succession made these points. (1) The ancient nation of Israel is no pattern for any modern nation, since the shadows of Moses "vanished at the coming of the Lord Jesus." (2) Religious persecution is a violation of the Christian spirit and, beyond that, "opposite to the very tender Bowels of Humanity." (3) State-required conformity hinders the conversion of the Jews since it does not allow them "a civil life or being." (4) Religious warfare is the chief disturber of civil peace, the chief murderer of men, women, and children. (5) The soul is violated, "ravished into a dissembled Worship, which their Hearts embrace not." (6) And last, although leaders profess to seek more light, in fact they persecute and suppress those from whom new light might come. After sixteen hundred years of bloodshed, it was time for the Christian churches to forsake Moses and follow Christ.

Dominated by Presbyterians, Parliament chose not to heed Williams' concerns. Because a military alliance with Scotland was necessary to defeat the forces of King Charles, that nation's Presbyterian church model was pressed upon England. In September 1643 the Solemn League and Covenant was adopted by Parliament and the Westminster Assembly meeting in joint session, the thrust of that Covenant calling for a close conformity of England to the Church of Scotland in doctrine, discipline, and form of government. Henry Vane protested that England should be bound only by the Word of God, but others argued that, while of course this was clearly understood, nevertheless Scotland's military support was critical; if it took the Covenant to gain that support, well, it would not be the first time that politics triumphed over religion.

In the spring of 1644, when Williams' *Queries* could be found in London's bookstalls, Parliament demonstrated that it was untouched by his hard questions or his sharp answers. That body passed strict rules for observance of the Sabbath, a Puritan sabbath, with no games or sports, no trade or travel. All maypoles were to be immediately removed. Sectarianism erupted everywhere, to the consternation of both Parliament and the Assembly. Greater conformity was demanded in order to control the plague of "erroneous opinions, ruinating schisms, and damnable heresies." Preaching, like printing, had to be licensed by the state; individual congregations would not be allowed "to take up what form of [worship] service they please." Cromwell's army exemplified what had gone wrong: even Baptists were becoming captains. Cromwell, however, steadily resisted the demands for conformity among his soldiers: a free conscience made a better fighter. The rest of England, however, resisted only minimally the "second tyranny" being imposed upon them. Williams' twenty-page pamphlet, a mere musket shot, had stopped nothing; the time had come to roll out the heavy cannon.

THE BLOUDY TENENT OF PERSECUTION

In mid-July 1644 Roger Williams published *The Bloudy Tenent of Persecution, for cause of Conscience*. It has become Williams' most famous book—more from a quoting of the title than from a reading of the contents, for it is a messy book. Williams acknowledged its roughness when he later explained that these "meditations" were prepared for the printer while he was on the move, "in change of rooms or corners" in London, and even when he was out in the country gathering wood "for the supply of the poor of the City." Amid all that and fighting for a charter and anxiety about his wife and children, Williams had "been forced to gather and scatter his loose thoughts and papers." Under the best of circumstances, Williams was not a great stylist. Under these far from ideal circumstances, style suffered even more.

Even the organization of the book presents problems. Williams clearly decided that he had to get as much as possible into this book while he was still in London, since when he returned to Rhode Island he would once again be "incommunicado" so far as the larger world was concerned. So he began *The Bloudy Tenent* with an Anabaptist "letter" (part of a larger work published in 1620) together with John Cotton's response thereto (written around 1632). Each item occupied only about a half-dozen pages, setting the stage for Williams' protracted response (about one-half of the book) to Cotton. The second half of the book consists of Williams' response to a "Model of Church and Civil Power" drawn up in Salem in 1635 but not previously printed. These two lengthy responses, one to Cotton and one to the model of church order put forward by Salem (after having been advised by Boston), are presented not in straightforward logical discourse but in the form of a dialogue between "Truth" and "Peace." Religious or philosophical dialogue in the hands of a master (Plato, for example) is a joy to read. Williams was no master. Yet, somehow the message survives the medium.

Williams also included three prefaces—the first, a general foreword addressed to no one in particular; the second, a respectful address "To the Right Honorable, both Houses of the High Court of Parliament"; and the third, a few pages inviting "every Courteous Reader" to consider the gravity of the subject presented and the necessity for all ordinary Christians to stand fast in a time of extraordinary testing. In the first preface he explained that mere toleration was not a worthy goal: only freedom would suffice. And freedom was worthy of the name only if it were extended without qualification to all consciences: "Paganish, Jewish, Turkish, or Antichristian." At the conclusion of this preface, he made the startling assertion that "true civility and Christianity may both flourish" in that state or kingdom which had the courage to guarantee liberty to "diverse and contrary consciences, either of Jew or Gentile."

In his second preface Williams intensified the debate by

the audience he chose. His book was not for John Cotton alone, or for the churches in Salem or Boston, or for the five Independents: he was ready to take on Parliament itself. And his arguments to them would be drawn from religion, reason, and experience—all three testifying to the dreary fact that, even in the midst of civil war, the greatest yokes lying upon English necks were "of a spiritual and soul nature." Williams would not inquire into their private religious views, for these were indeed private, but only into their civil actions with respect to religion. His most fervent hope was that the lawmakers would not be a party to any act of violence to the consciences of its citizens. May it never be told at Rome or Oxford, Williams begged, "that the Parliament of England hath committed a greater rape, than if they had forced or ravished the bodies of all the women in the World." On occasion, Williams' message came through with all the clarity and shock of a lightning bolt.

At last, in his preface to the "Courteous Reader," Williams raised the question of how the English would respond if Jesus "were present here at London." If asked which religion Jesus would endorse, each citizen would shout for his own option to be chosen. But then if Christ should be asked about what weapons he would provide to that religion for which Parliament ultimately voted, all England would learn that no weapons of steel would be provided, only the instruments of persuasion and love. There was irony, tragic irony, Williams noted, in the fact that Parliament had taken great pains to see that the English Bibles were made available even to "the poorest English houses," that the "simplest man or woman" was encouraged to search the Scriptures, and yet these simple folk were forced to believe as the national church believed. Why, said Williams, one might as well live in Spain or Rome, where no pretense was made that people read their Bibles and inform their own consciences. The Christian religion was too precious a commodity to be traded for a vote or an office or even a crown. If persecution comes, so be it. "Having bought truth dear," Williams wrote, "we must not sell it cheap, not the least grain of it for the whole world."

71

Identifying himself once more with the Baptist radicals, Williams opened his volume with a selection from *A Most Humble Supplication of Many of the King's Majesty's Loyal Subjects*, published in 1620 when Parliament resumed meeting for the first time since 1614. The author, Williams tells us, was a prisoner in Newgate who, having neither pen nor ink, wrote his manuscript in milk, permitting his followers to bring out the "invisible ink" later. This author, assumed to have been John Murton, wrote on behalf of those "falsely called Anabaptists" to let the king know that they were indeed "loyal subjects" in all civil things, but that final qualification was of course the critical one. Other aspects of Murton's work were likewise congenial to Williams: civil and ecclesiastical spheres must be kept separate; religious liberty does not defeat domestic tranquillity, but promotes it; and Old Testament kings are no proper model or justification for the powers of contemporary kings. No wonder that Williams wanted to begin with some of Murton's words. And no wonder that John Cotton assumed it was Williams who sent this "letter" to him, though Williams denied it. When Cotton wrote his response, however, he did send that to Williams, and no one tried to deny that.

In dealing with the issue of religious freedom, no scriptural passage received more attention or more strained exegesis than the parable of Jesus dealing with the harvest of wheat and tares. Because it surfaces again and again, the passage is worth quoting from the Gospel according to Matthew:

> The kingdom of heaven is likened unto a man which sowed good seed in his field: But while men slept, his enemy came and sowed tares among the wheat, and went his way. But when the blade was sprung up, and brought forth fruit, then appeared the tares also. So the servants of the householder came and said unto him, Sir, didst not thou sow good seed in thy field? from whence then hath it tares? He said unto them, An enemy hath done this. The servants said unto him, Wilt thou then that we go and gather them up? But he said, Nay; lest while ye gather up

the tares, ye root up also the wheat with them. Let both
grow together until the harvest: and in the time of harvest,
I will say to the reapers, Gather ye together first the tares,
and bind them in bundles to burn them: but gather the
wheat into my barn. (Matt. 13:24-30)

Parables are told to illuminate and clarify, but they sometimes
also obscure. In view of the extravagant attention given to this
one story in the seventeenth century, one can only conclude that
in this instance, at least, not all was made clear.

John Murton started out with the wheat and tares in order
to argue that Christ's followers should not be in so great a hurry
to separate the good from the bad. For one thing, those who have
been blind might learn to see; tares might become wheat; idolaters today may become true worshipers tomorrow. For another
thing, Christ's own command was to persecute not and, if
persecuted, to pray. As all know, the Christian church did not
persecute in the time of Christ, but was itself persecuted. What
better, what more commanding example can be put forward?
Or are there those who have not read the New Testament lately,
who think that Paul traveled about "with Regal Mandates, or
Kingly authority, to gather and establish the Church of Christ."
No, the heavenly appointed means for bringing men and
women to Christ were humility, patience, and charity. Jesus did
not send his followers as wolves among sheep to kill, spoil, and
devour; rather, he said, "Behold, I send you forth as sheep in the
midst of wolves" (Matt. 10:16). The king of England should
know that even the Caesar of Rome left his subjects undisturbed
in their "Consciences toward God."

John Cotton, having first distinguished between those
differences in doctrine and worship that are fundamental and
those that are less important, also distinguished between the
ways in which a church member might assert even the lesser
differences—"in a meek and peaceable way" or with "arrogance and impetuousness." And in all the talk about conscience,
it was vital, Cotton noted, to know whether we are talking about
"Conscience rightly informed" or about an "erroneous and

73

blind Conscience." As long as all this is clearly understood, then Cotton was prepared to deal with the substance of the Anabaptist complaint against persecution.

Treating the substance meant getting to the wheat and the tares, along with all other scriptural references and appeals to history. Cotton explained that biblical words had been taken out of context, that historical examples had been cited very selectively and often inappropriately. Christians who embrace false doctrine may certainly be censured by the church, or even excommunicated. If such persons corrupt others, or are in danger of doing so, then the "Civil Sword" may also be used against them. Cotton ended by asking "Whether an Heretic after once or twice Admonition . . . , or any other scandalous and heinous offender, may be tolerated, either in the Church without Excommunication, or in the Commonwealth without such punishment as may preserve others from dangerous and damnable infection." If ever Cotton phrased a purely rhetorical question, this was surely it. For who could imagine that the church had no right, the state had no power, to deal severely with "scandalous offenders"? Moreover, who could imagine the very survival of any society where such a right was denied?

For Williams the questions were far from rhetorical. On the contrary, they demanded answers—answers not for academic debate but for determining death and life. All the John Cottons of the world (and they were the vast majority, Williams knew) must somehow be convinced that a loving God did not condone all that shedding of blood in his name. Williams would try to make the point as clearly, as emphatically, as he possibly could. He would restrain his prolixity (his own word) and endeavor to do something about those sentences (as he had earlier observed to Winthrop) "that are as thick and over busy as Mosquitoes etc." He might even try to do something about those "etc.'s" and his parentheses within parentheses. But whether he succeeded or not in trimming the style, he would state the case so forcefully, so repeatedly, that only the obstinate and perverse would fail to get the point. He would use dramatic figures of speech, resort

74

to wit and sarcasm, and favor bluntness over politeness in his choice of language. So far as the argument itself was concerned, he would rely upon every authority that the seventeenth-century English would accept: the Bible, classical history, Christian history, reason, and experience. The argument would need to be both intense and sustained, for Roger Williams was out to do nothing less than alter the institutional structure of the Western world.

Williams slyly noted that treatises on behalf of peace and liberty were written in milk, while books proposing conformity and persecution were written in blood. His own language was filled with blood, but he preferred a blood-spattered page to a blood-spattered land. "Who can but run with zeal inflamed," Williams asked, "to prevent the deflowering of chaste souls, and spilling the blood of the innocent?" Any zeal, even impetuosity, seemed perfectly justified when one considers "the whole earth, made drunk with the blood of its inhabitants." Religious wars have darkened Europe's soils, and threatened to darken all England's as well. Are not we all obliged to listen to the "fearful cries" of the many thousands of "men, women, children, fathers, mothers, husbands, wives, brothers, sisters, old and young, high and low, plundered, ravished, slaughtered, murdered, famished?" John Cotton's questions were not rhetorical; they were genocidal.

Nor were his careful delimitations and definitions all that persuasive. He distinguished between matters fundamental and matters circumstantial but failed to see that one cannot find agreement even on this classification. Is the form of church government a "fundamental of the faith"—or no? It must be fundamental, since both Old England and New persecute those who do not conform to the fixed pattern. And about putting forth one's views with arrogance and impetuosity, these labels (Williams wrote) can be too loosely and freely applied. Consider, for example, the early apostles who traveled all over Galilee, uprooting the old religion and proclaiming a new. Was this arrogance and impetuosity? Or consider the case of Elijah confronting

Ahab, or Paul confronting Herod—were these instances of arrogance and impetuosity? When the apostles proclaimed that they owed allegiance to another king, namely Jesus Christ, were they too being arrogant and impetuous? It is true that Christian preaching through the ages has often been accidentally "the occasion of great contentions and divisions, yea tumults and uproars," yet this is no evidence of arrogance or impetuosity. In truth, these are mere names, scare words, to be thrown at those whose message we deplore and whose silence we seek. The real issue, said Williams, is not the manner in which truth is proclaimed but whether or not what we proclaim is truth.

One more qualification Cotton sought to make—that between a sincere and an obstinate conscience. This was pure artifice, Williams responded, for every persecutor invents some "mask or covering" to conceal his true motive in persecution. "Search all Scriptures, Histories, Records, Monuments, consult with all experiences," and you will find, without fail, that persecutors will never admit to persecuting Christ. Someone blasphemes; "therefore, stone him." Christ betrays Caesar; therefore, crucify him. John Hus is possessed by the devil; therefore, burn him. "Christians are schismatical, factious, heretical; therefore, persecute them." And so with respect to Williams himself: he was exiled not because he believed in liberty of conscience but because he sinned against his own conscience. An ugly doctrine is thus "painted over with the vermillion of mistaken Scripture, and that old dream that the Crown of Jesus will consist of outward material gold, and his sword be made of iron or steel" is revived once more. From this dangerous dream, Williams would awaken the world.

Persecutors, whose hands are filthy, denounce sober seekers after God, whose hands are clean. The situation, said Williams, can be compared to that of Potiphar's wife, who accused Joseph of adultery when, in fact, Joseph was innocent and the would-be seducer guilty. "So commonly the meek and peaceable of the earth are traduced as rebels, factious, peacebreakers," when it is those who hold civil and ecclesiastical

76

power who are divisive and disruptive, disturbers of all peace and order. That which they fear in others they could, if only they would, find in themselves.

Typically persecutors defend their practice by an appeal to Scripture. So, said Williams, let us consider the biblical condemnations of or proscriptions against Christian persecution, Scriptures that John Murton had initially put forward and which John Cotton had, in one way or another, dismissed. Naturally, the wheat and tares require close examination once again. If the sinners (that is, the tares) infringe upon the "peace and welfare" of the state, the civil magistrate has every right to restrain or punish them for any *civil* offenses. But in matters of worship and belief, in *spiritual* offenses, "let their Worship and Consciences be tolerated." The church, which has its own spiritual weapons to use against error, has even been promised that the gates of hell will not prevail against it. What more than that does the church need? Why call upon a weaker force than the arm of Almighty God? The parable is clear: leave wheat and tares until the harvest, when God's judgment will be made known. Unfortunately, kings and governors, bishops and priests, have fallen fast asleep in "Delilah's lap," failing to recognize the clear command "to let the tares alone."

Similarly, Jesus' comment to his disciples to leave the Pharisees alone, for "they be blind leaders of the blind" (Matt. 15:14), reveals that Jesus was more tolerant than his latter-day followers. Not so, said Cotton, for this comment was made privately, not publicly, and besides the import was simply for the disciples not to trouble themselves unduly. But note, said Williams, that civil government was never appealed to, never invoked in any way. The discussion was totally in the spiritual realm, as it were, within the church. Jesus, in saying that the blind leading the blind will all end up in the ditch, passed a spiritual judgment only. "Such a sentence no Civil Judge can pass, such a Death no Civil sword can inflict." But should we not protect those who are about to be led into a ditch? We have, Williams responded, all the "spiritual antidotes and preservatives against

77

spiritual sicknesses" that we need; no need to call in the state, for Christ "never appointed the civil sword for either antidote or remedy" where the church or its own flock were concerned.

John Murton had also argued from an episode in the Gospel according to Luke where Jesus had not been properly received by the Samaritans (9:54-55). His disciples urged him to call down fire from heaven to devour his enemies, but Jesus rebuked them, saying, "Ye know not what manner of spirit ye are of." Cotton responded that such a verse dealt with real outsiders, not with troublemakers in the church. Nothing in Jesus' reply hinders the ministers from proceeding "in a Church way against Church members, when they become scandalous offenders," said Cotton, much less does it address the issue of the civil magistrate. This "perplexed and ravelled Answer," Williams noted with some irritation, has to be unpacked in order to figure out just what John Cotton was trying to say. When he is pressed on the question of civil persecution, he retreats to the question of church censure—which is not the issue. Cotton seems to imply that the magistrate, if a Christian, has a duty to purge the defiler of orthodoxy. But if a Christian, said Williams, his real duty is to be like Christ and not turn into a destroyer of "the bodies of men."

So the Scripture references flow back and forth, the exegesis becoming precious, the tuning very fine. If a single verse seems hard to interpret in support of one's position (either Cotton's or Williams'), then a dozen other verses could be called upon to shore up a weakening defense. But Scripture offered not the only ground upon which the battle was to be waged. Williams never tired of appealing to history, especially the recent history of Europe and of England, for there the clearest evidence could be found of persecution's folly. "To seek no further than our native Soil," just in the space of a few years, what "wonderful changes in Religion hath the whole kingdom made!" Henry VII "finds and he leaves the kingdom absolutely Popish." Henry VIII "casts it into a mold half Popish, half Protestant." Edward VI "brings forth an Edition all Protestant," while Mary I returns to the all-Roman Catholic pattern of her grandfather, Henry VII. Then Elizabeth revives the model of Edward VI, all Protestant. What may one conclude from this dreary recitation? "It hath been England's sinful shame to fashion & change their Garments and Religions with wondrous ease and lightness, as a higher Power, a stronger Sword hath prevailed." More than a century later, Thomas Jefferson wrote that the only effect of official religion was to make one half of the world fools, the other half hypocrites. Williams phrased it this way: The sword may make a whole nation hypocrites, but it cannot bring one single soul in genuine conversion to Christ.

Beginning with Constantine in the fourth century, it has become the habit to defend spiritual truths with civil force. This introduced a Tower of Babel into Christianity, said Williams, a costly confusion that turned "the Gardens of the Churches of the Saints . . . into the Wilderness of whole Nations." As a consequence, genuine Christianity was eclipsed as the whole world became "Christendom." Perhaps some emperors and bishops of the Middle Ages intended to do the right thing, but the result was nonetheless tragic for true religion, fatal for thousands of men, women, and children. A Christian church, by definition, does not persecute; a church that does persecute is, by definition, anti-Christian.

Struggling to avoid the label of anti-Christian, John Cotton would allow liberty of conscience to those who truly fear the Lord. But there is the rub, Williams responded. Who is to decide who truly fears the Lord? New England can offer many examples of God-fearing souls being denied their "civil being" on no grounds other than "this man differs from us." Though "godly, useful, and peaceable," he obviously did not qualify for liberty of conscience. But beyond all that, Cotton's limitation would seem immediately to deny such liberty to all non-Christians, to all Turks and infidels. And to do that is to "confound Heaven and Earth together"; it is, moreover, to take Christianity out of the world and all civility as well. The world is reduced to a battlefield.

79

Which is why persecution for cause of conscience is a "bloudy tenent." Not only does it directly contradict "the spirit and mind and practice of the Prince of Peace," but beyond that it destroys all civil peace of kingdoms, countries, and commonwealths everywhere. Christ is not delighted with the blood of others, Williams concluded, but "shed his own for his bloodiest enemies." And so the civil sword, repeatedly brought down upon tender consciences, must now be sheathed. If this could be achieved, Williams affirmed, then all England would have a new "Magna Carta of highest liberties." Then every humble cottage in the land, with a new security and a new freedom, could place olive branches over its doorposts. Then at last would be stilled "the doleful drums, and shrill sounding trumpets, the roaring murdering Canons, the shouts of Conquerors, the groans of wounded, dying, slaughtered, righteous with the wicked."

CHURCH AND CIVIL POWER

And so Williams ended the first half of his passionate protest. He had perhaps said enough so far as Parliament and Old England were concerned. With respect to New England, however, more needed to be clarified regarding that Salem document, that "Model of Church and Civil Power." For it was the relationship between those two awesome powers that troubled Williams and that, in his view, troubled the whole world. Williams assumed that the document had been written by John Cotton, but Cotton denied it and the evidence supports his denial. For Salem was attempting to prove that it had "fallen into line" in its theories of government, while Cotton in a sermon preached in Salem the following year and in major treatises written later set down his own views in considerable detail. Authorship aside, however, Williams found the arguments pernicious and dangerous, reacting with a certain amount of personal pique since Salem was telling its side of the struggle with, and ultimately against, Roger Williams. Now, almost a decade after Salem had its say, Williams would have his.

Salem was quite prepared to admit that civil and church government were distinct entities. The trick was to determine precisely how they related to each other. Relate they must, the Salem clergy stated, since "every soul in the Church is subject to the higher powers of the Commonweal, and every member of the Commonweal . . . is subject to the laws of Christ's Kingdom." But there's the problem immediately at hand, Williams responded. Yes, every church member is subject to the civil magistrate, *in civil things only,* but only redeemed, regenerate persons are "subject to the laws of Christ's Kingdom"—not the multitudes at large, not the regenerate and unregenerate all thrown together in an undifferentiated glob.

It was true to say, as Salem did, that the magistrate was supreme in civil affairs, the church in spiritual affairs. Fine, said Williams. But then Salem and Boston denied that separate supremacy by making the civil magistrate the enforcer of the purely spiritual matters of the First Table. How absurd! This is to make the governor both the judge and the one being judged. Simultaneously he is "to sit on the Bench, and stand at the Bar of Christ Jesus." So much authority is given to the civil magistrate as "to make him absolutely the Head of the Church." If he is the reformer of the church, the suppressor of schismatics and heretics, the protector and defender of orthodoxy, "what is this in true plain English" but to make him the judge of all truth, be it spiritual or civil?

Christian liberty, Salem argued, is not a liberty to disobey civil authority, but only a liberty "from enthrallment and bondage unto sin." True, Williams agreed, but the civil authority has no "commission from Christ Jesus" to declare what is a true church or a false one, what a true ministry or a false one. Only the church can make such judgments, and only the church may punish (never by sword) the spiritual offender. And if the church is so misguided as to surrender to the magistrate its own authority over the spiritual, then the church must claim that only Christians of their own particular order can be magistrates. But this is an absurdity, Williams countered, for many states and kingdoms exist where Christianity is unknown; yet, they have legitimate rulers and an ordered civil society. To argue that only Christians can be governors is to argue that only Christians "should be Husbands of Wives, Fathers of Children, Masters of Servants."

If one's reasoning leads down a path toward absurdity, it is time to rethink the reasons. The church and the civil authority are not inconsistent, Williams argued, but they are and must be independent. One evidence of their independence is that "the Commonweal may be in perfect peace and quiet" even though the church is embroiled in bitter dispute. Likewise, the church may pursue its spiritual business though kings fall and civil strife ensues. Consider Geneva, said the Salem ministers: church and state worked together to punish heresy and enforce godliness. I've considered Geneva, Williams in effect responded, and I reject it. For it implies that the ordinances of the church may be "given by Christ to any Civil State, Town, or City," and that, said Williams, "I confidently deny." The state may assist the church only in the sense that it maintains peace and order. The church may assist the state only in the sense that it "may cast a blush of civility and morality" upon the citizens.

On the one hand, Massachusetts Bay talked about Christians separating themselves from the world. But on the other hand, they made such separation impossible by requiring all persons, regenerate and unregenerate alike, to support the ministry and to conform to the externals of church worship. In this manner, Williams added, employing a favorite image, they make the garden and the wilderness all one. The Roman Empire may turn out to be a better model than Geneva or London or Boston, for Jesus never sent any of his disciples to the civil authorities, seeking their help in the Christian cause. But Paul appealed to Caesar, someone has pointed out. So he did, Williams acknowledged, but in civil matters only. If he had appealed in a spiritual cause, he would have "overthrown his own

Apostleship and Power given him by Christ Jesus in spiritual things." In fact, Christianity may never have shined so brightly as in those days of Roman persecution, as stars shine brightest in the darkest night, as spices give off their finest aroma when ground, pounded, and burned.

Anticipating John Locke, Williams argued that all civil power originates with the people. Williams would have nothing to do with the so-called divine right of kings. And if the people create a government most suitable for their civil condition, it follows that governments "have no more power, nor for no longer time" than the people "consenting and agreeing shall betrust them with." It is otherwise with the church: this is ordained of God, chartered by Christ, under the rule of the Emperor who is above all emperors. Therefore, to take an institution such as the church that does have "divine right" and place it in the hands and under the authority of "natural, sinful, inconstant men, and so consequently to Satan himself" makes no sense whatsoever. In this manner, said Williams, one has pulled God, Christ, and the Holy Spirit right out of heaven.

If one followed the New England rule, Christ was demoted, as the spiritual was subsumed under the civil and polluted thereby. Religion, moreover, was debased by being turned into a matter of outward observances only. And if the state can compel one to attend church, why not compel one to participate in the Lord's Supper? Why not compel one to be converted? If people are forced to conform to a particular religion, the end result is that they shall "be of no Religion at all, all their days." Consider that when Paul entered the city of Corinth, he did not invite the magistrates of that city to use the sword to compel all people to come to hear him. That must be because Paul did not understand the New England rule, did not follow their "model of church and civil power."

But if Williams could cite the example of Paul in Corinth, his opponents could cite the words of Jesus in another parable: "Go out into the highways and hedges, and compel them to come in, that my house may be filled" (Luke 14:23). One must

83

distinguish, Williams responded, between moral and civil compulsion. The former, which is accomplished by "powerful argument and persuasion," was wholly appropriate, while the latter, which is accomplished only by armies and courts and prisons, was as perverse as it was pointless when dealing with spiritual matters. Compelling an unregenerate person to attend church to be spiritually fed is like commanding "a dead child to suck the breast, or a dead man [to] feast." Oh, it is true, Williams conceded, that men can be forced to attend, pray, contribute, and go through the proper motions. They may be told that thus they aid religion; but they may then conclude that such externals are the whole of religion, effectively shutting themselves off from the possibility of any genuine conversion.

New England was still hung up on Moses, Williams contended, still hypnotized by the examples of churchly states in the Old Testament. What New England refuses to accept is that there really is a New Testament, a new covenant, a new dispensation, that Old Israel is passed away, now replaced by not a nation but a church. The New Israel is the Christian community, spiritual alone, not physical. Canaan is a pattern for no other land at all: "It was a nonesuch, unparalleled and unmatchable." Under the dispensation of the gospel, nations are not churches; no nation can now claim the command "That whosoever would not seek the Lord God of Israel should be put to death, whether small or great, whether man or woman" (2 Chron. 15:13). That age is past, superseded by a new dispensation, a new gospel. And yet, after sixteen hundred years, kings and parliaments and governors and sheriffs refuse to get the message. As a consequence, "what slaughters of the innocent and faithful witnesses of Christ Jesus, who choose to be slain all the day long for Christ, his sake, and to fight for their Lord and Master Christ only with spiritual and Christian weapons."

A Christian must obey his ruler in civil matters, but in spiritual matters a Christian must judge his ruler as he would all other persons. A physician, Williams noted, must obey "the Prince in a Body politic," but in prescribing for the prince's body, the latter must obey the physician. So the distinction between civil and spiritual: the magistrate attends only to the bodies and goods of his subjects, but he is (if a church member) subject to the same "power of the Lord Jesus" as all other Christians are. For the magistrates to put themselves above all other Christians in the practice of their art (namely, religion) is as though they put themselves above all physicians in the practice of theirs (namely, medicine). To act in this way is "to turn the World upside down"; it is to destroy "all common society in the World, to turn the Garden and Paradise of the Church and Saints into the Field of the Civil State of the World." And to act in this way is also to open ever wider the doors to religious persecution, soaking the earth with more and more innocent blood. "The Doctrine of Persecution for cause of Conscience" remained, for Williams, the very bloodiest of all foul and bloody doctrine.

Published in London, *The Bloudy Tenent* was first answered in London—initially by being publicly burned. The book was published in July; by August Parliament ordered the volume to be destroyed. Nevertheless, enough copies fell into the hands of Parliament's sympathizers to guarantee that it would be answered, and enough copies were kept in the hands of Roger Williams, now safely on board a ship bound for America, to guarantee that it would not be totally lost. It proved not an easy book to ignore, nor an easy one to destroy.

Leading Presbyterians of the Westminster Assembly quickly let their horror of Williams' views be known. The learned Robert Baylie thought religious toleration so abhorrent an idea that the very words themselves should not be voiced aloud. If a state were to grant liberty to religious errors, it should then in all consistency grant liberty for every form of vice or crime, Baylie asserted. England had to choose between order on the one hand and religious chaos on the other, and Williams' book directly promoted the latter. Williams would trade divine certainty for "the reelings of windmills, fair forms and dreams, beliefs bottomed on fallible opinions."

85

Even more critical of the notion of toleration, to say nothing of full religious freedom, Thomas Edwards contended that the magistrate's duties included the suppression of heresy and the protection of religion. Far from being none of his affair, such was in fact his highest duty and noblest calling. The judicial laws of the Old Testament had never been repealed, Edwards declared, nor was the example of ancient Israel irrelevant to the structure of the modern state. The magistrate, basing his action on an infallible Bible and guided by pious and learned men who may resolve all doubt, "can infallibly and certainly know such and such doctrines to be false, and such true." In fact, the devil could hope for no better assistance in supporting his "tottering kingdom" than that provided in *The Bloudy Tenent*. Roger Williams made few converts in England's or Scotland's Presbyterian ranks. Nor did he gain many allies in the ranks of New England's divines, though their responses took somewhat longer to reach the printer.

In the twelve or fourteen months that he had been in England, Williams had accomplished much: he had cut wood to help the poor through the winter of 1643-1644, he had obtained a charter for his colony, he had managed to get two books and one large pamphlet published, and he had taken time to tend to some family affairs. Williams had two brothers, Sydrach, a widely traveled merchant who traded with the Near East and elsewhere, and Robert, who had up to this point stayed close to the family home and become executor of the estate thereby. But the execution of the estate had not gone well, owing chiefly to Robert's bankruptcy. Both Sydrach and Roger had been entitled to an inheritance, one hundred pounds for Sydrach and two hundred for Roger. The two were obliged to go to court for recovery of these sums, but Roger—who felt strongly about oaths—lost out in court since he would not testify under oath concerning the legacy left by his mother, who had died nearly a decade before. However, if Robert were in some measure at fault in the entire debacle, Roger was ready to forgive, even inviting his brother to join him in Rhode Island, which he did. Robert may have accompanied Roger in the August trip back home, along with his (and Milton's) printer, Gregory Dexter.

This time the ship headed for Boston, not New Amsterdam, for Williams carried with him at least one letter from highly placed members of Parliament to the governor and assistants of Massachusetts Bay. The letter spoke in warm tones of Williams' work in London and in disconsolate tones of the estrangement between Williams and the officialdom of Massachusetts. The common enemy, all must remember, were the high-handed bishops of the Church of England, and Williams and the Bay Colony could make common cause on that point. The letter healed no wounds, but it did render the authorities a bit more willing to consider Williams' request for safe passage from Boston back to Providence—that is, some assurance that he would not again be placed under arrest the moment that he left the wharf. London had in August been glad to see him go; Boston in September was no less happy to speed Williams on his way.

So, with some families and friends from England, Williams set out on foot for Providence. If Boston had been frigid, even in September, Providence planned a proper welcome. As Williams and his party crossed over the Seekonk River, fourteen canoes crowded about to give their occupants the opportunity to shout greetings and cheering words. Upon returning home, he also could feast his eyes on a son born while he was away. For him and Mary there was glorious reunion; for him and his colony, there was much work to be done. By November he had been elected "chief officer" of the colony, a position that he would maintain for the next three years. For those years and for several beyond, Williams struggled to determine just what liberty of conscience meant, both for the church and for the civil order. Winning such liberty was only half the battle; using it properly called for even more discernment, struggle, and sacrifice.

4 Exile from the Church

In 1639, well before his first trip back to London, Roger Williams was excommunicated by his old church in Salem. The church had preferred to call their action a "great censure," but to Williams it was nothing less than a "bull of excommunication." Williams did not suffer alone. His wife and eight others fell under a similar sentence, this definitive action being taken when word reached Salem that their members had formed a church in Providence and had even indulged in the scandal of a second baptism, thus discrediting the baptism administered in Salem and in all of Massachusetts and the entire nation of England as well. So the church in Salem had little choice.

Williams preferred to think that they had no choice at all, for (he later wrote) "I first withdrew Communion from Your Selves for halting between Christ and Antichrist." Nonetheless, the formal excommunication was bitter as gall to Williams, especially when he considered that Salem and the other Bay churches continued in communion with the national church to which "all are forced by the Bishops." So Williams concluded that he was dealt with "more cruelly" than all the "Profane Protestants and Papists too." In the same letter to John Cotton, Jr., written years after, in which Williams conveyed these sentiments, he also indicated that the Bay authorities had even considered executing him but resorted instead to the "Dry Pit of Banishment."

THE CHURCH IN PROVIDENCE

In the earliest days in Providence, little organization of any sort could be found: no charter, no government, no written titles to the land, no church. All was informal, casual, improvised. This applied to religion as well as politics, as Williams gathered friends and neighbors together in his home for preaching, praying, and testifying concerning God's gracious goodness toward his scattered sheep. "No man should be molested for his conscience," these neighbors had agreed. Did that include women too? The question quickly became more than academic.

Joshua and Jane Verin, who had moved from Salem with Roger Williams, built their home just to the north of Roger and Mary's dwelling. Jane Verin attended the many informal religious meetings next door with great faithfulness and regularity, so much so that Joshua decided she was giving more attention to religion than to him. He forbade her to go any more. When she refused to obey, he beat her, so savagely that the neighbors could hear her screams. At length, the heads of households met to reprove the husband for his brutal behavior and for violating his wife's liberty of conscience by preventing her attendance at religious meetings. Joshua replied that *his* liberty of conscience was being interfered with, since the Bible clearly declared that a wife should submit to her husband. He was only seeing to it that she submitted. A majority of the settlers decided otherwise, voting to "discharge him from our Civil Freedom," as Williams reported to John Winthrop in May 1638. Compelling his wife to accompany him (hauling her "with ropes," Williams

89

wrote) Joshua Verin returned to Salem, where its court could decide just what to do with such a "foul and slanderous and brutish" fellow. Liberty of conscience, as would be repeatedly demonstrated, could mean many things.

Later in 1638 Williams joined with others in organizing a church along strict Separatist lines (not halting between Christ and Antichrist), a church that rejected all civil jurisdiction over laws of the First Table and that embraced the Baptist principle of adult baptism. One member baptized Williams, who in turn baptized all the others. About twenty persons joined in the creation of this, the first church of Baptist identification not only in Rhode Island but in all of North America as well. At last Williams might find a fellowship in which he would be subjected to no scorn, no reprimand, no exile. And yet he could continue to subject himself to reprimand and subject his ecclesiastical views to ever closer examination. For Williams, who wrote of the "restless unsatisfiedness of my soul," found no enduring peace, not even in the church molded by his own hands. What authority did he have to be baptized or to baptize others? What line of apostolic continuity could be traced to that score of Bible believers who agreed to worship together? What biblical commission or divine command set this church apart or perhaps even above all others? The church must be pure, unsullied by the world: that he knew. The garden must be walled off from the wilderness of the world: that he also knew. But how did one achieve such purity, and how did one fully protect and preserve that garden?

THE TRUE CHURCH

In this quest, as in so many others, Williams began with the New Testament. If one yearned to find the pattern for the true church of Jesus Christ, only a single source sufficed. Salem had offered its "Model of Church and Civil Power," but that was not the one true model for the church, "that first and ancient pattern" laid down in Scripture. In writing to John Winthrop as early as 1636, Williams bemoaned the spiritual nakedness of New England's churches but added the hope that within a few years the Lord would reveal "the first and most ancient path" more plainly "to you and me." More than a dozen years later, in a letter to Winthrop's son, Williams indicated that he found no churches organized "after the first pattern"; instead, he saw only disputing, separating, and contending, with "the breaches and Divisions wonderful." As he came to appreciate the New Testament pattern more fully, Williams gradually reached a much-dreaded conclusion—namely, that no true church of Jesus Christ was possible, at least not until Christ came again.

His growing unease about the nature of all man-made (as opposed to Christ-created) churches led to his departure from the Providence church after only a few months of fellowship in that congregation's midst. The New England churches had halted halfway between Christ and Antichrist. The Providence church had moved closer to Christ and further from Antichrist, but it had not moved far enough. What would it take to leap the whole way, into perfect and pure congruence with the ancient pattern? It would take, Williams reluctantly concluded, more than mere mortals by themselves could ever achieve.

For what was the New Testament church but one called by Christ out of the world? Christ's appointed apostles, commissioned directly by him, could establish a true church, with true acts of worship, with a congregation of the purified and redeemed. But how, sixteen hundred years later, could such a church be formed? The doctrine of apostolic succession might seem to be the answer: that the authority and commission of Christ had been transmitted, generation by generation, from his own time to the present. But that would mean that a wholly false church, the papal Antichrist, could in its impurity faithfully preserve and rightly pass on a wholly pure power. And that made no sense at all. After Constantine, a true ministry no longer existed, and none but God could now bring it back.

Williams did not come to this position easily, nor did he

91

find it easy to persuade others that recreating the true church of Christ was a vain pursuit—apart from direct divine intervention. In a tract entitled *The Hireling Ministry None of Christs,* Williams labored to explain the defectiveness of the current ministry and its ordinances. In four ways, he wrote, the modern ministry fell short of its New Testament pattern: in gifts, in calling, in work, and in wages. With respect to the first, Williams argued that the greatest gift of all was missing—namely, an apostolic commission, a discipleship like that enjoyed by those whom Jesus appointed. A simple proof of this lack was that present church leaders could not even agree on such matters as the proper baptism or the ceremony of laying on of hands for ordination or even church membership.

Second, concerning the call to the ministry, it could not come through some apostolic succession, for this would force current clergy to "run into the Tents of Antichrist, and to plead Succession from Rome." Or it would force them to declare that "two or three godly persons might first make themselves a church, & then make their Ministers." But nowhere "in the first institution and pattern" do we find "any such two, or three, or more did gather and constitute themselves a Church of Christ, with a Ministry sent from God." And if the ministry is not sent of God, then how can the church be of God? If someone says the Bible justifies this method of forming a church, then, said Williams, "let one instance be produced in the first patterns and practices of such a Practice." On the contrary, the Bible informs us that there can be no marriage feast without a messenger "from God to the Souls of Men, Matthew 22, Luke 14, Romans 10."

Third, those who claim the command of Jesus in Matthew 28 ("Go ye therefore, and teach all nations, baptizing them in the name of the Father, and of the Son, and of the Holy Ghost") involve themselves in a contradiction. For, on the one hand they claim that their English nation is already Christian, yet on the other they fail to see that the Great Commission was intended for witnesses to nations that knew not Christ. The official clergy cannot have it both ways: they cannot pretend to preach to the unconverted when at the same time they worship and pray with them as though they were already converted.

But it was the fourth point that attracted Williams' chief attention: the matter of wages, and more particularly of wages paid by means of a forced tithe collected by the civil power. The ministry was a calling, not a trade, Williams argued, noting that Jesus drew a clear distinction between the true shepherd on the one hand and the mere hireling on the other (John 10:11-13). The first truly cares for his sheep, while the latter flees at the first sign of danger. "I am bold to maintain," Williams wrote, "that it is one of [the] grand Designs of the most High to break down the Hireling Ministry, that Trade" by which one chooses to live off the job of preaching. He who haggles over his wages, who bargains for his keep, who "makes the cure of Souls, and the charge of men's eternal welfare, a trade, a maintenance, and living" was never sent of God to be a laborer in his vineyard.

Like servants hired by the year, today's clergy leave one parish for another the minute they hear offers "of more Ease and better Wages." Indeed, they even leave one religion for another, "from Popery to Protestantism, from Protestantism to Popery, from Popery to Protestantism again!" in order to keep their comfort and their salary. This they do, Williams noted with rich sarcasm, so that they will not lose the "Liberty of Preaching!" Now, in the mid-seventeenth century, it was happening all over again, and would continue to happen as long as the nation maintained its "hireling ministry." England had rejected Anglicanism in favor of Presbyterianism in 1645; then in 1648 Parliament rejected Presbyterianism in favor of Independency. In 1652 a committee of Parliament went so far as to call for a limited toleration, but it still insisted on a ministry paid by the state, chosen by the state, certified and approved by the state. True messengers are such because of a greater spiritual power in "the Sender than the Sent." Parliament has no such greater spiritual power; Christ does.

Roger Williams acknowledged that he had himself been a hireling minister in days past, but he would be one no longer.

93

He had known what it was to study, to preach, "to be an Elder, to be applauded." But he had also known what it was to "tug at the Oar, to dig with the Spade and Plow," and on the whole he found the latter a more honest form of labor than the former—so much so that he counseled those considering the professional ministry to turn to law or medicine or teaching or even digging, "rather than to live under the slavery, yea and the censure . . . of a mercenary and Hireling Ministry."

If this seemed hard, one had to recognize that the New Testament was hard. No model can be found there of wages and salaries, benefices and livings, Williams observed. But this may all seem hard only because we inheritors of the gospel have made such "great mistakes," have wandered so very far "from the Patterns and Institutions of Christ Jesus." Indeed, this wandering has gone on for so long that the church is like an "Army routed, and can hardly preserve and secure itself, much less subdue and conquer others." Or, to change the figure, Williams compared the church of his own time to a "Vessel becalmed at Sea." It may be possible to budge it a little, this way or that, by rowing or towing, but neither of these desperate human actions could compare with the filling of its sails with "the mighty gales of God's holy Spirit [or] breath."

But was there not great danger in suspending all ministry, all administration of the ordinances, all claims for the visible church? Yes, Williams acknowledged, but there was far greater danger in perpetuating a false or counterfeit ministry. Williams had nothing against university education, nothing against the "training up of Youth in Languages and other humane Learning," but he emphasized that all this was no substitute for godliness, for Christ's own calling. A degree in divinity did not imply divinity, or even saintliness. And Williams took delight in contrasting the pomp of seventeenth-century England with the simplicity of first-century Galilee. In England one confronted the clergy's "holy Gowns (black and red), holy cassocks, holy caps, holy scarfs, holy Rings, yea and holy boots also." All this, he added, was "as far from the purity and simplicity of the

Son of God" as was the sober attire of a chaste matron from the "flaunting vanities of some Painted Harlot."

God, however, had not left the world without some testimony in all those centuries since Constantine. Williams wrote of a "Ministry of Witnesses," prophets or witnesses who had stood firm for a purified Christianity even as they had testified powerfully against the pollutions of a corrupted church. Called directly by the Holy Spirit, such men as John Hus, John Wycliffe, Martin Luther, and John Calvin were "holy Prophets of Christ Jesus." They did much good, but they were no more able to restore the New Testament church in their time than we are in ours. Every attempt to reproduce the primitive church was, said Williams, like an almanac that is calculated for only "one Meridian and Climate." The universal pattern, the true model, has eluded all, and continues to elude.

But we must have a ministry, many contended, if for no other purpose than to record the births, perform the marriages, and bury the dead. But these were purely civil actions, Williams responded, and the state should assume responsibility in these matters, thereby removing "the soul yokes from the Necks of all that do or may inhabit this Nation, Jews or Gentiles." In fact, many had suffered unduly from these services being strictly under the control of the church. Those who had not "been able to walk in the Parish ways" had been forced to find burial grounds wherever they could, to live in marriages not recognized by the state, to record the births of their children only privately within their own homes. Again the civil and the ecclesiastical had been confounded and confused.

A "hireling ministry" was always bad, but far worse when the wages were exacted by civil power. Tithes should never be forced, nor should the state prohibit the tithe when (and only when) the free conscience of the people voluntarily offered it. The evil was not the tithe but the coercion. This was only one more example of state's meddling in affairs that were none of its proper business. When it came to religion, the duties of the magistrate turned upon two hinges, Williams wrote. The first

95

was to remove all spiritual yokes "that pinch the very Souls and consciences of men." This included taxation for the support of ministers that the people have no faith in, along with forced oath-taking and "holy Marryings, holy buryings, &c." The second hinge, as every reader of the *The Bloudy Tenent* already knew, was the "free and absolute permission of the consciences of all men" in matters purely spiritual—*all* men. And so that none would misunderstand, Williams spelled it out: no one was to violate the "consciences of the Jews, nor the consciences of the Turks or Papists, or Pagans themselves excepted."

If no state-enforced religion, then voluntary religion must become the norm. If no hireling clergy, then all men and women as clergy must become the norm. And if no true church, the faithful must, nonetheless, pledge all their talents, spiritual and temporal, for the advantage of "their Lord and Master." They must still witness, still prophesy "in sackcloth," bemoaning the absence of a full churchly ministry, regretting the continued strength and presence of the Antichrist. This is the best one can do in such dark times, Williams wrote, for there "is but one God, Lord and Spirit, from whom those Gifts, Administrations and Operations proceed," as we are told in 1 Corinthians 12. Without those divinely bestowed gifts, we may think that we glorify God when in fact we only blaspheme him. To put it most bluntly, one cannot reproduce the New Testament church without the presence of the New Testament Christ.

This conclusion intensified the millennialism of Roger Williams. He looked with even greater expectancy toward the return of Christ, who alone could restore his true church. The only apostolic succession worth believing in was Christ's own restoration of the apostolic age. Then the ordinances of the church could be reestablished and a pristine Christian community reborn. Then the outward and visible signs of church order would truly reflect inward and invisible spiritual grace. Then God's dominion over history would be made evident to all.

Williams, like most Puritans, believed in the Second Coming of Christ. Williams, like most Puritans, believed that this

Advent might be soon. But unlike the Puritans, Williams removed himself from the visible worship of his time and place, awaiting that day of glorious restoration of the "first Pattern." Also, unlike some, he thought that the millennium really would be a restoration, not a new type of Christianity, not a new kingdom where both political and spiritual power would be brought together. In England, the radical millenarian Fifth Monarchists asserted that Christ would establish a temporal kingdom, replacing Rome, the Fourth Monarchy. But Williams believed that the coming kingdom of God would be like the New Testament kingdom, bringing not a sword but a message of ringing clarity to the poor, weak, and despised among humankind. Christ exercised no civil power in his First Coming; he would exercise none in his Second.

Nor did the approach of the millennium bring great joy to the saints. On the contrary, in Williams' view, the millennium would be ushered in by persecution and slaughter of the faithful, for so the book of Revelation had predicted: "And when they [the prophets in sackcloth] shall have finished their testimony, the beast that ascendeth out of the bottomless pit shall make war against them, and shall overcome them, and kill them. And their dead bodies shall lie in the street of the great city" (11:7-8). Some were all too ready to interpret the victories of Cromwell or the execution of King Charles (in 1649) as signs of the coming kingdom. Roger Williams, however, envisioned different signs: widespread suffering, deep despair, calamity and chaos. "In these searching times," Williams warned, the faithful can only look toward that day when they shall see Christ himself, shall "reign with him, eternally admire him, and enjoy him, when he shortly comes in flaming fire to burn up millions of ignorant and disobedient."

Meanwhile, one's task was not to found churches but to judge the false churches, to witness or become a martyr to that which the world once knew but had spurned. In trying to cleanse the church of centuries of corruption, the witnesses and prophets helped prepare for the millennium. But apart from the miracle of divine intervention, no true church was possible again. Meanwhile, the faithful must wait in hope and work in love—and, if necessary, wait and work alone.

When Williams left the Providence church in 1639, the most obvious question was what other church he would join. It was unthinkable that a Cambridge graduate and ordained minister would not affiliate with some ecclesiastical institution, even if one had to be invented for him. But Williams, on the basis of his theological convictions, was not interested in exchanging one imperfect entity for another. For perfection he would wait. Others, less willing to wait, branded him a Seeker. William Hubbard, in his *General History of New England* (1680), declared that Williams, having doubted the validity of his second baptism, did with some others turn "Seekers, and so continued ever after." While others in the seventeenth century and beyond found this label convenient as a way of classifying the unclassifiable, there is no evidence that Williams joined this or any other group. English Seekers did argue that no true church existed at this time, but they also presumed to enjoy an intimacy with God that Williams would have found abhorrent. Once again, Williams preferred simply to wait—in exile, an exile of his own choosing.

LIBERTY OF CONSCIENCE REVISITED

By 1647 John Cotton had found time to reply to the barrage that Roger Williams had aimed at him in 1644—namely, *Mr. Cotton's Letter Answered* and *The Bloudy Tenent.* Cotton's response took the form of separate replies that were published together under the title of *The Bloudy Tenent, Washed, And Made White in the Bloud of the Lambe.* The great questions, said Cotton, were these: "How far Liberty of Conscience ought to be given to those that truly fear God? And how far restrained to turbulent and pestilent persons, that not only raze the foundation of Godliness, but disturb the Civil Peace where they live?" One other question, involved in the effort to answer the first two, was "how far all

Magistrates may proceed in the duties of the first Table." For nearly two hundred pages, Cotton loaded his charges and fired back at his voluble opponent. Cotton not only disagreed with Williams but had become irritated with him for "going public" with communications that Cotton regarded as essentially private. But if Williams would attack him before the whole world (i.e., London and environs), then Cotton had no choice but to defend himself before that same forum.

Cotton regarded Williams as an unfair debater who, at every turn, misinterpreted his words, ignored his careful qualifications, and concealed or simply forgot the point of a specific difference between them. He did not obey the rules of civil discourse as a good Christian should. But what would one expect? A man who looked for new apostles "must seek also for new Gospel, before this manner of dealing can be justified." And since Williams' book began by disobeying gospel rules, it was "no marvel if it swerve from the truth of the Gospel all along." Nor was it any marvel that the two men found it increasingly difficult to conceal their irritation with each other.

Once past the contentions about words, motives, and rules, differences of substance remained. Williams, for example, had argued that a church was like a private society of physicians or lawyers or merchants, and the breakup or dissolving of such a society in no way affected the civil peace of a government. Well, Cotton rejoined, such societies may not be the essence of a city, but they certainly had something to do with the integrity of a city. Civil government, moreover, should be concerned for the peace and welfare of such societies; why then should it not be concerned for the peace and welfare of the church? Besides which, the whole analogy was strained, Cotton declared, because one must "consider the Excellency and Preeminence of the Church above all other Societies." The world would not survive, Cotton continued, except for the church. "And can the Church then break up, into pieces, and dissolve into nothing, and yet the Peace and welfare of the City not in the least measure [be] impaired or disturbed?" The question answered itself.

Cotton conceded Williams' point that some civil societies prospered "for a time" without the presence of a Christian church. But this was utterly irrelevant to the situation in New England, where the church was planted and could not, therefore, be neglected. If the civil magistrates allowed the churches to become corrupt and to "annoy themselves by pollutions in Religion," then the peace of the commonwealth would be disrupted just as surely as the purity of the churches was despoiled. Consider the example of Rome, Cotton advised. When Roman emperors failed to maintain the purity of the Christian churches, God allowed the Turks and others to destroy not only the churches but the civil order as well. "Go now, and say, the estate of the Church, whether true or false, pure or corrupt, doth not concern the Civil Peace of the State."

Massachusetts Bay was not intolerant, Cotton explained. It allowed the Indians to remain in their paganism, compelling them by neither force nor law to the "Profession or acknowledgment of our Religion." So also, we could tolerate Jews or even atheists in our midst, just so long as they did not "openly blaspheme the God of heaven, & draw away Christians to Atheism, or Judaism." But when Christians began subverting other Christians to novel and dangerous opinions, then toleration ceased. "I would not account them either vigilant or faithful Christians, that were not troubled at such a destroying of the true Religion." And if troubled, then the faithful and vigilant magistrate must do his duty to punish, banish, or destroy that which polluted the Christian church. King David, Cotton explained, did not punish those outside of Israel who failed to worship Jehovah, but if an Israelite abandoned Jehovah, the matter was entirely different. Then punishment, swift and sure, must fall.

Cotton and Williams agreed that one should never persecute "a conscience rightly informed." But what of a blind and erroneous conscience? Even here Cotton argued that the punishment should normally be that of the church only (for example, excommunication) and not necessarily of the state. But exceptions do occur. If one has been excommunicated and yet persists in his errors, his blasphemy, or his idolatry and, most of all, if one seduces "others to his Heretical pernicious ways," then indeed the civil authority must get involved. Moreover, if the heretic, after being carefully admonished, persists in his heresy, then he condemns himself, he sins against his own conscience. Cotton found the scriptural warrant for his position to be so clear as to admit of no refutation: "A man that is an heretick after the first and second admonition reject; Knowing that he that is such is subverted, and sinneth, being condemned of himself" (Tit. 3:10-11). Such a person errs not because of ignorance but from sheer willfulness. And such a person deserves not only the censure of the church but the penalties imposed by the state as well.

When arguing the parable of the wheat and the tares, John Cotton examined carefully the Greek words as well as the agriculture of first-century Palestine. Tares, he pointed out, were not just any kind of weed, but a very special sort of weed: "having a narrower leaf, fatter, and rougher, and a leaner seed in a prickly bark, bearing a purple flower." Tares also greatly resembled the wheat until all became mature; this was why one could not deal with them until harvest. The point of the botany lesson was to make the spiritual lesson plain. Tares—that is, hypocrites who greatly resemble true Christians—cannot be rooted out immediately. "They cannot easily be discerned one from another, till in process of time, the difference of fruit discover them." Once they were discovered, however, the good husbandman, the good farmer, would uproot them for the sake of his crop. Roger Williams should certainly know, Cotton declared, that it was contrary to "all piety, order, and safety, that hypocrites . . . be tolerated in the Church 'til the end of the world." To act otherwise was to turn the church into a spiritual Babylon.

In Cotton's response to Williams' answer to his earlier letter, the tone of the argument became more personal and sharp. Cotton defended himself in the role that he played (or did not play) in Williams' banishment from Massachusetts, explaining that Williams managed sooner or later to become a thorn in everyone's side with his "self-conceited, and unquiet, and unlamblike frame of his Spirit." "Unlamblike" probably does describe accurately the personality of Roger Williams, but John Cotton, for his part, could also be "self-conceited" as he justified himself and his fellows in every action taken against Williams. Banishment was not really punishment, Cotton argued, for Williams was sent out of a small territory into a large country "where a man may make his choice . . . of more pleasant and profitable seats than he leaveth behind him." Banishment was not a confinement but an "enlargement," Cotton pointed out, "where a man does not so much lose civil comforts as change them." And so far as spiritual liberty was concerned, Williams had perfect liberty to accept the church ordinances of the Bay Colony. But he found them "a burden and a bondage," casting off not only those of Massachusetts but of Rhode Island as well, waiting "till Christ shall send forth new Apostles to plant Churches anew." Even in his own town, even in his own church, the unlamblike Williams became a thorn and an affliction.

So there was some fine justice, Cotton wrote, in the subsequent fortunes of this "backslider." He had brought forth no good fruit, only "bitter and wild fruit." Such was especially dangerous when all Englishmen were distraught, when "their hearts are become as Tinder, ready to catch and kindle at every spark of false light." Antinomians were doing their worst, along with antisabbatarians and papists; then came "Mr. Williams" to challenge and question all "instituted worship of God," to undermine all Christian magistrates, and to refuse all "Communion with the Churches of the Saints" for himself. If I alone were under attack, said Cotton, "I should have been as a deaf man, and a dumb man that openeth not his lips." But too much was at stake now. When a man under the pretext "of maintaining Liberty of Conscience" attacked the very truth and righteousness of God and God's people, that man must be answered.

So for nearly another 150 pages, John Cotton defended the Bay Colony, its magistrates, its churches, and its integrity. Mr. Williams, if he had an eye to see and an ear to hear, would be admonished, as the Scriptures required, yet again.

Cotton and Williams shared much: a common respect for the Bible and the conviction that truth could be wrung from every verse, every precedent, every instruction—if not in English, then in Hebrew or Greek. They also shared a veneration for the early church fathers, for their testimonies and interpretations. And of course they shared a Cambridge University education. But Cotton was Williams' senior by about twenty years, and when he published *The Bloudy Tenent Washed*, Cotton was only five years away from his death. By the time Williams was able to issue his reply to the reply, Cotton was in the final year of his life. Had it not been for his death, the argument might have gone on for another thirty years, each convinced of the rectitude of his own position, each convincing the other of very little.

It was only Cotton's death that granted Williams the last word in this arena, or the last stroke of the sword of the Lord. In 1652 he published *The Bloudy Tenent Yet More Bloudy: By Mr Cottons Endeavor to Wash it White in the Blood of the Lambe*. And, as with the treatise he wrote some eight years before, although John Cotton was unmistakably the target, Williams took time to write a preface for England's Parliament in order to make timely points to those "Most Noble Senators" as they labored still to soothe the nation's political and religious distresses. The Long Parliament had indeed been a long one, having met from late in 1640 to now, the early summer of 1652. "Your tired spirits," Williams wrote, "after so long and troublesome a Term," deserve a break, even a vacation, from all their anxieties and travails.

Williams complimented the members for two specific deeds, one of mercy, the other of justice. First, Parliament had taken steps toward a broader religious toleration—not a full and absolute religious freedom, to be sure, but more "mercy and moderation" than had been the case under either the Anglicans

103

or the Presbyterians. Second, Parliament had seen to it that Archbishop Laud had met his just end, having been beheaded in 1645; King Charles had suffered a similar fate in 1649. Now, Williams observed, the "most High Eternal King of Kings" was more England's true king than ever before. So the noble senators had done well, in Williams' eyes, and deserved much praise—as well as much rest.

Of course Williams did not let the matter stop there. Parliament needed to be even bolder in its embrace of religious freedom and its forthright rejection of religious persecution, the latter being like a "notorious and common Pirate" that sets fire to and sinks all ships—spiritual ships, that is—"the Consciences of all men, of all sorts, of all Religions and Persuasions whatsoever." All rulers hesitate to embrace a full freedom in religion because, as common wisdom had it, society would suffer and the state would fall. Not so, said Williams: look at Holland. Having removed the yoke of persecution from the necks of all (Dutch, English, French, "yea, Popish & Jewish consciences"), what was the result? Prosperity, not despair; civil peace, not war. From all over Europe, the persecuted fled to Amsterdam, "a poor fishing Town," and turned it into a center of wealth, commerce, and greatness—to the astonishment of Europe and the world. "Why should not such a parliament as England never had," Williams asked, "out-shoot and teach their Neighbors" by framing a constitution that guaranteed freedom of conscience? To take such a path was not to court danger and disaster, as so many supposed; on the contrary, it would prove "beneficial and marvelously advantageous." It would also endure, Williams noted, whereas any form of national worship endorsed and established today would come tumbling down tomorrow.

A second preface fixed New England and its General Courts in Williams' sights, "especially that of Massachusetts." New England sat far away from England's civil strife, yet the issues in Boston were connected to the issues in London. Great principles were at stake, especially since New England "professeth to draw nearer to Christ Jesus than other States and

Churches." If it was to be a model, it was critical that the model be correct in all respects, but particularly with respect to one special "Bloody Doctrine." And that doctrine was like a sly serpent that had managed to creep under the "shade and shelter of Mr. Cotton's Patronage and Protection."

Even in this preface, Williams laid down two "fundamentals" to which he would repeatedly return: first, that government was derived from the people and had, therefore, no authority from God to rule or reform or discipline God's church; and second, that the Old Testament pattern of a national church, unique to that time and place, was now "unimitable by any Civil State in all or any of the Nations of the World beside." To be sure, he had made that point before in the portion of *The Bloudy Tenent* that dealt with the Salem model of church and civil power. But John Cotton, on the ground that he had no hand in writing that "model," declined to answer that large segment of Williams' treatise. Perhaps he declined even to read it. Better not take a chance, Williams thought; he would make the argument again. (For Williams, repetition was no sin.)

A third preface, "to the Merciful and Compassionate Reader," enabled Williams to take up at least two additional tasks. The first related to John Cotton himself. Professing respect for his person (even though some Rhode Island friends characterized Cotton's 1647 "washing" reply as having washed Jesus in blood and Williams in gall), Williams had little respect for his arguments or his position. If Cotton objected to the debating techniques of his adversary, the adversary returned the favor. Whenever Cotton took a stand, Williams noted, he always provided himself with some escape, "strange Reserves, and Retreats." When pressed as a persecutor of men's souls, Cotton retreated, explaining that he did not persecute, but sometimes obstinate consciences convicted themselves. When pressed about the magistrate's interference with the church and laws of the First Table, Cotton ran as fast as he could "into the Land of Israel, and call[ed] up Moses and his Laws." And when pressed concerning civil powers all over the world persecuting and murdering, Cotton escaped to his last refuge, clarifying that magistrates must not meddle in religion until they were properly informed. What this meant, Williams wrote, was that they must not act until Cotton "is sure they will draw their swords for his Conscience" and his church.

The second task related to the nature of the church. Williams was now convinced that one must restore the original institution as revealed in "the last will and Testament of Christ Jesus." But churches in the present day could come closer to that pattern, if they would. And the four marks of the primitive church for Williams were these. (1) The Christian members and ministers are "content with a poor and low condition in worldly things." (2) The church purges itself of "the filthiness of false worships." (3) Simultaneously, it strives for as near approximation as possible to New Testament forms and ordinances. And (4) this church, as one would expect Roger Williams to declare, will never kill or wound those who believe otherwise, but on the contrary, these saints "resolve themselves patiently to bear and carry the Cross and Gallows of their Lord and Master, and patiently to suffer with him." If for Williams there was no true church, there were nonetheless churches that more nearly approached the exalted heights of righteousness and truth.

All three prefaces only raised the curtain on the main event: another dialogue between Peace and Truth, this one even longer than the 1644 publication. And more repetitious. Since Cotton's 1647 reply reproduced most of the argument of Williams' 1644 treatise in order to answer line upon line, biblical text upon biblical text, and since Williams treated *The Bloudy Tenent Washed . . .* in similar fashion, repetition was unavoidable. If either opponent misquoted a verse of Scripture, this had to be noted. If either failed to answer a particular argument but hurried on to the next, much was made of that fact. And should one get his chapter titles or page numbers wrong, there was no escape. *The Bloudy Tenent Yet More Bloudy* is yet more painstaking, yet more insistent, yet more familiar. One can expect to read again about the wheat and the tares, at extraordinary length.

One will encounter the first and second admonitions recorded in Titus 3, the distinctions between civil and ecclesiastical power, the limitations upon the magistrate, the lessons of history after Constantine, the instructions of Scripture before. But some novelties and emphases nonetheless deserve notice.

Williams' 1644 book also had a preface to Parliament. John Cotton, in his reply, ignored it. For Williams, this omission was pregnant with meaning. Cotton did not want to involve Parliament in his defense of "the New England Way," for while the former body moved in the direction of ever more toleration, Cotton and company moved in an opposite direction. "Master Cotton is wise, and knows in what door the wind blows of late," Williams wrote, adding that many letters and tracts in England poured forth in protest "against New England's persecuting." Cotton was forced to respond to *The Bloudy Tenent,* but the times advised him to do so "with as little noise as may be," for he had "no great willingness" for Parliament to probe his reply too closely. Therefore, let's ignore Parliament, Cotton in effect says, confining the quarrel to just the two of us.

While Williams was not prepared to ignore Parliament (thus another preface in 1652), he was willing to engage Cotton directly. Hardly a page (in a book of more than 300 pages) fails to mention "Master Cotton" once, and on many his name appears several times. It was Cotton's reading of the Bible that was under attack, Cotton's reading of history, Cotton's running and retreating, jabbing and feinting, as he defended what Massachusetts thought and did. But this was only to give Williams' argument more precision and focus; the battleground for "soul-freedom" was worldwide.

Should dissenters or false worshipers be tolerated in Massachusetts? "Master Cotton" says no, because they will cause mischief. Well, replied Williams, if they break civil law, then the civil state, which is "strongly guarded," can take appropriate action. But what if they break church law? In that case, Williams wrote, the guard was even greater: the whole army of heaven, with its mighty, but purely spiritual, weapons. Perhaps so, conceded Cotton, but superstition will still spread like a plague, infecting all. Has Cotton no confidence in spiritual weapons? asked Williams. Is he turning the powerful swords of Christ Jesus into mere "wooden daggers" or "scarecrows"? Does he really think it necessary to take spiritual swords to the black-smith's shop in order to purge the church of "idolatry and superstition"? A failure of confidence in an omnipotent Deity is suggested in one who hides behind the puny defenses erected by man.

When cornered, Cotton said that only rightly informed magistrates should meddle in religion. But "Master Cotton can-not deny but that most of the Magistrates of the world . . . are such as Herod, Pilate, Caesar were, without God, and enemies to him, yea also in that part of the world which is called Protes-tant." Now if only godly and Christian magistrates should rule over the church, how is it that Christ Jesus made so serious a mistake? For note that through all history and over all the world "how poorly hath Christ Jesus in all ages provided for and furnished his people with such main pillars" as godly rulers. The wolves rule the world, not the sheep. So Cotton's civil state was more a dream, a fantasy, than a fair description of how civil and ecclesiastical power do in fact operate. "Master Cotton and those of his bloody judgment" do not appreciate the awful conse-quences of their doctrine. Let's not blame the magistrates, how-ever, for the clergy are really responsible. Everywhere they stir up the princes to come to the rescue of their religion, or in "plain English," to the rescue of "their profits, honors, and bellies."

If Williams was "unlamblike," Cotton's doctrine was even further removed from the gentleness and softness of the lamb. Resorting to one of his favorite though disturbing images, Wil-liams wrote of the violence done to the human conscience, forced against its will to support a church that it did not attend, to attend a worship it did not trust, to pay for a ministry it did not call. It is like "some lustful Ravisher" dealing "with a beau-tiful Woman, first using all subtle Arguments and gentle per-suasions," and when these do not work, turning to violence and

108

force. Protestant and papist alike have been so ravished. "What is it now to force a Papist to Church, but a Rape, a Soul-Rape?" In order to save his career, or his estate, or his life, he "comes to that Worship which his Conscience tells him is false." Similarly, Protestants, Thomas Cranmer and others, "were forced or ravished by the terror of Death" and so they "subscribed, abjured, went to Mass, but yet against their Wills and Consciences." Cotton cannot possibly defend this sort of thing, whether it be Protestant or papist, nor can he deny the grossest violence done to that innermost holy of holies, the human soul.

So, after a long journey, "after all our tempestuous Tossings in the boisterous Seas of this bloody Tenent," Williams at last ends his treatise with a devastating description of why that bloody tenent is in fact so bloody. It is, said Williams, a "high Blasphemy against the God of Peace, the God of Order," even as it wars against the Prince of Peace, "denying his Appearance and Coming in the Flesh." For Christ Jesus came not to destroy people's lives for the sake of their religion "but to save them." This bloody tenent, moreover, has cut throats, torn out hearts, and poured forth blood in all the ages—so much so that one cannot conceive of any crime, no matter how obscene or outrageous, that has so brutally devastated humanity. And where it has not slain, it has robbed nations of their best citizens, who have been forced to flee their own homelands for freedom of conscience.

The bloody tenent remained bloody despite Master Cotton's greatest efforts. "Let Heaven and Earth judge of the washing and color of this Tenent." The stain has not been, can never be removed. In a mighty burst of rhetorical power, Williams concludes, "I must profess, while Heaven and Earth lasts, that no one Tenent that either London, England, or the World doth harbor, is so heretical, blasphemous, seditious, and dangerous to the corporal, to the spiritual, to the present, to the Eternal Good of all Men, as the bloody Tenent (however washed and whited) I say, as is the bloody Tenent of persecution for cause of Conscience."

109

This book was not burned in London, Parliament having already moved somewhat nearer to the position of Roger Williams. Nor was it burned in Boston, but it was scorned—and would continue to be throughout the colonial period. Rhode Island in general and Roger Williams in particular stood for that which Massachusetts in general and John Cotton in particular condemned and despised. By the time that copies of this volume reached American shores, Cotton was only a few months from death. He had spoken his last words on the subject. Likewise, on that same subject Roger Williams had spoken his last—almost.

Parliament had moved, it was true, but perhaps with just another nudge or two, it could make that wonderful jump from mere toleration to absolute freedom. The first implied special favors graciously granted; as such, they could be abruptly withdrawn, or the conditions of toleration could be constantly redefined (and in fact Parliament was in the process of making just such ongoing changes). But absolute freedom in religion placed all on an equal plane: no gracious indulgence on the one hand, no fawning gratitude on the other. A fundamental, essential, irrevocable right had been recognized, not as the pleasure of Parliament but as the will of God.

So Williams took pen in hand one more time, though much more briefly on this occasion, to answer a tract for the times circulating in London in the spring of 1652. Earlier that year, a pamphlet entitled *Zeal Examined* appeared, defending the position taken by Williams. He could only rejoice to receive the overt support contained in this publication, which may have been written by his good friend Sir Henry Vane. His rejoicing turned to anger, however, when that tract was refuted by another under the title of *The Examiner Examined.* This anonymous work carefully posed twenty-two questions that again threw the principle of religious freedom into serious doubt. For all of England, the timing was too critical to leave such doubt hanging in the air. So Roger Williams responded with *The Examiner Defended*, a pamphlet that demonstrated the author's sincere effort to compress

110

his ideas and avoid redundancies. Few new points were made, though Williams did reveal an antipathy toward long-haired men.

He also explained the accidental dangers of religious persecution. Once one was fired with the zeal of using the civil sword against nonconformity, it was difficult to know when or where to stop. "Into what furious Extremes do we run and leap." Mary, the mother of Jesus, giving birth in our day "without the company of her Husband," would have been an object of attack. "For how fiery would we be to condemn such a Birth as spurious, the Parents and the child unclean," and harsh punishment would swiftly follow. Similarly, we condemn the socially despised Ranters, those "poor deluded . . . Mad Folk." But a far worse and much more pervasive "ranting" is that of nations who persecute: this "mad flinging about of Firebrands, Arrows, and Death" turned the whole "world topsi-turvy."

In a move meant truly to stagger the imagination, Williams asked Parliament to consider what would happen should England defeat France, or vice versa. "What should the Catholic conqueror do with so many thousand Protestant heretics, so accounted? And what should the Protestant conqueror do with so many hundred thousand Popish Idolaters in France and Spain, yea suppose all the world over?" How horrifying the result! This might seem altogether fanciful or hypothetical, but Williams knew it was not. "I know what some furious Zealots would say, on either side." What Williams wanted to know was "what Christ Jesus would do, what the meek Lamb of God would do, who tells his fiery Disciples in such cases (Luke 9), You know not what Spirit you are of."

Here and elsewhere Williams made much of "civility," giving emphasis to the word's original meaning. For Williams, civility (in addition to being common courtesy) pertained to the civil state. The magistrate had every right to require civil behavior: incivility was properly punished. Impiety, on the other hand, was none of his affair. That was the province of the church or the private person. And if we all could only understand the clear line between incivility on the one hand and impiety on the other, the world would be a far safer place in which to live. We might then even understand "the Mystery and Tyranny" that is New England.

ECCLESIASTICAL CONCERNS

Though Roger Williams questioned the legitimacy of every visible church (until Christ comes again), he did not question the right of others to create what they regarded as the best approximation of the true church. Nor did he cut himself off from the ecclesiastical interests and efforts of others. He remained a student of the Bible, a critic of church polity, a theologian wrestling with the wonders of the cosmos and of Infinite Wisdom. He also confronted in his own colony zealous efforts, perhaps even more zealous than his own, to arrive at religious expressions pure and undefiled.

Samuel Gorton represented one such effort. Gorton's career often paralleled that of Williams himself. As noted earlier, he was ejected from the Bay Colony, fled to Plymouth and was ejected from there, and then went to Aquidneck and later Providence. Arrested in Rhode Island by Massachusetts men, he was tried and condemned. Then, like Williams, he made his way to London in order to tell the story of his indignities (in *Simplicities Defence*, published in 1646) and to seek some guarantees regarding the large tract of land that he and his friends had purchased from the Narraganset sachems. Also like Williams, he courted the favor of commissioners who held in their hands the full power of decision regarding his request. He won their favor, particularly that of the Earl of Warwick, who decided that Massachusetts had no valid claim to the land of Shawomet that Gorton and his followers had occupied in Rhode Island since 1642. Gorton received clear title as well as safe passage through Massachusetts when he returned. In gratitude for the favors of his patron, Gorton in 1648 gave the area of Shawomet the name of Warwick, so by that date the colony of Rhode Island had four towns: Providence, Portsmouth, Newport, and Warwick.

When Williams was fighting factions within Providence itself, he found Gorton's presence no great help. Later, however, he found that he could not continue to hold a grudge against a man who made Massachusetts so angry, nor against a man who also condemned civil interference in spiritual affairs. In 1652 he publicly complained about all the suffering to which the Gortonites had been subjected, their being captured, condemned, imprisoned, chained, and abused. And had all this changed the mind or heart of a single Gortonite? Not at all. If anything, it brought more sympathy to them and their cause. In truth, Williams wrote, "I am no more of Master Gorton's Religion than of Master Cotton's." But this was just another excellent example of how religious persecution "doth give strength and vigor, spirit and resolution to the most erroneous."

Gorton supported Williams in his effort to keep Rhode Island lands out of the clutches of Massachusetts and, later, Connecticut. He stayed on in London for a time to publish more against the Bay Colony and to keep the title to Warwick from being challenged or clouded. Most of all, however, he advocated positions that Williams could, in many instances, support. This cannot be very surprising, since Gorton emerged from the same tradition of Anabaptist separatism that appealed to Williams. Nor can it be surprising that Massachusetts continued to view both men with alarm, since the Puritans saw Anabaptism as inevitably leading to skepticism about all forms of government, civil or ecclesiastical.

Sounding very much like Roger Williams, Gorton in 1647 contended that the magistrate must be carefully confined "within the compass of civil things." He may regulate relations between citizens, but never the relations between creatures and the Creator. New England seized power that belonged only to Christ, forgetting or denying the great gap between the heavenly and earthly spheres. Gorton questioned civil authority so severely that many wondered if he did not reject all government,

113

but he contended that his only concern was to see that such authority stayed within its "proper confines and circuits." For Gorton as for Williams, of course, this question had utmost pertinence.

Gorton also questioned too great a reliance upon learning, especially if this seemed the essential qualification for the ministry. A man may be filled with knowledge, yet empty of spirit, and this could only lead to religious desolation for those dependent on him. A ministry "that spends its time, study, and care in seeking and hoping for the transfusing Spirit of Christ" is chasing a rainbow. One might as well spend one's time trying to "teach a dog the art of arithmetic, Astrology, or navigation." Reproved for his lack of "humane learning," Gorton happily confessed that he had not been "drowned in pride and ignorance through Aristotle's principles and other heathen philosophers, as millions are and have been."

One needed only the spirit of Christ dwelling within, whether clergy or laity. Indeed, the difference between those two "classes" was essentially meaningless, as it was between the ruler and the ruled. Gorton went so far as to suggest that the very notion of sin might have been an invention of the professional and learned clergy, designed to keep the masses in subjection, oppressing "the poorer sort with burdens of sins, and such abundance of servile obedience, as to make them slaves to themselves and others." Nietzsche could not have said it better, adding to the charge that ethical terms were only tags of social oppression and division. By questioning all class structures, Gorton came close to being a Leveler, a social radical who (in the words of Edward Winslow, a Massachusetts agent and apologist) treats every man as a brother, "whether rich or poor, ignorant or learned." From this it naturally follows, Winslow added, that "every Christian in a Commonwealth must be King, and Judge, and Sheriff, and Captain, and Parliament-man, and ruler." Massachusetts had done right to get rid of Samuel Gorton.

Williams, uncomfortable with Gorton in Providence, apparently had no difficulty with him after he and his followers gathered in a legally recognized Warwick. And in fact, once the Gortonites were no longer harassed and jailed and chained, they settled down to a quieter, less contentious way of life. Which, of course, was the very point that Williams had tried to make in 1652: persecution promotes even greater zeal and stiffer determination. That Williams did not agree with Gorton in all respects was irrelevant to the determination of the former to leave the latter in peace "in all civil things." After Samuel Gorton died in 1677, his followers did not long survive as a separate sect. But Gorton had helped prepare Rhode Island for the coming of the Quakers in large numbers. That sect did survive, and about them at a later date Roger Williams had much to say.

The group that held his attention more closely in the 1640s and fifties continued to be the Baptists. Departing from the Baptist church in Providence did not lead to any sort of "apostate syndrome": he did not denounce, ridicule, or turn sharply away from the denomination with which he had been identified. On the contrary, he continued to defend the Baptist interest and follow closely developments in their doctrine and worship. Most of all, he kept a wary eye on Massachusetts and what it would do about this suspect and potentially subversive religious body. He had reason to do so.

In 1644 Massachusetts outlawed Baptists. From the Bay Colony's point of view, there were several good reasons for doing so. First of all, they were really "Anabaptists," and everybody knew what went on in Münster: anarchy, polygamy, revolution; all Anabaptists were "incendiaries of commonwealths." Second, they denied infant baptism, and (employing the camel's nose in the tent argument) Massachusetts argued that people who do such a thing as that "have usually held other errors or heresies together therewith." Third, they gave magistrates a bad time, some by denying the "lawfulness of making war" and others by objecting to civil inspection "into any breach of the first table." Fourth, they insisted on increasing in number, making Massachusetts anxious about its own safety or serenity in the years ahead. As finally published the next year, the law provided for banishment as the fit punishment for those who denied infant baptism or who "went about secretly to seduce others from the approbation or use thereof" or who even walked out of a service when infant baptism was being administered. With equal force, however, condemnation fell upon the Baptists for their objecting to the civil magistrate's doing what Massachusetts had elected him to do—namely, enforce all the Ten Commandments, the First Table no less than the second.

Unfortunately, any letters in which Williams might have given his immediate reaction to this law have been lost, though we learn later in unmistakable terms of his repugnance when that law was specifically applied. We also learn from Williams in 1649 that the Baptists not only persisted in rejecting infant baptism but came to require that adult believers be fully immersed. Not content with sprinkling, as was the case with infants, Baptists now wanted all members "dipped," symbolically buried with Christ in baptism and raised with him into a new life. "I believe," Williams wrote, that this baptism "comes nearer the practice of our great Founder, Christ Jesus, than other religions do, and yet. . . ." For Williams, always that "and yet." His qualification pertained, of course, to his conviction that until Christ came again and created new apostles, all church ordinances lacked full validity.

The new mode of baptism had been introduced from a Calvinist English Baptist church into John Clarke's Newport church in 1648, then into Providence soon after, and then beyond the safe borders of Rhode Island into Plymouth Colony. Plymouth had no law against Baptists as Massachusetts did, but the General Court in Boston advised that that defect should be rectified as quickly as possible. Plymouth, having entertained such as Roger Williams and Samuel Gorton, required supervision—obviously. Massachusetts was ready to provide it—generously. Rumor had it, said the Boston Court, that some thirteen or fourteen persons had within a few weeks been rebaptized (dipped) in the single town of Rehoboth; such swift in-

116

crease terrified. And, said Boston, "to our great grief, we are credibly informed" that the Plymouth General Court has done nothing, enduring all patiently. "Consider our interest," Boston begged; "the infection of such diseases, being so near us, are likely to spread into our jurisdiction." Plymouth caught the hint, arraigned the malefactors before them, and ordered them to cease and desist, to ordain no clergy, "not to baptize, nor to break bread together, nor yet to meet upon the first day of the week."

Some ceased and desisted, but the majority did not. After further harassment, they left in 1650 for the freer air of Newport, Rhode Island, where liberty of conscience could be embraced and a welcome fellowship in John Clarke's baptizing church enjoyed. Newport was far from the jurisdiction of the Massachusetts General Court, which may have had some hope for reforming Plymouth but had none whatsoever for reforming Rhode Island. Newporters were safe, at least so long as they remained in Newport.

On July 16, 1651, John Clarke along with two other members of his church, Obadiah Holmes and John Crandall, decided on a fateful trip from Newport to Lynn, Massachusetts. After a three-day walk, they arrived in Lynn for the immediate purpose of bringing spiritual comfort and communion to a blind and aged Baptist who, since Baptists were outlawed, had no local church that could minister to him. More broadly, of course, the three traveling evangelists wanted to proclaim to others the good news of Jesus Christ as they understood it, new baptism and all. Clarke, from his brief experience in Massachusetts more than a decade before, knew what that colony needed most to hear. Holmes, a recent convert in Rehoboth, had all the passion of the new and true believer, while Crandall, a son-in-law of Samuel Gorton, had zeal from more than a single source.

So the three men preached, privately to be sure (in the home of that blind Baptist); they also baptized some present and served communion. The law against "Anabaptists," however, specifically prohibited all seducing of others to their opinions. The three were arrested, imprisoned (for a week or more), tried, and found guilty—to the surprise of no one. That 1645 law had specified the penalty for their offenses—namely, banishment. But banishment would be no punishment at all for these three intruders, who would like nothing more than to be "banished" back home. Something obviously had to be worked out; the wording of the law had to be adjusted. The Court in its wisdom decided that each criminal should be fined, with the proviso that if the fine were not paid, each would be "well whipped." After another week or so in jail, Clarke was released when friends paid his fine. Crandall put up bail and returned to Newport, it being unclear whether he "jumped bail" or not. Only Obadiah Holmes obstinately stayed in prison, refusing to pay his fine or to let others pay it for him.

From mid-August to early September, Holmes languished in a Boston prison alone, awaiting the whipping that was now inevitable. On the day set for the public event in Boston's marketplace, friends came to Holmes to offer him some wine to lessen the pain. He refused it and all other comforts, lest the world say, he wrote, that he was sustained by anything other than the spirit of God. When the time came, Holmes was tied to a post and the "executioner" instructed to "Do your office!" As his clothes were being stripped from him, Holmes said: "I am now come to be baptized in afflictions by your hands, that so I may have further fellowship with my Lord. [I] am not ashamed of His suffering, for by His stripes am I healed." The executioner spat on his hands, then laid thirty lashes "with all his strength" across the exposed back of the prisoner. Later, returned briefly to his prison cell, Holmes received an old friend who, "like a good Samaritan, poured oil into my wounds and plastered my sores." The entire episode that September morning was over in less than an hour, but it would not be soon forgotten.

For Rhode Island had its cause celébré and Roger Williams his unmistakable evidence that in the fifteen years since his own banishment Massachusetts had not learned anything at all. The Bay Colony had learned nothing from his long letter to Cotton, nothing from *The Bloudy Tenent*, nothing from the liberalizations

Parliament introduced in England, and most of all nothing from the New Testament. It was time to write another letter. As soon as he heard of the events in Boston (John Clarke brought the news to him), Williams wrote—as much in dismay as in fury—to the governor who passed the sentence, John Endecott, an old friend from Salem days. But friendship was at this point not uppermost in his mind.

Violation of conscience was uppermost, and no excuses, please, this time. No pretext that people like Holmes sinned against their own conscience, for "this is the Outcry of the Pope and Prelates, and of the Scotch Presbyterians, who would fire all the world." No pretense that you, Endecott, do not know better, for you have confessed the contrary to me, Williams noted. But now your eyes are blinded once again, so that you must be instructed once again. "Be pleased, then honored Sir," Williams wrote, with hand and teeth clenched, "to remember that that thing which we call Conscience is of such a Nature (especially in Englishmen) as once a Pope of Rome . . . himself observed that although it be groundless, false, and deluded, yet it is not by any Arguments or Torments easily removed." Nations do what they will about religion; there is no constancy or faithfulness there. But conscience, said Williams, is "a persuasion fixed in the mind and heart of a man" that requires him to maintain a position of truth, especially "with respect to God, his worship, &c." Williams then reviewed the arguments against religious persecution, arguments that he hardly dreamed he would need to elaborate so soon again.

He wished, however, to make the case personal, not theoretical. And he did so in language of enormous force. Do you not hear a voice, Williams asked, from the king of kings: "Endecott, Endecott, why huntest thou me? why imprisonest thou me? why finest, why so bloodily whippest, why wouldest thou (did I not hold thy bloody hands) hang and burn me?" Even the wisest of the world cannot discern the Christ, especially when he appears among the poor and despised. Even the wisest ask: "When did we see thee naked, hungry, thirsty, sick, in prison?"

119

That being so, "I beseech you" to consider this awful possibility, asking yourself: Is it possible "that since I hunt, I hunt not the life of my Savior, and the blood of the Lamb of God?" Is it not possible, Endecott, that since you "have fought against many several sorts of Consciences" that you have not, in fact, fought against God? Moreover, such indiscriminate persecution, once begun, knows no end. "Like stones once rolling down the Alps, like the Indian Canoes or English Boats loose and adrift, where stop we until infinite mercy stop us?" To give even more emphasis to this letter, Williams the next year appended to it *The Bloudy Tenent Yet More Bloudy*. Perhaps together they would send the message that the world so sorely needed in "these wonderful, searching, disputing, and dissenting times."

If Massachusetts was offended by the further interference of Roger Williams in their purely internal affairs, they soon had yet more reason to be offended, even embarrassed. John Clarke, who had been denied the opportunity to present his case (and his beliefs) before the General Court in Boston, resolved to present it before an even wider audience. In London in 1652 he published a book, the title of which made part of his case: *Ill Newes from New-England; or, A Narative of New-Englands Persecution. Wherin Is Declared That while old England is becoming new, New-England is become Old*. Clarke put his finger on a very sore spot. As Parliament under the Independents moved toward greater toleration, Massachusetts under Endecott and others moved toward harsher repression. Clarke's report would not endear Massachusetts to Parliament in general nor to Oliver Cromwell in particular.

When a former Massachusetts magistrate living in London wrote back to the Bay Colony to protest this spirit of persecution, John Cotton, in the final months of his life, could restrain himself no more. Our enemies are clearly out to get us, and we're not as bad as portrayed, Cotton wrote. So what if our laws make hypocrites? At least "hypocrites give God part of his due—the outer man, but the profane person gives God neither outward nor inward man." We are willing, said Cotton, to tolerate persons who dissent "privately or inoffensively," but not the flagrant and scandalous dissenters. As for keeping Clarke, Holmes, and Crandall in prison so long, Cotton offered the opinion that a jail in Boston was no doubt more comfortable than a house in Newport. With respect to Holmes in particular, imprisoned longer than the others, the guards fed him and clothed him, and "I am sure [he] had not been so well clad for many years before." Cotton was not dead yet.

Nor were the ideas for which he fought, though John Clarke did his part in *Ill Newes* to subject those ideas to further blows. Conscience, said Clarke, is that "sparkling beam from the Father of lights and spirits that . . . cannot be lorded over, commanded, or forced, either by men, devils, or angels." Before another decade had passed, Massachusetts demonstrated that it still had not gotten the message by hanging four Quakers in Boston Common.

Williams, who questioned the validity of the visible church, never questioned the necessity of a visible government. From the founding of Providence, from the securing of the first charter, from the time he was chosen "chief officer" of the colony, and for years thereafter, Roger Williams found himself totally engaged in, caught up by, the world's daily business. That prison restrained him; it threatened to defeat him.

5 Exile from the World

Roger Williams spent much of his time criticizing civil magistrates and trying to circumscribe their activities. The rest of the time he spent assisting such magistrates or becoming one himself. Of his surviving correspondence, the greater segment by far is to officers of the state, notably to John Winthrop and (when that friendship cooled in the late 1640s) to his son, John Winthrop, Jr. The former was governor of Massachusetts, the latter of Connecticut. In addition, Williams wrote to civic bodies such as the towns in Rhode Island, the General Court of Massachusetts Bay, the Commissioners of the United Colonies, and other governing authorities. A strong critic of governmental practice, Roger Williams was nonetheless a chief practitioner.

When one launches a new enterprise, one has to accept responsibility for the survival of that enterprise. Williams could not escape his responsibility in Rhode Island any more than the senior Winthrop could in Massachusetts or William Penn in his colony. In addition, Williams' unique relationship with the Indians in New England repeatedly thrust larger chores upon

him. Then, too, he had valuable contacts both in England and in America that enhanced the worth of his services—contacts, it must be said, that he carefully cultivated. Finally, his "humane learning" gave him an elevated status, however much he might deny or regret that fact. Williams did not lust for political office; he simply could not escape it.

PROVIDENCE PLANTATIONS

When Roger Williams returned in the fall of 1644, he quickly assumed the role of leadership that awaited him. By the following August, if not well before, he was officially designated "chief officer." Chief officer of Providence, clearly, but of what other towns? The charter specified that Portsmouth and Newport would be part of the colony, and soon Warwick needed to be added to the list. But each town guarded its independence jealously, as did the thirteen colonies later when a federal union was under consideration. Each town, often each family, had its own economy: no "common market" was required. Each town controlled vast unoccupied acreage: no "zoning laws" or "spheres of influence" had to be defined. Each town thought of itself as self-sufficient militarily, at least in the absence of organized military attack. And each town had been settled by the most rigorously independent men and women that the New World had ever seen: cantankerous, ill-tempered, suspicious, and righteous in their own eyes. It would not be easy to bring Rhode Islanders into a single colony.

And it was not easy. It took Roger Williams nearly three years from the time he returned to consummate the reluctant—and incomplete—union in May of 1647. The General Court, meeting that month in Portsmouth, agreed to a "democratical" form of government, defining this to mean that laws and judicial system and nature of representation would be set "by the free and voluntary consent of all, or the greater part of the free Inhabitants." The four towns took this bold step not so much

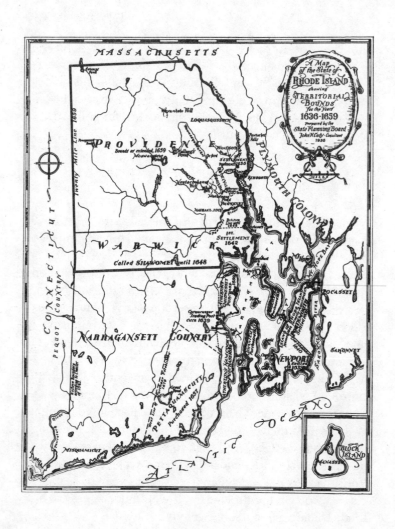

Colony of Rhode Island, 1636–1659

Courtesy of the Rhode Island Historical Society

out of brotherly love for each other as out of mutual anxiety about their colonial neighbors. Neither Massachusetts nor Connecticut, nor even Plymouth for that matter, ever quite conceded that the rich lands all around Narragansett Bay were forever beyond their jurisdiction or control. Rhode Island possessed a charter, to be sure, but it had been granted merely by the hand of a Parliament committee, and committees and politics in England in the 1640s seemed to rise and fall with the daily tides.

In August 1645 the General Court of Massachusetts officially informed Roger Williams that the Bay Colony had received a charter "from the Authority of the high court of Parliament" by terms of which all the lands of Providence, Portsmouth, and Newport now fell within the jurisdiction of Massachusetts. Therefore, said the General Court, "forbear to exercise any Jurisdiction therein." If Rhode Islanders wished to challenge this directive, they must "appear at our next General Court . . . to show by what right you claim any such Jurisdiction." And the Court, to show its generosity, would grant, even to those under sentence of banishment, a "free liberty to come, stay, and return" for the purpose of attending this hearing. Even in the chaotic days of England's civil war, could such a thing possibly be true? Was all of Rhode Island to be at the mercy of an unforgiving General Court?

The Massachusetts charter, however, turned out to be a fraud. Never had a majority of the London commissioners signed this "Narragansett Patent," nor had the document ever been formally registered on the agenda of the Commission on Foreign Plantations. The charter that Williams had brought back, on the other hand, had been duly signed and sealed by a majority gathered in a regular meeting of the Commission. Of course, it did not have royal approval, but when the king and Parliament were at war, such was more than even Massachusetts could expect or demand. So this Massachusetts challenge failed. Nevertheless, it would be many years yet before Rhode Island's borders were secure against grasping neighbors.

Meanwhile, Indian conflicts threatened to engulf the small

colony, and the danger would increase if the rest of New England joined in the dispute. Warfare erupted between the Narragansets and the Mohegans, a warfare that had its origins in the settlement after the Pequot War of 1637. Roger Williams urged that the English stay out of this tribal conflict, as both sides (Williams wrote Winthrop in June 1645) "have deeply implunged themselves in Barbarous slaughters." Williams urged that Massachusetts and Connecticut "improve all Interests and opportunities to quench these Flames" rather than take sides and thereby enlarge the war. "My humble requests are to the God of Peace," Williams added, "that no further English blood be spilt in America." To that end, he called for "loving Mediation or prudent Neutrality."

But Massachusetts had already taken sides—with the Mohegans and against the Narragansets. Two years earlier Miantonomo, leader of the Narragansets, had been captured by the Mohegans in a brief skirmish. (That Samuel Gorton had given him wholly unsuitable heavy armor to wear did not help.) The Mohegan chief, Uncas, curried favor with the English by not killing Miantonomo on the spot, but turning him over to the United Commissioners of the New England Confederacy (formed in 1643). All except Rhode Island were members of this Confederacy. The Commissioners met, decided that Miantonomo deserved to die, decided that they wanted no part in the execution, decided finally that Uncas was best fitted to carry out the vengeful task. On the way back from Hartford, where the Commissioners met, Uncas more than satisfied the judgment of the court. When the aggrieved Narragansets sought revenge for this murder in 1645, Massachusetts decided to take military action against the tribe that Roger Williams had so carefully cultivated.

In July 1645 the Confederacy formally declared war upon the Narragansets, immediately dispatching soldiers from Massachusetts, Plymouth, Connecticut, and New Haven to rendezvous in Rehoboth and then proceed to the attack. A proviso was included for one more attempt at diplomacy, Massachusetts again enlisting the services of Roger Williams as interpreter and negotiator. Thanks to Williams, war was avoided, the Narragansets agreeing to send emissaries a few days later to Boston, where the terms of peace would be discussed. Those terms, when finally agreed upon in late August, represented a total victory for the United Colonies of New England and a total, humiliating defeat for the Narragansets, who were required to pay a large fine to the English plus a reparation to the Mohegans and a return of all captives to their hated enemy. They were also required to relinquish all claims to land formerly possessed by the Pequots. Bitter resentment over these harsh terms was to explode in calamitous tragedy thirty years later.

Roger Williams had dealt fairly with the Narragansets, and he firmly believed they had dealt fairly with him. His relationship was especially close with the now aged chief, Canonicus, who had initially given Williams land for the Providence settlement but who later accepted "presents and Gratuities" in view of his generous donation. In June 1647 Canonicus died, having earlier asked that he be buried in cloth from Williams and that the Englishman attend his funeral. Williams did attend, later testifying that "when the hearts of my countrymen and friends failed me," the "infinite wisdom and merits" of Canonicus sustained him, adding that the chief loved him as a son "to his last gasp." Both Canonicus and Williams had hoped that the English and the Indian could live together in peace, generation after generation. When Canonicus died, much of that hope died with him.

For the saints of God, the whole question of war was a troublesome one. Some solved it by refusing ever to engage in any war at any time. Others solved it by distinguishing between good wars and bad, just and unjust, holy and unholy. Still others solved it by surrendering conscience to the demands of the state. Though Roger Williams did not reject all war, he deplored all war, viewing it as one of God's "most dreadful earthly and temporal Judgments upon the children of men." Since it was a "sore plague," prudent and God-fearing men would not resort to it lightly or without considering every possible alternative. But of one thing Roger Williams was sure: men's wars were just that—wars of men, not of God. No war was holy or blessed of God, no army wielded its sword on behalf of Christ. No divine right of kings, no divine right of government, no divine right of admirals or generals. "I must be humbly bold to say," Williams sternly informed John Endecott in 1651, "that 'tis impossible for any Man or Men to maintain their Christ by the Sword." To believe or behave in this fashion was to worship a false God, to follow a God of wrath, not of love.

The United Commissioners, nonetheless, resolved once more to declare war, a war "called by God," against the Narragansets and their close allies, the Niantics, led by Ninigret. In 1653, hearing of Ninigret's slaying of some Indians on Long Island, the Commissioners decided that this sachem had become too proud and insolent, especially with respect to their authority. For a time Massachusetts held back from this declaration, but by the next year it was ready to join in a military action against this proud chief. Roger Williams agreed that Ninigret was both "proud and fierce," yet he pleaded with the General Court of Massachusetts (in October 1654) to avoid this war if at all possible. "I never was against the righteous use of the Civil sword," Williams wrote in his official capacity as "Providence Colony president," and defensive wars can often be justified. But was this a defensive war? "I humbly pray Your Consideration whether it be . . . not only possible but very easy for the English to live and die in peace with all the Natives of this Country." Besides which, Williams added, Ninigret had a point.

Who made the United Commissioners rulers over Ninigret? He was settling a dispute between Long Island Indians and his own tribe, a dispute stemming from the killing of one of his men by the Long Islanders. When rebuked for his action, Ninigret asked, if a New England governor were slain, "would you ask Counsel of another Nation how and when to Right yourselves?" The question struck Williams as right on target, as he put to the General Court a query of his own: "I question whether any Indians in this Country, remaining Barbarous and pagan, may with Truth or Honor be called the English subjects." But Williams persuaded no one outside of Rhode Island, and not even all there, so relationships between the English and the Indians continued to deteriorate.

Nor was Roger Williams' success in dealing with his own citizens much greater. Governing a colony brought him little but trouble and heartache. No sooner had the towns agreed in May 1648 to abide by the 1644 charter than factionalism broke out. The most threatening rift was led by William Coddington of Portsmouth. This man, who had political ambitions of his own, resented the official recognition given to the Gortonites in Warwick and resented the authority granted to Roger Williams. Others complained that pure democracy was being compromised, that land allocations were unfair. At times, it appeared that the "islanders" (Newport and Portsmouth) would in all cases be divided against the "mainlanders" (Providence and Warwick). Should that division persist, the colony would collapse, to be hungrily devoured by its neighbors.

By the end of August 1648 Williams wondered what he could possibly do to "bring Water . . . and not Oil or Fuel to the Flame." He suggested to the town of Providence that the colony needed to find some way to settle its disruptive disputes—some peaceable way. To try to do it through written petitions was, said Williams, an endless process. To prove the stronger argument "by Arms and Swords is cruel and merciless." To appeal to England "is most unseasonable," for the very charter itself might be withdrawn. And, finally, "to trouble our Neighbors seems neither safe nor honorable." Especially unsafe, since those neighbors would seize upon any sign of Rhode Island's weakness to move in for the kill. In other words, Rhode Islanders had to solve their problems themselves; they had to prove themselves to be "loving friends," however unlikely that prospect appeared.

So Williams proposed that ten men be chosen from each

of the four towns to form a grand committee of arbitration "to examine every public Difference, Grievance, and Obstruction of Justice, peace, and Common safety." This committee would then consider the debated point and, by majority vote, issue its "final sentence." In this way, Williams dared to hope, the representative body would "set the whole into an Unanimous posture and Order." But it did not work. By September, William Coddington was carrying a petition to Plymouth Colony, asking that all of Aquidneck Island be placed under the authority of that civil entity. Williams managed to squelch that move by explaining that Coddington spoke mainly for himself, or perhaps for a majority in Portsmouth alone, but nowhere else. The other three towns, he reported, agreed that "they dare not . . . depart from the Charter."

But what if the charter was in some way nullified? That would remove what little solid ground that Williams had to operate on, placing the colony once more on a sandy foundation. Coddington, reasoning that he had to do something about Roger Williams' precious charter, sailed for London early in 1649 to obtain a charter of his own. Yet Coddington's absence brought no great calm to Rhode Island, just more turmoil. The settlement of Pawtuxet, just south of Providence, repeatedly sought an alliance with Massachusetts Bay. Just as repeatedly, the town of Warwick voiced its anxiety about being taken over by that colony to the north. From another quarter the Niantics, under Ninigret, continued to agitate for hunting rights in Pequot Country, land that both Massachusetts and Connecticut regarded as ripe for their plucking. The Indians quarreled among themselves, even as the English quarreled among themselves, with Roger Williams trying desperately to mediate, conciliate, and avoid the increasing threat of bloodshed. On every side, Williams was besieged and battered.

In addition to the larger affairs of state, Williams found time to worry about widows and orphans left uncared for, as he solicited the town of Providence in January 1651 to settle the matter of a widow's grist mill, to make certain that an orphaned daughter now of marriageable age found a groom worthy of her, and to act as a conservator for an elderly "distracted woman" who could no longer manage her own business affairs. At the same time, Williams brought up a delicate matter concerning himself—namely, that he had never been paid the one hundred pounds voted him in 1647 as his due for expenses in connection with procuring the charter. Now, four years later, he urged the towns of Providence, Newport, and Portsmouth (Warwick had not been part of the original agreement) to press on with respect to "that money due unto me about the charter." The towns pressed on a bit more earnestly, though the full amount was never paid.

By mid-summer of 1651 William Coddington was back in Rhode Island. That news alone was bad enough, but it quickly became worse: Coddington had indeed gotten his own patent. In London, he had laid his appeal before the Council of State, representing himself as the sole discoverer of the Island of Aquidneck and the sole purchaser of this impressive bit of real estate from the Indians. After nearly a year of deliberation, the Council granted Coddington his request, in addition naming him governor of the island for life. Even those who formerly supported Coddington—and presumably pure democracy along with it—found this too much. Outside of Portsmouth, recognition was swift that the rights of the towns had to be protected, to say nothing of the survival of Rhode Island itself. In Newport, pressure was brought to bear upon John Clarke "to do his utmost endeavors in soliciting our cause in England." And on the mainland, the person to feel the pressure was, of course, Roger Williams.

Williams was not eager to return to London, especially since he still had not been fully paid for the costs of the trip he had taken seven years before. On the other hand, he was not eager to see his hard-won charter so flagrantly violated or his colony so swiftly doomed. "My Neighbors of Providence and Warwick," he wrote John Winthrop, Jr., in October 1651, "with Importunities have overcome me to endeavor the Renewing of

131

their Liberties upon the occasion of Mr. Coddington's late grant." In order to finance another trip, Williams sold his Indian trading post in Narraganset country and disposed of other properties, keeping only his house in Providence. If that were not sacrifice and indignity enough, he then had to compose a polite letter to the General Court of Massachusetts Bay asking if, this time, he might be permitted to take a ship from Boston.

"The humble petition of Roger Williams" began with a reminder that, since his banishment, he had been a faithful servant not simply to Rhode Island but to "all the Colonies of the English in peace and War, so that scarce a week hath passed but some way or other I have been used as instrumental to the peace and spreading of the English plantings in this Country." His statement hardly exaggerated, since, with respect to Indian affairs in particular, Williams' involvement was virtually continuous. But he would abase himself further by promising the "honorable General Court" that he would go straight to Boston wharf: no preaching, no seducing of others, no visits to old friends. "Inoffensively behaving myself," Williams wrote, he asked only to pass "without molestation . . . through Your Jurisdiction as a stranger for a night to the ship." Some, nonetheless, might object on the grounds that Williams was still opposed to the Bay Colony's way of worship and that he was making this trip in an attempt to secure Rhode Island's claim to the town of Warwick. With respect to the first point, Williams acknowledged that he was indeed still opposed to their form of worship, but he asked them to remember that "many millions of our Father Adam's children . . . are not of your persuasion." On the second point, Williams would be glad to debate with any two or three persons that the Court might choose in order to clarify that he sought only "a peaceable and honorable end of that sad Controversy." No debate took place. After due deliberation, the Court decided that Roger Williams could embark from Boston, "provided he carry himself inoffensively according to his promise." In November 1651 he and John Clarke sailed for London.

LONDON AND THE LARGER WORLD

Rhode Island was fortunate in being represented by two such able men, one an islander, the other a mainlander. These two, probably the only university-educated persons in the whole colony, could move with some ease in London's upper political echelons where crucial charter decisions would be made. Clarke, who had been born in Suffolk, England, in 1609, was Roger Williams' junior by about a half-dozen years. The relationship between the two men remained close until Clarke's death in 1676, Williams presenting him with personally inscribed copies of both *The Bloudy Tenent* and its sequel published while the two men were together in London. This latter book bore the inscription, "For his honored and beloved, Mr. John Clarke, an eminent witness of Christ Jesus against the bloody Doctrine of Persecution." But should not his title have been "The Reverend John Clarke"? Not for Clarke, and not for Williams.

Educated in law, medicine, and theology, Clarke regularly referred to himself as a physician, not a clergyman: he made his living in the former capacity, not as a "hireling minister." The title page of *Ill Newes* identified him only as "Physician of Rode Island in America." And during his long stay in London, Parliament's minutes refer to "John Clarke, the physician." While his university has not been positively identified, Leyden—noted for its medical faculty in the seventeenth century—is a strong possibility. But educated he clearly was, for he worked with both Hebrew and Greek in preparing a concordance to the Bible that Parliament in 1655 approved for printing (it "may prove singularly conducive to the help of those who desire to try all things in these trying times by that touchstone of truth," the Bible). If it was ever printed, however, no copy has survived.

Roger Williams knew his way around London, of course, both from his boyhood days and from his previous visit in 1643-1644. Many friends who had helped him before stood ready to help him again. He soon accepted the hospitality of Sir

133

Henry Vane, Jr., who had a home in Charing Cross. He also accepted the political influence of Vane, hoping that with such help the Coddington patent would be quickly overturned and the Williams charter quickly reconfirmed. But in England in the 1650s, nothing came quickly.

Meanwhile, Roger Williams had many works to deliver to the printer (most of which are discussed in Chapter 4). He also sent communications of encouragement or advice back home, expressing his uncertainty about how long the Council of State or the Committee for Foreign Affairs would keep him and John Clarke waiting and his concern that Cromwell's army would succeed in dissolving Parliament—a move that would bring all their efforts to a halt. In October 1652 Williams wrote to his good friend (and former printer) Gregory Dexter in Providence, telling him that it looked like he would have to remain in London for some time. "I see now the mind of the Lord to hold me here, one Year Longer." In light of the likely delay, Williams noted that he had raised the possibility of having his wife join him in London. It was a prospect not without difficulties, however, including the expense of maintaining a large family abroad and "the danger of the Seas, and enemies." Everything considered, "I freely leave her to wait upon the Lord for Direction," he told Dexter, "and according as she finds her Spirit free and Cheerful, so to come or stay."

Williams was able to report, however, that the Council of State that month had at least nullified the commission earlier granted to William Coddington. The Council further instructed Providence Plantations to proceed as before in the governance of the colony, "until further direction and order be given by the Parliament, or this Council." In other words, Coddington was out, but the 1644 charter was not yet absolutely back in. And Williams, seeing the confusion in Parliament, the outbreak of war between England and Holland the previous summer, and the highly placed adversaries opposed to him and sympathetic to Massachusetts, recognized that neither a new charter nor a reconfirmation of the old one would soon be obtained. We have,

Williams said to Dexter, an "Interim Encouragement," but anything more definitive would be "a work of Time."

In that same October the General Assembly of Providence Plantations finally got around to writing its agent in London, urging him to "make firm the fabric unto us about which you are employed." Making that fabric firm meant, of course, "laboring to unweave such irregular devices wrought by others among us." That would include Coddington, to be sure, but also Massachusetts trying to annex Pawtuxet and Connecticut trying to extend its eastern border closer and closer to Narragansett Bay. Were that not enough distraction, the Dutch in New Netherland looked upon every tumult and quarrel in Rhode Island as an open invitation for them to move up from Long Island into the southernmost lands of the vulnerable colony.

The Rhode Island assemblymen, who had every reason to be nervous, came up with a plan. Perhaps Parliament would be so good as to appoint Roger Williams directly "as Governor of this Colony for the space of one year." This would have the effect, the General Assembly wrote, of settling the minds of lots of people, especially those who have been "refractory." One year of sweet stability might be enough "to add much weight forever hereafter" to the tricky business of governance of a colony that still might not make it. To make this offer more enticing, the Assembly promised that it would do all that it could to compensate Williams for his time and labor abroad: "We are resolved to stretch forth our hands at your return beyond our Strength for your supply." It was a nice thought. Five months later, however, the towns of Providence and Warwick reported, "to our grief," that because of internal distractions "we cannot at present supply you with money as we ought." They would, however, look after his family.

Though he was grateful that his family was being looked after, Williams wanted to be with them himself. Either he should be discharged from further duties in London or he wanted his family to join him there. In April 1653 he wrote the mainland towns in poignant terms: "Remember, I am a father and an husband; I have longed earnestly to return with the last ship, and with these." Yet, without a formal discharge from them, he would not remove his shoulder from the burden lest it "fall heavy upon all." But, "pray you consider, if it be not convenient that my poor wife be encouraged to come over to me," since none of us really knows how long this complex business is going to take. For all kinds of reasons, he would hurry home. But for other heavy reasons—estates, peace, liberty—he would remain, until instructed otherwise, "your most faithful and affectionate friend and servant. Roger Williams. P.S. My love to all my Indian friends."

In the midst of political and personal anxieties about home, and in the midst of snail-paced negotiations in London, Roger Williams wrote to the eldest daughter of his old friend, employer, and patron Sir Edward Coke. He told the daughter, Anne Sadleir, that her "dear Father was often pleased to call me his Son, and truly it was as bitter as Death to me" when he had to sail for America without having the opportunity to bid his benefactor good-by. During his years in America, Williams noted, "how many thousand times since have I had the honorable and precious remembrance of his person, and the Life, the Writings, the Speeches, and Examples of that Glorious Light." This high compliment, plus his gift of a noncontroversial book that he just published ("a plain and peaceable discourse," to be considered in Chapter 6), would be enough to melt the heart of any daughter proud of her father's memory. But not Anne Sadleir's. For she was also proud of the monarchy and of the Church of England, and she saw Roger Williams as enemy to both.

She returned the book unread. She had time only for the Bible, she observed, together with writings of such loyal sons of the national church as Richard Hooker, Lancelot Andrewes, and Jeremy Taylor. "These lights shall be my guide; I wish they may be yours." All the new lights with which England was afflicted would turn out to be only "dark lanterns," she wrote in a note both curt and sharp. Despite the rebuke, Williams sent a reply, once more in most deferential terms, once more extending his "humble Respects to that blessed Root of which you Spring"— and once more daring to send her a book, this time the totally controversial *Bloudy Tenent Yet More Bloody*. She returned that one too, unread, except for the title page. She wrote that she could not think of any who had been put to death for their religious beliefs: "some few that went about to make a rent in our once well governed church were punished, but none suffered death." What caused most bloodshed, she added, was leaving "to every man's conscience to fancy what religion he list." She closed her quick note, "intreating you to trouble me no more in this kind." Before her death, she wrote on the back of one of Roger Williams' letters that "if ever he has the face to return into his native country, Tyborn may give him welcome." At Tyborn criminals were hanged.

While he was in London, Williams enjoyed better fortune with Oliver Cromwell, who invited him to join in many entertaining "Discourses." They frequently discussed Indian affairs, with Cromwell raising many questions and Williams giving weighed answers, usually taking the side of the Indians against Massachusetts. They also discussed the millennium and what the signs were of its near or distant approaching. That Cromwell in 1652 or 1653 could have any time for "entertaining discourses" in the maelstrom of political struggle and military mayhem staggers the imagination, but Williams clearly had some friends in high places, Cromwell being in the loftiest during these London years.

Williams also found time for activities beyond the affairs of state, such as teaching Dutch to John Milton. (In March 1649 the Council of State appointed Milton as Secretary of Foreign Tongues; clearly, Milton wished to add Dutch to his already impressive linguistic repertoire.) How far the personal association of these two men extended beyond this cannot now be reconstructed. What can be reconstructed, however, is the intimate association of their ideas. Before the decade of the 1650s ended, Milton—like Williams—addressed Parliament regarding his political and ecclesiastical concerns. In a *Treatise of Civil Power*, Milton began with a neat summary of England's current religious difficulties: "Two things there be which have been ever found working much mischief to the church of God, and the advancement of truth; force on the one side restraining, and hire on the other side corrupting." In this essay, Milton concentrated on that force which restrained, declaring what a civil magistrate or group of civil officers could or could not do.

Like Williams, Milton frequently quoted Scripture to make his point, but beyond that he argued that the only foundation of the Christian religion was the Bible as illuminated "within us" by the Holy Spirit. Matters of religion cannot be understood apart from this illumination granted to those who are children of God, and even they cannot be certain at all times that they possess the truth, much less can they be certain of others. From this "it follows clearly, that no man or body of men in these times can be the infallible judges or determiners in matters of religion to any other men's consciences but their own." Even the church must limit its punishment to spiritual means only and to those only who "have willingly joined themselves in that covenant of union." A church can separate persons from its fellowship, but beyond that it can do no more. No fines, no corporal punishment, for in spiritual things these "are the two arms of Antichrist, not of the true church." No councils, no edicts, no "canons of any visible church," but only the Bible can be the "final judge or rule in matters of religion, and that only in the conscience of every Christian in himself."

Like Williams, John Milton was persuaded not only that this course was right, but that the opposing course was disastrous. Force created hypocrites even as it degraded "a divine and spiritual kingdom to a kingdom of this world." Besides, state coercion in religion demonstrated a pathetic lack of faith; its enforcers failed to recognize that the gospel "began and spread over the whole world for above three hundred years under the heathen and persecuting emperors." Somehow, our modern enforcers think that without their sword and their armies the Christian church would collapse. History demonstrated the contrary, and true faith should believe the contrary. Respect for conscience was respect for true religion. But, Milton said, he would not labor the point for hundreds of pages, for the message, being so clear, could be stated briefly and without pomp. "In matters of religion, he is learnedest who is plainest." There are those who think that only great books can settle great matters, but "I rather chose the common rule, not to make much ado where less may serve."

With such dispatch, therefore, Milton treated the first item that brought "much mischief to the church of God." The second item had to do with "hire," or to quote the title of his additional essay, *Considerations Touching the Likeliest Means to Remove Hirelings Out of the Church*. England, Milton contended, was among the last of all Protestant nations to get rid of the compulsory tithe for the support of the ministry—a tithe which represented not a point of conscience but a point of covetousness. "Hire of itself" was not unlawful, Milton wrote, but hire in the church was both dangerous and evil, because of the manner of collecting the money and the manner of receiving it. As for Williams, so for Milton: coercion was the problem and corruption the result. As for Williams, so for Milton: the New Testament had replaced the Old. Under the law of Israel, God commanded the tithe, but under the gospel freedom of Christ, all was left to charity and voluntary offering.

It upset Milton, moreover, that having exacted the tithe from all, rich and poor, the clergy then proceeded to exact even more in the way of "fees for christenings, marriages, and burials." The Council of Trent proscribed Roman Catholic priests from requiring payment for such services. Should English clergy do less? In the early Christian church, before Constantine, no fees were collected. Indeed, the New Testament instructions were still clear: "And as you go, preach, saying, 'The kingdom of heaven is at hand.' Heal the sick, cleanse the lepers, raise the dead, cast out devils: *freely ye have received, freely give*" (Matt. 10:7-8). It was bad enough that the minister already lived off the gospel, unlike the apostle Paul, who made his living as a tent maker (Acts 18:3-4). But to charge fees on top of all that revealed a "greediness lower than that of tradesmen."

But we must be compensated for our expensive university education, the clergy say. A pox on your formal and elaborate learning, Milton responded: "It were much better that there were not one divine in the university, no school-divinity known, the idle sophistry of monks, the canker of religion." Let ministers be educated by the church and in the Scriptures. "Neither I speak this in contempt of learning or the ministry, but hating the common cheats of both." Milton did have contempt, however, for those "notorious hirelings" who cry out, "If ye settle not our maintenance by law, farewell the gospel." "Nothing can be uttered more false, more ignominious" than this, Milton added. It was a blasphemy "against our Savior, who hath promised, without this condition, both his holy spirit and his own presence with his church to the world's end." Most of all, let us remember, that there is a spiritual priesthood to which all Christians alike are called, that all Christians have their own liberty, their own dignity, their own adoption, "whereby they all have equally access to any ministerial function whenever called by their own abilities and the church, though they never came near commencement or university." If Christians will but remember this, the days of the hirelings are over.

John Milton and Roger Williams shared much in the realm of ideas and of radical religion. Williams, however, remained the more radical of the two, for his liberty extended equally to "Papist, Turk, Jew, and infidel." Not so for Milton, who presented these two tracts to Parliament primarily to free Protestantism from those two great mischiefs: civil force restraining and compulsory tithes corrupting. In the 1650s that no doubt seemed a task daunting enough, so daunting that Milton's liberties were taken no more seriously by the populace at large than Williams' had been. Anne Sadleir could rest more easily.

By the time Milton's tracts appeared, Roger Williams had long since departed from London. Providence needed him. So great were the distractions and divisions in the Plantations that both the town and colony needed more than that. Indeed, as Williams prepared to leave England early in the spring of 1654, he thought it wise to arm himself with a letter from Sir Henry Vane, one of the colony's most valued friends, but one who also grew weary of hearing from Rhode Island nothing but tales of faction, feud, and endless discord. In April of the previous year, Williams wrote the towns of Providence and Warwick that "Under God the sheet anchor of our ship is Sir Henry." What Williams had in mind at that time was that on Vane rested Rhode Island's best hope for getting the original charter strengthened and confirmed. He would, wrote Williams, "observe the motion of our New England business." But if a sheet anchor in London, perhaps Sir Henry could also be a large anchor in Providence, securing that rocking ship in the midst of furious storms.

So Roger Williams prevailed upon his friend to write a letter to Providence Town, a letter that Williams would carry with him when he sailed. It seems most likely that Williams actually wrote the letter himself (a copy exists in his handwriting) and presented it to Sir Henry for his signature. In any case, the letter of stern if paternal reproof could come with better grace from an elder statesman, now in a "private and retired condition which the lord of mercy hath brought me into." It was Oliver Cromwell more than the lord of mercy who brought about Vane's retirement, for Sir Henry had protested most vigorously Cromwell's shutting down of Parliament the previous year. But still Vane could make the point better than most others that the woes of Providence echoed far beyond Narragansett Bay or even all of New England; doleful news reached England "by Every return of ships from those parts," creating great consternation among Rhode Island's few friends and great rejoicing among her many enemies.

So Vane (and Williams) inquired of Providence, "Are there no Wise men amongst you, no public self-denying Spirits that at least upon the grounds of Common Safety, Equity, and Pru-

dence can find out some Way or Means of Union and reconcil-
iation?" That was a tough question, the answer by no means
sure. This letter (dated February 8, 1654) referred to that earlier
Council of State notice to Providence that they had full freedom
to operate under the old charter until informed otherwise. But
of what advantage had that freedom been? One would suppose
that a "better use would have been made of it than there has
been." The situation was critical, no less in London than in
Rhode Island. The advice, therefore, was direct: get together in
some sort of united and general meeting, and do it now. Only
in this way can you "put a Stop to your growing breaches and
Distractions, silence your enemies, Encourage your friends,
[and] honor the Name of God which of late hath been much
blasphemed by reason of you." Strong medicine, but never more
needed.

After more than two years away from wife and children,
without oft-promised pay, without a definitive charter, Williams prepared to leave. John Clarke would stay behind to finish
the task the two of them had begun together; just how long that
would eventually take, neither Clarke nor Williams dreamed.
Williams also had to arm himself with a letter from Cromwell's
council that would instruct Massachusetts to grant him, once
more, safe passage from Boston to Providence. Sometime in
March he sailed from Portsmouth, arriving in Boston in the early
summer. He made it home to Providence as soon thereafter as
his feet could carry him.

THE ART AND SCIENCE OF POLITICS

After greeting friends and family, Williams quickly settled
down to the political task of bringing some order out of the
turbulence that bubbled over during his long absence. A first
order of business was a polite response to Henry Vane, written
in August 1654. (Again, since there is a copy of this letter in
Williams' own hand, he may be assumed to have been the

142

guiding force behind it.) From the moment the colony was founded in 1636 until now, nearly two decades later, we have, said the town elders, "reaped the Sweet Fruits of Your Constant loving kindness and favor toward us." Your "sharp and bitter Arrows" have found their target, the town confessed. All we can say in our defense is that we have been the victims of persons who lacked all public spirit, notably William Coddington, who "procured by most untrue information a Monopoly of part of the Colony"—namely, all of Aquidneck Island (Portsmouth and Newport, and all land in between).

But the fathers admitted (with Williams prompting them all the way) that they could not put all of the problems "upon other men's backs." "We have long drunk of the Cup of as great Liberties as any people that we can hear of under the whole Heaven." That "sweet cup," it turned out, "hath rendered many of us wanton and too active." Liberty of conscience, as Williams and others discovered, exacted a high price. Providence settlers needed to count their blessings, which were many: no "wolfish Bishops" ruled them; no popish or Anglican ceremonies were shoved down their throats; no bloody civil war afflicted them, but "we have sat here quiet and dry"; no "New chains of the presbyterian Tyrants" and no tyrannies from what some were pleased to call the "Godly and Christian magistrate" bound them; and best of all, "We have almost forgot what Tithes . . . or Taxes are, either to Church or Commonwealth." A multitude of blessings, to be sure, yet unaccompanied by the acceptance of responsibility that all freedom imposes. But the town promised Sir Henry that he had awakened "our sleepy Spirits by Your sweet Alarm."

Williams was less sure that sleepy spirits had awakened, or if awake knew in what direction to walk. About the same time that this message was dispatched to Henry Vane, Roger Williams composed—and dispatched—an even stronger message to his "well-beloved Friends and Neighbors" in Providence. Since his return, Williams had listened to nothing but complaints and charges, many of them directed against himself, and he had reached his limit. If he were to start complaining, Williams observed, his list would be so long as to drown out all those of others. "I am like a Man in a great Fog," he wrote. "I know not well how to steer. I fear to run upon the Rocks at home," having already endured many sore trials abroad. Furthermore, "I fear to run quite backward (as men in a mist do), and undo all." At the end of his tether, Williams would strike out at the factionalism that had divided even his own town into two warring parties for nearly a year. The time had come—indeed, it had long since passed—for healing and forgiveness. "Love covereth a Multitude of Sins."

To the extent that he was the focus of resentment and grumbling, Williams tried to answer fairly but "boldly" his critics. "I have been charged with Folly for that Freedom and Liberty which I have always stood for. . . . It hath been told me that I have labored for a licentious and Contentious people." He had even been accused of treason, and the two factions seemed able to agree on only one point: they "wished I might never have landed, that the Fire of Contention might have had no stop in burning." What a bitter homecoming for Roger Williams. And what a feeble response for him to be able only to say that for the last eighteen years he had fought unceasingly on their behalf, without any fortune or riches coming to him. On the contrary, he had been dispatched from his trading post and his family "to do your work, of a costly and high Nature," and there in England he was left to "starve or steal, or beg or borrow." Despite the lack of support from home, despite the rumors and tales of chaos in Providence, despite his enemies everywhere, this town and this colony, "and that Grand Cause of Truth and Freedom of Conscience hath been upheld to this day," no thanks to his well-beloved friends and neighbors.

It was as sour a letter as Roger Williams ever wrote to his fellow colonists. And it had a sobering effect. He called for Providence, first, to settle its feuds, if the town in his absence had not "disfranchised Humility and Love." Next he called for the colony to bring the four towns back together in something resembling a genuine union: islanders and mainlanders, saints and sinners. By September Williams had been elected president of the colony, a position he would hold for three years. Perhaps there was at least one wise man among them after all.

It would take all of the art and science of politics as well as the help of friends abroad and at home to pull off the magician's trick of finding civic unity hidden under the hat of licentious liberty. Roger Williams would call upon Massachusetts to calm the warfare among the Indians. He would call upon John Clarke and Oliver Cromwell to frustrate the aggressive efforts of the Dutch out of New Netherland. He would write to John Winthrop, Jr., to bring him up to date on events in England (while Williams was there) and events in Rhode Island upon his return. He would organize, once again, a Court of Commissioners with representatives from each of the four towns to act in the name of the whole—the once more whole—colony. And he would reflect on the nature of government itself, there being nothing like the dirt of daily politics to concentrate one's mind.

His most famous reflection is found in a letter to the Town of Providence in January 1655, only four months after his election to the presidency of the colony. The immediate provocation for the letter remains unclear, but it may have pertained to disagreements about compulsory military service in the colony. The long-range provocation, of course, was the effort to clarify just what authority government did have, why that authority did not extend to religion, why that authority could appropriately restrain the vicious or wanton, and why all exercise of civil authority was not automatically "tyranny." (Some even complain about the rules of grammar as being a tyranny, Williams wrote to the younger Winthrop in 1654.) Liberty of conscience was not infinite, Williams explained, and he had never written "a Tittle" to suggest that it was. Some of his fellow colonists, however, acted as though liberty had no limits and government no valid place in the affairs of humankind. Perhaps, thought Williams, an analogy might help.

"There goes many a Ship to Sea," he began his letter to the

town fathers, "with many a Hundred Souls in one Ship, whose Weal or Woe is common." The ship was like the commonwealth or state. Now consider this, said Williams: the passengers aboard the ship may include "Papists and Protestants, Jews and Turks"—all on this one vessel. "Upon which Supposal, I do affirm that all the Liberty of Conscience that ever I pleaded for, turns upon these two Hinges: [first], that none of the Papists, Protestants, Jews, or Turks be forced to come to the Ship's Prayers or Worship; nor, secondly, compelled from their own particular Prayers or Worship, if they practice any." This was the liberty for which he had fought: a freedom from religion, a freedom for religion. That's all there was to it. But there was a corollary, and here he hoped that his fellow Rhode Islanders would pay special attention.

"I further add that I never denied that, notwithstanding this Liberty, the Commander of this Ship ought to command the Ship's course; yea, and also to command that Justice, Peace, and Sobriety, be kept and practiced, both among the Seamen and all the Passengers." Are you listening Providence? Will these words even reach all the way south to Warwick, and across the water to Newport and Portsmouth? And if any passengers or crewmembers refused to obey the lawful order for the safe running of the ship, or if they refused to pay their way "in Person or Purse," or if any should threaten mutiny, or if any (Samuel Gorton, pay heed) "shall preach or write that there ought to be no Commanders, nor Officers, because all are equal in Christ,"—if any of these conditions obtain, what is the prerogative and duty of the captain? It was manifestly clear: he "may judge, resist, compel, and punish such Transgressors, according to their Deserts and Merits." That was the burden of his message early in 1655, and it took only a page to say it, Williams having at last learned the beauty of brevity. But he hoped it was enough to "let in some Light, to such as willingly shut not their Eyes."

The message contained both art and science, just as the navigation of a ship, especially through dangerous shoals, called for both. Liberty was not the equivalent of anarchy, nor did soul freedom imply civic irresponsibility. In the realm of religion, each individual was a law unto himself or herself. In the realm of politics, each individual had positive duties to perform, positive restraints to observe. All had an obligation to the common defense, and if that meant compulsory military service, so be it. All had financial commitments to the colony, and if that meant laws of taxation and penalties for failure to pay them, then so be it. And the commander or governor was no thin reed to be blown and bent by the strongest wind, no passive keeper of the minutes or counter of votes. He had a duty to discharge, a duty that included, when necessary, both compulsion and confinement. The science of government required obedience to the law; the art lay in getting the people to accept it.

Of course, the government was of the people, as Roger Williams had explained many times over. God did not institute it; men and women did. Though it lacked sanctity, it possessed necessity. Being of the people, it could be dissolved, but not upon the fanciful notion that one could then construct a government that never required taxes or jails. The ship at sea had to move safely from one port to another, and that ship included a brig where all those who interfered with the safe passage would be locked away. The captain had his duty, the crewmen theirs, and the passengers theirs. Could any shut their eyes so tight that this simple truth would not penetrate?

The people had the power to create a government. Yet they did not have the power to baptize that government—that is, to make it a Christian civil order. Roger Williams did not leave Massachusetts so that he could show the whole world what a truly Christian commonwealth should look like. He left the Bay Colony in order to show the whole world (if eyes were not tightly shut) that a commonwealth was never Christian: no Christian country, no Christian England, no Christian Rhode Island, no Christian town of Providence. God redeemed men and women, not empires and dominions. Christendom was still the enemy. But this was not to dismiss government: it was to clarify its purposes and specify its motives. Justice, peace, and the common good—these were the charges under which a civil order operated.

Williams had spent much time explaining what government must not do, how it must not invade or violate that most precious sanctum that humanity possessed, the individual conscience. But now he must explain what the magistrate *could* do, *must* do, if civility were to displace barbarism. It was not enough to drink deep draughts from the sweet cup of liberty. At some point citizens must put their hands to the plow, to the spinning wheel, to the fishing nets, to the shovels and oars. And if they failed to carry their proper load, then the civil magistrate must compel their obedience and their service—though in civil things only, as the very first Providence compact had declared. At the same time, citizens had a right to expect the civil authority to protect them from unfairness and injustice, from robbers and murderers. After all, the apostle Paul had appealed to Caesar, rightly so, to protect him against slander and the anger of the mobs. He did not appeal to him in spiritual things, for that would have been both a tragic mistake and a blasphemy against God. So God's people, like any other people, could appeal to the state—but in civil things only. And the magistrates, whether Christian or no, should look after the citizens' bodies and goods, but leave their souls to God.

THE HARSH REALITIES OF POLITICS

In March 1655, no doubt at the urging of John Clarke (still in London), Oliver Cromwell wrote to all inhabitants of Rhode Island and Providence Plantations, reminding them that they did have authority, under the 1644 charter, to set up a civil government and, more importantly, to make it work. Williams no doubt welcomed this word from "His Highness." Cromwell urged those in authority to resist both domestic disturbances and foreign invasions, "as Far as you by your Care and diligence Can prevent." Cromwell apologized that no further progress had been made on a new and stronger charter, explaining that "other, great and weighty Affairs" had occupied his attention. That was his excuse, but this did not provide Rhode Island with any excuse for not proceeding to rule with vigor and effect, even now. And that was precisely what Roger Williams endeavored to do.

In November of that year, Williams wrote to the General Court of Massachusetts, seeking its cooperation in settling long-standing grievances between Rhode Island (or some portion thereof) and the Bay Colony. He asked for arbitration between Warwick and the Court to settle the former's claim of damages to the extent of £2,000. In Pawtuxet, Indians pretended to be under Massachusetts' authority and therefore defied the locals and stole their cattle, while four English families in that same settlement "live not by your laws . . . nor ours, but evade both under the color of your authority." This continued pretense that Pawtuxet was part of Massachusetts simply had to stop, Williams warned. It might be a "rich mercy," Williams noted ironically, if the whole country of North America were under the authority of the Bay Colony, but that was not the way that Parliament, or before that the king, had chosen to operate.

As for Rhode Island itself, not to speak of other North American charters and lands, Massachusetts should remember what had so recently transpired: "since it pleased first the parliament, and then the lord admiral and Committee for Foreign Plantations, and since the Council of State, and lastly the Lord Protector and his Council, to continue us as a distinct colony," that should be enough to settle the matter. Williams urged that the General Court not persist in being "the obstructer of all orderly proceedings amongst us." And though he did not say it, Williams might well have added that he had problems enough trying to get Rhode Islanders to unite and agree without neighboring colonies doing all in their power to muddy the waters concerning the true center of their civil government and authority.

One other matter troubled Williams: the unwillingness of the Bay Colony to allow citizens of Rhode Island "to buy of you all means of our necessary defence of our lives and families." Massachusetts had passed a law making such purchases illegal, the point being that if Rhode Island could not defend itself from the Indians or its neighbors, then that plum was ripe for picking. The Indians were armed, Williams pointed out, making purchases largely from the Dutch, but also "by stealth" from the English. The Dutch were armed, of course, as were Massachusetts and Connecticut. Only Rhode Islanders operated under an unfair and even murderous scheme to keep them hopelessly exposed. Just within the last few weeks, Williams told the Court, Indians had attacked New Amsterdam and subjected its citizens to a cruel siege. Will we not be next? Will Massachusetts not relent? Receiving no reply to his urgent request, Williams had to depend on John Clarke in London to send arms and supplies to his beleaguered colony.

Six months later (May 1656) Williams wrote to the General Court again, repeating his requests, all of which had been ignored. He pointed out that people who claimed they were under the jurisdiction of Massachusetts and not Rhode Island managed to avoid paying taxes to either. These artful dodgers deserved to be punished, and so they would be if the Bay Colony would simply renounce its claims to any lands within the bounds of the Rhode Island charter. To urge Massachusetts along that path, Williams enclosed a copy of the Committee for Foreign Plantations' declaration to Samuel Gorton regarding the Warwick land. That response stipulated that the territory in question was "wholly without the bounds of the Massachusetts patent"; therefore, the Bay Colony was explicitly enjoined against "extending your Jurisdiction to any part thereof, or otherwise disquieting them in their Consciences or Civil Peace." That clear declaration, made on May 15, 1646, should have settled the matter; ten years later, it still had not.

Williams also made his request for arms and supplies quite specific: four or more barrels of powder per year, "with some convenient proportion of artillery." True, Williams said, some of your people still look upon us as a "thorny hedge" at your side. Even so, he wrote, a hedge needed to be maintained if it was to serve as any sort of barrier. Rhode Island, moreover, could act as a kind of early warning system of Indian uprising, but sentinels

150

needed to be armed. It was clear from Williams' strong comments as well as from his anxiety that relations with the Indians were rapidly deteriorating. He found arbitration less and less effective, and armed conflict more and more probable against those native Americans who, in his judgment, had grown "exceedingly insolent, provoking and threatening," especially those migrating from the interior of upstate New York.

Meanwhile, Roger Williams' problems of civil authority at home only grew. Cattle rustling had to be stopped, horse thieves had to be restrained, and persons who defaced or weakened jail houses must themselves be sentenced to "sit six hours by Estimation in the stocks and make Reparation of [all] that is spoiled." Fines had to be levied, and some remitted. Laws on selling strong drink to the Indians had to be more finely tuned. All the while, Roger Williams kept an eye on what was happening in England, not just with respect to Rhode Island, but with respect to Spain and Holland, with respect to Cromwell and the rumors of a return to monarchy. He wrote letters to John Winthrop, Jr., who was soon (1657) to become chief officer of Connecticut, trying to protect his colony's flank to the west. Government was of the people, Williams never tired of saying, but he sometimes tired of the people.

And, oh, what people. In the troublesome settlement of Pawtuxet more was at stake than just the jurisdictional quarrel between Rhode Island and Massachusetts. No law, moral or civil, was honored. Some settlers "made a trade of selling powder and shot to the barbarians," while others shielded from justice a certain Richard Chasmore, accused of the capital crime of buggery with one of his heifers. It was unthinkable that such could be tolerated or the crime concealed. Williams confessed that "I was and am in a Straight what to do in these cases," partly because he did not want to upset the delicate negotiations with Massachusetts over that territory and partly because he was not sure of his own civil authority there. Maybe the good citizens of Pawtuxet would help him out, but more likely not.

Williams first heard of the Chasmore incident in August

151

1656. Receiving help from no one, he decided in late September to take action, issuing a warrant for Chasmore's arrest and writing to Governor John Endecott about how best to proceed in a case that now began to take on a life of its own. Williams explained his dilemma to Endecott this way: "We can neither proceed" in these Pawtuxet matters without offending you, nor can we "Wink at them without great Scandal." The warrant issued, however, led to Chasmore's flight to New Netherland, so for a time the issue was moot. Williams wrote to the Dutch governor, Peter Stuyvesant, telling him that he now harbored a fugitive from justice. Then in November, accompanied by some men from Pawtuxet, Chasmore surrendered himself to Roger Williams at his home. All this prompted Williams to write Endecott once more, trying to get clearance to go ahead. "I was not willing," he wrote, "to proceed with him in a Common way of Trial, but took bond of him to appear at Newport at our General Court in May." Chasmore and others pressed for a speedier trial. Williams balked. When pressure mounted, Chasmore was called before the General Court of Trials meeting in Newport in March 1657.

Inexplicably, Williams absented himself from the proceedings, the result being that the Court, with no testimony offered against the defendant, found him "Not Guilty of the fact." By keeping Massachusetts so carefully informed, Williams may have improved relations there; the Bay Colony, moreover, having learned more about Pawtuxet than it really wanted to know, ceased pressing its claims for jurisdiction—a clear benefit for Williams. A clear debit, however, was that his whole handling of the case aroused murmurings of dissatisfaction, not just in Pawtuxet, but throughout the colony.

The Chasmore case may have been complicated, but its entanglements were small in comparison with contentions about land. In that same March meeting in Newport, Williams brought charges against ten of the colony's prominent citizens, notably against William Harris "for his open Defiance under his hand against our Charter, all our Laws and Court, the Parliament, the Lord Protector, and all government." Harris, one of the wealthiest men in the colony and one of Williams' oldest friends (they had emigrated to New England on the same ship), was being charged with treason. The animosity between Harris and Williams had been building for some years, always concerning land, and by 1657 it reached the point of fury. Williams, never interested in acquiring for himself large tracts of land or great wealth, came to despise Harris, who, it seemed, was interested in little else. One of the original settlers of Providence, Harris pressed for that town's boundaries to be extended as far to the interior as possible. Williams preferred to keep the limits carefully defined, so that land would be available to future refugees "distressed for cause of conscience." But deeper moral issues were lost in the flurry of charges and countercharges of deception, malice, unlawful authority, and more. It was too much for the General Court of Trials to deal with, so all the testimonies and evidence were shipped off to John Clarke in England, where it was hoped a definitive decision might be reached. No decision ever emerged, however, for the ship carrying the evidence sank at sea. Nor did settlement ever come to the disputes between Harris and Williams, these continuing until the deaths of both men, and indeed even beyond.

Harris, who led a faction opposed to Roger Williams, passed up no opportunity to heckle him, belittle him, or organize plots against him. In the course of the Chasmore trial, Harris shouted, "Roger Williams—what is he? He is but our fellow creature and one of us, and hath no more power than any of us have." Other citizens joined in the rallying cry. "What is Roger Williams" that he would set himself up as a superior magistrate, wiser and stronger than us all? In May 1657 Williams did not stand for reelection as the colony's president; it is unlikely that he would have won had he done so. Three years of trying to pacify and control a restless populace had been enough for him, enough for them. On May 19 Williams was elected to no office whatsoever in his colony. "What is Roger Williams?" Once more, an outcast, an exile.

RHODE ISLAND MADE SECURE

Through all of Roger Williams' tribulations at home, John Clarke faced his own assortment of enemies and critics abroad. Still struggling to find a clear channel through the turbulent waters of English politics in the late 1650s, Clarke hung on in London year after year after year. He had watched, as indeed all English in North America watched, as Parliament searched for ways to bring the nation from an absolute monarchy to a representative republic without falling into radical sectarianism. Before Clarke and Williams even arrived in London, they—along with thousands of others—held their breath as Charles I allied himself with the Scots in 1648, thereby gaining the support of the Presbyterians in his opposition to Cromwell's "New Model" Army. In response, Parliament purged itself of royalists and Presbyterian sympathizers, and the resulting Rump Parliament formally charged the king with treason. After three weeks of trial, Charles was found guilty and was beheaded on January 30, 1649.

At that point England became a commonwealth, at least in name, though the real authority resided with Oliver Cromwell and his army. By the time Clarke and Williams arrived in England, Cromwell had dismissed the Rump Parliament, creating a new one (largely out of his army) that history has nicknamed the "Barebones Parliament" after one of its members, who bore the memorable name of Praise-God Barebones. In 1653 Cromwell became Lord Protector, and he ruled England with virtually unchecked powers until his death five years later. In 1658 Clarke, like all others in England, waited to see what would happen next. Cromwell's eldest son, Richard, served briefly and unsuccessfully as Lord Protector. His resignation led to a resumption of parliamentary rule. But England, at this juncture thoroughly exhausted by war (both foreign and domestic), by political unrest, and by religious controversy, was ready to welcome a return to monarchy and stability. In 1660 the son of the beheaded king was called from the Conti-

nent to restore the monarchy; in 1661 he was formally crowned
Charles II.

Clarke lived through all this and much more, wondering
when, where, and how to press the claims for Rhode Island.
The friends of the past were now powerless; former enemies
now dominated Parliament. Sir Henry Vane, for example, had
been arrested, and in June 1662 he was beheaded. A king with
some reputation for debauchery and none for spiritual conviction now sat on the throne. Where to turn in such a time?
Through all these years of parliaments coming and going,
Cromwell rising and falling, alliances forming and dissolving,
Clarke had another problem that Williams understood well:
what to live on. Williams reported that he had, during his
London stays, been reduced to begging and borrowing. Clarke,
whose stay was far longer, had similar problems, though he
was able to practice some medicine and do some preaching.
Chiefly, however, he depended on those back home, whose
patient and long-suffering agent he was, to provide support.

Those back home were sympathetic but not especially
forthcoming, despite the twelve long years that Clarke spent in
London. Under Williams' constant goading, Providence did
more than the other towns, but even there it was tough sledding.
In August 1661 the colony ordered its four towns to raise two
hundred pounds for Clarke's expenses, Providence's share
being forty pounds. When after several months even that
amount had not been collected, Roger Williams wrote to his
town that something more had to be done. Perhaps land, in more
bountiful supply than cash, could be given, a suggestion followed up by the Quarter Court the following April when that
body offered Clarke or any friend or friends of his from England
the privilege to be "freely accommodated amongst us, with a
full purchase Right of Land, as of gift." Six months later that
same court ordered a tax rate to be levied "upon the inhabitants
of this Town [Providence] to be sent to England, unto Mr.
Clarke." The money, moreover, was to be collected in only
fourteen days, suggesting that urgent appeals may have been

received from Clarke, who had, in fact, been obliged to mortgage his house in Newport and much land besides.

When, still later, Warwick declined to raise its assessed share of money for Clarke, Roger Williams complained in a letter to the townspeople about their failure to abide by a minimal standard of simple fairness. "Common Honesty and Common Justice," he wrote, should govern all affairs among us. But this seems not to be the case in our dealings with John Clarke. The future, said Williams, "will cry shame upon us that Mr. Clarke should be undone, Yea, destroyed and ruined (as to this World) for his so great and so long pains, Faithfulness, and Diligence." Even the barbarians do better than we, Williams added. When they send forth a public messenger, they provide him with all necessary supplies, defray all payments, "and gratify him with Rewards." And should some injury or illness befall their agent, "they visit him and bring him home upon their shoulders (and that many Scores of miles) with all Care and Tenderness." Rhode Islanders were not even coming close. Though Williams did all that he could, Clarke years after still sought relief from his impoverished state.

In London, however, Clarke had more to concern him than mere money. Monarchy was the most pressing problem, for the nonroyalist posture of Puritans and Separatists and radical sectarians was well known. When Charles II ascended to the throne, Rhode Islanders back home considered sending another agent to London "to present our humble petition and Allegiance to the King's Majesty." But after receiving further communications from Clarke, the colony decided instead to renew his commission and encouraged him "to go on in our business." He had been about that business ever since 1652, when he and Roger Williams petitioned the Council of State to vacate William Coddington's patent. In January 1661 Clarke represented his colony before the Council for Foreign Plantations, arguing that Rhode Island continued to operate under the charter "received from the late King in 1644" and now greatly desired to be "sheltered under the wing" of the present king. All this to the end, said Clarke, that his fellow citizens "may be quietly permitted to flourish in their civil and religious concernments with freedom of conscience to worship the Lord their God." In February Clarke asked again for "a more absolute, ample, and free Charter of Civil Incorporation."

All appeared to be proceeding smoothly, if ever so slowly, when suddenly Roger Williams' old friend, John Winthrop, Jr., appeared on the scene to make as strong a case as he could for his colony of Connecticut. Unfortunately, that case was so strong that much of Rhode Island was being gobbled up. Connecticut's charter, granted in May 1662, defined its eastern border as extending all the way to Narragansett Bay, thereby "annexing" virtually everything but Aquidneck Island. Clarke swung into action immediately, urging the king to give swift attention to the still-pending business of Rhode Island's charter, along with another look at "the charter lately granted unto my neighbor Mr. Winthrop . . . for as much as he hath injuriously swallowed up one half of our colony."

The next months were Clarke's busiest, as he wrote, visited, lobbied, cajoled, and no doubt prayed. In October 1661 he tried direct diplomacy with John Winthrop, writing him that a committee of the Council of State would in a few days examine the boundary question. "I could wish," Clarke said, that "we might look each other in the face as persons agreed in that point, rather than to be found hotly contending each other." Two weeks later, Clarke wrote again, offering as a specific compromise that the western boundary of Rhode Island would be three miles west of the Pawcatuck River. "If you reject this friendly motion," Clarke cautioned, "do not blame me, whatever inconvenience may befall you." Meanwhile, Clarke warned that he would do everything within his power to serve "the Poor Colony, being founded upon so noble a Principle, from being swallowed up and totally ruined." The decision of arbitration, issued the following April, favored the claims of Rhode Island. John Clarke had won. Three months later, he won even more.

On July 8, 1663, King Charles II granted the "poor colony"

157

its first truly royal charter (in the midst of civil war, Charles I had neither inclination nor opportunity to sign the first one). That charter, which would endure through the rest of the colonial period and well beyond, guaranteed more than boundaries. It specified, in words that could only startle and shock, that "a most flourishing civil state may stand and best be maintained ... with a full liberty in religious concernments." A civil society, embracing religious liberty, could not only manage to survive: it could actually flourish. Who could believe such a thing? Who could have hoped for such a thing? True, Charles ruled a kingdom bone-weary of years of religious turmoil. True, he wished to prove that a restoration of monarchy was not necessarily a restoration of tyranny. True also that Clarke had labored tirelessly for a dozen years for just such language as this. Nonetheless, the guarantees granted at this moment in England's history were staggering in their sweep and momentous in their impact.

However surprised himself, Roger Williams, back in Rhode Island, must have felt enormous gratification, even vindication. For in 1644, nearly twenty years before, he had written that civil states which granted liberty of conscience did indeed prosper, did indeed flourish. Consider Holland, he advised, where one saw "Shipping, Trading, wealth, Greatness, and Honor" descending "as out of Heaven in a Crown or Garland" upon that fortunate land. If there, then anywhere that courage abounded: courage and a clear sense of what civil government was all about.

6 "Beloved Privacie"

A man driven by absolute principle, Roger Williams might better have been a hermit, a celibate, a solitary monk. He was none of these. Caught up in the political and ecclesiastical whirlpools of his day, burdened with the support of a large family and the governance of an ungovernable colony, Williams had little time to himself. What little he did have, he deeply cherished as a "beloved privacie." Then he could read (especially the Bible), write (especially his letters), and meditate (especially a "holy meditation into the valley of the shadow of Death"). He found this privacy most often not in London or Salem or Plymouth or Providence but in closest proximity to the Indians.

THE TRADER

Perhaps as early as 1637 Williams established a trading post near the main Narraganset village, about twenty miles south of

Providence. The site, laid out for him by his good friend Canonicus, was on a cove of Narragansett Bay, giving it a great
advantage for shipping; the post also led to many Indian trails
in the immediate neighborhood. Here at Cocumscussoc he later
built a house and carried on a trade with the English and Dutch
as well as the Indians. And here he proved himself no "hireling,"
as he lived off the earnings (about one hundred pounds per year)
of his enterprise.

He traded cloth, seed, cooking utensils, tobacco, and
simple tools, but rigidly resisted the opportunity to engage in
the lucrative business of buying and selling arms. He also refused to sell strong drink to the Indians, except small amounts
in cases of serious illness. Indians paid for their goods with furs,
skins, or baskets, which Williams could in turn sell both locally
and abroad. Sometimes the Indians, especially those on most
friendly terms with Williams, did not pay at all. Canonicus, who
had granted the land for Providence and perhaps for the trading
post as well, accepted "payment" in the form of whatever struck
his fancy that Williams happened to have. "Canonicus laid me
out Ground for a trading house," Williams wrote, "with his own
hand, but he never traded with me, but had freely what he
desired: Goods, Money, &c." He had taken so much that none
would have viewed Williams at fault if he had denied the
Indian's last request—namely, that he be buried "in my cloth of
Free gift." But Williams could not turn down his old friend; he
reported simply, "and so he was."

All of his commercial activity, together with his raising of
crops in Providence and goats on an island in the Bay, went a
long way toward supporting a family of six children and making
possible a life devoted—to such a considerable degree—to
public and religious service. It also helped relieve the poverty
that had attended him ever since the banishment from Boston,
a poverty so humiliating that Mary Williams had once been
obliged to accept a piece of gold pressed into her hand by the
governor of Plymouth Colony.

But the trading post provided him with more than a living:

it was an escape from contentions and quarrels among his fellow English, their irascibility making the Indians by contrast appear downright placid. When disputes in Providence grew especially intense in 1648, Williams retreated to Cocumscussoc. "I have kept myself unengaged," he wrote, except for a proposal that some outside arbitrator, for example John Winthrop, Jr., be chosen to help his difficult neighbors to arrive at some peace. In this temporary retirement, Williams corresponded with the younger Winthrop on terms ever warmer and more wide-ranging. A man skilled in medicine, chemistry, and astronomy (and a member of the Royal Society of London by 1663), Winthrop enjoyed hearing news from Williams pertaining to England or the Indians or the Dutch or whatever. The two men, far removed from the centers of civilization, even exchanged pamphlets and books with each other to keep the intellectual life alive.

Williams often invited members of his family to join him in his remote dwelling, particularly when he thought the salt breezes and country air might do them good. He was especially concerned about the health of his eldest daughter, Mary, who (he wrote Winthrop in June 1649) stayed with him along with a younger sister, Freeborn, but did not show any significant improvement. She had headaches so severe that even one eye was affected. She had taken purgatives and had her blood let—standard treatment, unfortunately, in the seventeenth century—"but yet no change." The concerned father had several years earlier asked Winthrop for his own remedy: "If your powder (with directions) might be sent without trouble, I should first wait upon God in that way." But Winthrop's combination of natural herbs and plants having had little effect, Williams now in 1649 asked Winthrop's advice concerning the best physicians in the Boston area. Mary did recover, either because of or in spite of the medical advice and treatment received; she later married and had a family of her own.

From 1647 to 1651 Roger Williams spent much of his time at this retreat, acting as interpreter and trader with and for the Indians, writing letters on their behalf as well as his own, making periodic returns to Providence (usually by water, for he owned a "great Canoe"), and composing treatises that might sometime find a publisher. Boston still declined to publish anything that Williams wrote, and Providence still lacked printing capability. Williams composed his *Bloudy Tenent Yet More Bloudy* during these years, sending it off to London for printing. He also wrote a tender tract of spiritual consolation to his wife, distressed as he was by his long absences from her and by news of her illness.

Solitude and privacy ended in 1651, however, when he was persuaded to return again to London to keep Rhode Island out of the clutches of William Coddington and the colony's "loving neighbors." The colony, having no reserve with which to fund his long journey, left its reluctant agent to his own devices. After considering all the alternatives, Williams made the painful decision to sell his trading post, along with some land and other items. In September 1651 the sale was made (to Richard Smith of Portsmouth). Many years later Williams wrote in doleful terms of the necessity, "for the public Peace sake," of his surrendering this "trading house" that had brought him some measure of private peace.

THE PIETIST

Williams, the controversialist and agitator, the disputant and antagonist, also had a private side. Like the Puritans and the Separatists, he never forgot that he was the puny creature of an omnipotent Creator. He never forgot that the purpose of the Christian life, as opposed to the purpose of the civil state, was to cultivate the closest relationship possible with that God, to please him through obedience, to serve him through love, to suffer for him when called upon to do so, and to rejoice that he had shown love first. Williams also endeavored to face life with eternity ever on his mind, with the foibles and fashions of this world never worthy to be compared to the glory that would be revealed. Such glory would be revealed to the saints in heaven, of course, but perhaps soon to the whole world when Christ came again.

Scholars read Williams' letters for the insights they provide into the politics and business, the controversies and charges of his day. But they can also be read for their piety, for their casual and habitual allusions to a God whose world this most manifestly is. If he and John Winthrop, Jr., failed to meet as planned, no matter: we can look forward to that "eternal meeting in the presence of him that sits upon the Throne and the Lamb forever." When writing in anger to John Endecott, Williams first disposed of "our transitory Earthly Affairs" that he might deal with issues that truly counted: heavenly and eternal things, in comparison with which all worldly matters "are as but dung and dross." Even in his unsuccessful correspondence with Anne Sadleir, he related his desire to replace all secondary and inherited religion with personal and experiential faith. He once read the same Anglican books that she did, but then "the Father of Spirits mercifully persuaded [me] To Swallow down no longer without Chewing; To chew no longer without Tasting; To Taste no longer without Begging the Holy Spirit of God to Enlighten and Enliven [me]." For Williams, religion had to be of the heart, not just of the mind—of direct, transforming experience, not "the Favor or Custom of any Men or Times." In other words, Williams was a pietist, one who counted the presence of God in his life as more valuable than all the world's riches and honors.

Much of his most intimate correspondence, to wife and children for example, has been lost. Otherwise, that private and quiet faith might be even more fully revealed. Fortunately, however, one tract written for his wife, around 1650, did get published two years later, thus escaping the fate of so many of Williams' letters. This "plain and peaceable Discourse" (as he described it to Anne Sadleir) was wholly lacking the contentiousness and adversarial tone that filled so many of his other published works. Entitled *Experiments of Spiritual Life & Health,* this little book revealed a Williams far different from the public man. Compassionate, tender, and full of faith, hope, and love, this peaceable discourse was designed first of all to cheer and strengthen his wife, second to repay Henry Vane and his wife, Frances, in some small measure for their many kindnesses (the work is dedicated to "Lady Vane"), and third, on behalf of "every truly Christian Reader," to sow "a little handful of spiritual seed while the short Minute of my seedtime (the opportunity of life) lasteth."

Mary Williams suffered some illness while her husband was away for long periods of time in 1649 and 1650, but more seriously, both from her point of view and that of her husband, she began to doubt the security of her spiritual estate as a child chosen and preserved by God for an everlasting fellowship in heaven with him. Puritans and Separatists had been carefully instructed in the ways of discerning the true signs of spiritual life and health, but they had also been repeatedly warned about the ways in which those signs could be counterfeited or mistaken. In her illness, despondency, and loneliness, Mary Williams was no longer sure of her salvation. Roger Williams could not provide her with medicinal powders, nor could he prescribe the best methods for purging and bleeding, but he could serve as a physician to her soul.

He went through the Bible, selecting passages of comfort and assurance, offering them to his wife as a bouquet, "a little posy," and organizing them all in such a way as to bring not just sympathy but strength, not just solace but cure. "My Dearest Love and Companion in this Vale of Tears," he began, "Thy late sudden and dangerous Sickness" and your deliverance from "the jaws of Death" should make you ever more ready for that "sudden call to be gone from hence." We all, said Williams, live "our short uncertain span more as strangers, longing and breathing after another Home and Country." Keeping that other home uppermost in mind was one of Williams' goals in writing, as it was to assure his wife that she had, without question, been chosen for that home. Therefore, Williams wrote, "I now send thee that which I know will be sweeter to thee than the Honey and the Honeycomb . . . this handful of flowers made up in a little Posy, for thy dear self, and our dear children, to look on and smell on, when I as the grass of the field shall be gone and withered." No last will and testament of Roger Williams survives, except for these fragrant flowers.

Williams started his words of consolation with a description of the true marks of the spiritual life, marks that he knew his wife could find within her own life. These were the "experiments," or, more properly, the experiences that could heal. He assured her that she was not mistaken in the reading of the signs or marks: her spirituality was genuine, not false; sincere, not hypocritical. God's true child, for example, longed "for more and more knowledge of God." But did not the hypocrite also desire this increase in knowledge? Yes, that may be true to a degree, Williams responded. "Out of an itching desire for knowledge and novelty, and out of self-love" the hypocrite may seek a selective sort of knowledge of God. But that desire was prompted by terror or fear of retribution, not by "hearty reverence and affection." So through a list of ten true signs Williams steadily moved, in each case claiming biblical promises that would be as familiar to Mary as they were to him. "These and many more discoveries of the life of Christ Jesus in the soul (though in the midst of weaknesses and spiritual sickness)" his wife could discern in herself, just as he "and others have discerned [them] in thee."

Beyond assuring her that she was not lost, Williams wanted to encourage her to even greater spiritual health and well-being. He noted several "particulars," setting them forth "as an holy looking-glass to discover to us our soul's spots & blemishes." But alongside that revelation of spots and blemishes, Williams offered "sweet cordial flowers to refresh and encourage our drooping spirits." One of those flowers concerned privacy: doing good for the eyes of God alone, being upright "in secret." Hypocrites do good to be seen of men, Williams reminded her, but God's own children do good "regarding no eye but the eye of the Heavenly Father."

Since Williams also regarded "frequent prayer" as an unfailing mark of spiritual health, it is reasonable to assume that prayer was much a part of his own private piety, though—being private—we have no record of it. Jesus provided the example of private prayer, Williams wrote, retiring from the crowd and even from his disciples to be alone. "And therefore is it true that all true Christians are the spiritual Israelites, that is, wrestlers and strivers with God in prayer, like unto their Father Jacob." True prayer, said Williams, is a "breathing of the soul to God, arising as incense and perfume to God." True prayer, moreover, brings the Christian a kind of "holy pleasure," like a man who "finds delight in casting off an heavy burden from his shoulder, or in the unbosoming of a grief into the bosom of a friend." Here, too, privacy had a spiritual value all its own: genuine religion begins in solitude and quiet, not in the midst of assemblies and noise. But after that private beginning with just a spark, "like marriage love," it bursts into "an open flame of public confession, without shame, before all men."

Saints are not chosen for ease and glory here on earth so much as they are chosen for persecution and humiliation. One must remember, of course, that this is only temporary, only for a moment or two—in God's eternal time. If we have worldly comforts, Williams said, they should be employed "with a weaned eye and mind, as if we used [them] not." Williams urged his wife (and "every truly Christian Reader") to live on this earth more like an English person lodging temporarily in the midst of the Indians' "wild comforts"—that is, ready to leave at any time—or "like passengers on a ship," more than willing and ready to go ashore "in our own country, to our own house and comfort in the heavens." Clinging to this life as though that were all there were could indeed cause despondency and melancholy, and rightly so, but looking forward to unceasing joys beyond this brief passage, however storm-tossed, would take one from despair to victory.

The pietist's assurance rested not on temporal but on heavenly rewards. Williams saw no guarantee that God would bless the pious with wealth, health, or worldly honor. On the contrary, as Christ suffered, so his disciples were called to suffer, to follow him in these steps also. As Christ was beaten with many stripes, so his people may expect affliction as their reward. And if, like Mary Williams, we are struck down by illness or disease, it could be God's way of softening our hearts, "like the ground moistened with storms and showers from heaven," making us ready for "the Lord's most gracious seed and heavenly planting." Though weak now, she would be stronger than before. Though searching for her sins and mistakes, what she shall find instead is her great good fortune in God's love: "frequent reckoning makes God and our souls true friends."

Many men, most men, said Williams, make the mistake of falling in love with the things of this world, not recognizing the fleeting, shadowy nature of all these passing images. "If riches, if children, if cattle, if friends, if whatsoever increase, let us watch that the heart fly not loose upon them." Worldly pleasures are so full of thorns and vexations, Williams noted, that we should dwell "upon their insufficiency to content and fill our hearts." The goods of this world are at best a kind of "stool or ladder to help us upward to heavenly comforts" that will not pass away. The soldier in battle looks forward only to his victory, the passenger at sea only to his safe arrival, the woman in childbirth only to her newborn, the farmer laboring in the field only to his harvest. "So let us sometimes warm and revive our cold hearts and fainting spirits with the assured hope of those victories, those crowns, those harvests, those refreshings and fruits . . . which God hath prepared for them that love him." Persecuted and martyred saints have sown the soil with their tears and their blood; they shall reap a "never-ending harvest of inconceivable joys."

Williams did not sentimentalize death. It was real, it was cruel. The corpse grew "loathsome, ugly, terrible" even to the closest family and friends. People should not ignore death; on the contrary, they should think about it steadily and often. Only in that way would they ever get the perspective right. Only in that way would men and women ever develop the proper attitude of thanksgiving that "we poor strangers" have been granted "any allowance of bread, of clothes, of friendship, &c." The other important perspective to keep in mind, dear wife, is that "our very life and being is but a swift, short passage from the bank of time to the other side or bank of doleful eternity." Doleful for those who have thought only on the things of this world, but blissful for those whose true home is heaven. Sweeter than the honeycomb, and "stronger refreshment than the strongest wines or waters, and of more value than if every line and letter were thousands of gold and silver"—so was this lovingly gathered bouquet of priceless spiritual truths.

Much later, as Roger Williams approached his seventieth year, his piety had not changed, nor his perspective regarding the temporal and the eternal. In our "calm midnight thoughts," if not in the hustle-bustle of daily affairs, he wrote then, we may best see the true nature of "these Leaves, and Flowers, and Smoke and Shadows and Dreams of Earthly Nothings." Concerning all these "we poor Fools and Children . . . disquiet ourselves in Vain." All the wars of the world were, at bottom, about "greater Dishes and Bowls of Porridge," Esau and Jacob setting the example for us long ago. In New England we fight, said Williams, about "these Children's toys of Land, Meadows, Cattle, Government &c.," forgetting the sweeter "Counsel of the Son of God to mind first the matters of his Kingdom [and] to take no thought for tomorrow." And that was why wars did not cease, nor cruel sufferings end.

THE WEARY NEGOTIATOR

The letter quoted above, to Colonel John Mason and Governor Thomas Prence of Connecticut in June 1670, concerned one of those problems that seemed never to go away. One might have thought that John Clarke had delivered a final answer to the question of the border between Connecticut and Rhode Island in 1661. Nearly a decade later, however, the issue clearly had not been resolved. When Clarke and John Winthrop, Jr., reached an agreement on the boundary between the two colonies, it entailed in part that Rhode Island would allow private owners in the southwestern corner of the state, the Narragansett Proprietors, to choose which of the two colonies they wished to affiliate with, although that part of the understanding never made it into the 1663 charter. When angry Proprietors voted themselves into Connecticut, Winthrop's colony quickly set up its own government in this Narraganset country, taking over the land on which Roger Williams' trading post had stood along with virtually everything south of Warwick. Rhode Island protested this as a clear violation of the boundaries set forth in their royal charter.

A royal commission sent in 1664 to settle the matter read both the Connecticut and Rhode Island charters, shrewdly concluded that they were incompatible, and calmly declared the disputed territory to be the king's province, but for the time being under the jurisdiction of Rhode Island. All this did was ensure that bitter debates between the two colonies would continue for years. In May of that year, Williams hastily wrote to his friend, now the governor of Connecticut, conceding that not much love was being demonstrated on either side. The Spanish in Central America made gold their god; the English in North America made land theirs. But Williams closed his letter with the hope that Winthrop, together with some of his sober and serious elders, would help solve the difficult dispute between them. In a reply written the following February (after the English had conquered the Dutch in New Netherland, promptly renaming it New York), Winthrop expressed gratitude to Williams for his spirit of moderation, a spirit that "doth well help to [provide] ballast in gusts and too high sails."

The spirit of moderation did not prevail, however. Each colony branded the other a trespasser, called for the arrest of illegal settlers, and appointed magistrates and countermagistrates. In June of 1670 a boundary commission consisting of delegates from the two colonies met in New London to try to reach some agreement. They failed, with the result that Roger Williams sat down to write that long letter to Mason and Prence. He would have preferred a personal visit, but his "old lame bones" prevented it. Not surprisingly, his sympathies lay entirely with Rhode Island, as he voiced his sorrow that his fellow English in Connecticut were "embarked in a Resolution to invade and despoil Your poor Countrymen . . . of our temporal and Soul Liberties."

Williams then launched into a lengthy review of how Rhode Island came into being in the first place, invoking the memory of the senior John Winthrop, who had privately encouraged him to settle around Narragansett Bay, assuring him that it was free of "any English Claims or Patents." Taking this as "an Hint and voice from God," Williams proceeded south, though he was uprooted again after Plymouth declared that he first settled within their bounds. When at last he came to the headwaters of Narragansett Bay, the governors of both Massachusetts and Plymouth promised him that he "should not be molested and tossed up and down again while they had Breath in their Bodies." Now it was time to claim that promise with respect to Connecticut.

Williams could also testify, of his own "ocular Knowledge of persons, places, and transactions," that Rhode Island's first charter (1644) did extend his colony's western boundary to the Pawcatuck River, a boundary reaffirmed in the 1663 charter. No English patent covered the territory that Connecticut now claimed, Williams asserted firmly, and it was only the greedy villainy of grasping men that would now overturn both history and law. Connecticut displayed, Williams wrote, "a depraved Appetite" for land, for more land, for "great portions of land." Christians were behaving toward each other in so un-Christlike a manner that the whole episode was like a bad dream, a nightmare. Here was a large colony with a great expanse of land that, not content with its platters "full of Dainties," would "pull and snatch away their poor Neighbor's Bit or Crust." Well, sirs, it shall not happen. King Charles II has given us this land "under his Hand and Broad Seal," with the guarantee that none of us would be molested for matters of consciences so long as we were loyal to him and kept the civil peace. And sirs, "We must part with Lands and Lives before We part with such a Jewel."

Weary of the continued strife, Williams noted that now, after the Restoration, the two sides should be standing together at a time when in England all sorts of consciences (Puritan and Separatist) were "frying in the Bishops' Pan and Furnace," when French Jesuits in the back country were conspiring with Indian tribes to resist the English, when New England's enemies abroad were waiting for a chance to pounce on a country that could not manage to keep peace among its own people. Williams would make one more effort at compromise and mediation, though he knew it, too, might fail. Life seemed filled with failure. "If I perish, I perish," he wrote at the conclusion of his letter. "It is but a shadow vanished, a bubble broke, a dream finished. Eternity will pay for all." Those were the words of a man who had very nearly reached his limit in the search for temporal peace. And it would not have greatly surprised him that, after his death, Connecticut and Rhode Island continued to pursue their border wars.

Even more exhausting were the apparently endless disputes with William Harris—land again, that great god land, being the crux of the battles. Harris still pushed for extending the original limits of Providence some twenty miles westward, and Williams still pushed for keeping the limits within the bounds of reason and moral law. The sachems, Williams wrote in 1669, granted land to the original proprietors sufficient for their livelihood—and not more than that. "I never understood infinite and boundless matters, no nor 20 miles, but what was usually accounted Sufficient for any plantation or Town in the Country." The agreement, to be sure, had been verbal and vague, with the inevitable result that the controversy would be endless and hot. It has reached the point, said Williams, where just about every other day somebody "had a terrible burning fit,

171

ready to come to blows about our Lines, about our Lands." The struggle focused particularly on Pawtuxet, where, if Harris had his way, the wealth accruing to him and his faction would be enormous.

Harris staked claims; opponents ignored or defied them. The central government, still struggling to assert its authority, at this juncture decided in 1670 to levy a colony-wide tax to raise £600 to repay John Clarke for his costs in obtaining the charter. Harris objected to that, too; in fact, he even objected to the charter, claiming that Charles II had granted more than he should, including liberty of conscience. But others, opposing Harris, reasoned that if Rhode Island had no charter, it had nothing. When Harris finally took the side of Connecticut in the boundary dispute, most Rhode Islanders had had enough. In 1672 they arrested and imprisoned him. And that would be the place to end the story, except that the story did not end. Within a few months, Harris was out of jail, his friends now in high office. And so the struggle continued, as did the Connecticut quarrels. Both quarrels, however, were soon swallowed up in a crisis of monumental proportion, where the failures of negotiation and understanding resulted in consequences of incalculable tragedy.

From the late 1660s into the 1670s rumors of Indians plotting against the English flew from one part of New England to another. Williams investigated many of these, sometimes questioning the integrity of Indian informers and on one occasion in 1671 even giving himself as a hostage to the Wampanoags to assure the safe return of their sachem, Philip, from Plymouth Colony. Negotiations at that point between Philip and Plymouth were successful, with Philip surrendering some seventy guns that had been in his possession and recognizing Plymouth's claims to yet more land. Philip returned safely to his home, and Roger Williams to his—one of many crises having passed, for the moment.

When the controversy between Philip and Plymouth erupted again four years later, it first appeared to be another local dispute. An Indian who had been converted by a missionary reported to Plymouth that Philip was preparing for war. When other Indians heard of this betrayal, they killed the informer. Three were charged with that crime, tried by a Plymouth court, and condemned to die. Whether Philip was directly involved in that murder or not, his honor and that of the Wampanoags was on the line. Tensions mounted, as Roger Williams wrote Winthrop on June 13, 1675: Philip was armed, Rehoboth was armed, even Providence was armed. "But," Williams wrote prematurely, "blessed be God the storm is over." It was not over. On June 17 Rhode Island officials met with Philip and some of his armed warriors to try to settle the matter of who had most injured whom. That was too tough a question to settle, but they did agree to mend their differences, not as dogs do, but by arbitration.

One week later, men from Massachusetts, deeply concerned that the Wampanoags would be joined by the more numerous Narragansets, hurried to Providence, where they pressed Roger Williams (with only a half-hour warning) to join them in a peace parley. The Narragansets, Williams reported, "professed to hold no Agreement with Philip in this his rising against the English." But they demanded to know why Philip was under so great a threat from Plymouth and why Massachusetts and Rhode Island bothered themselves with that cause at all: let Plymouth and Philip work it out. Williams answered the first question by pointing out that Philip had broken all laws that Plymouth had laid down and was in "Arms of Rebellion" against that colony. To the second question, he responded that since all of New England recognized the same sovereign, it was both the pleasure and duty of any one Englishman to stand to the death by all other Englishmen anywhere in the world. For the time being, Williams must have put Connecticut and William Harris out of his mind.

If peace had not been won, war had at least been contained—or so for the moment it must have seemed to Roger Williams. Before the day was over, however, he heard that five

Englishmen had been slain in Swansea (in fact nine were killed), and their heads had been carried triumphantly to Philip. As Plymouth readied itself for a full war, Williams felt that he could do little more to prevent whatever was to come. "Sir," he wrote Winthrop, "my old bones and Eyes are weary with Travel and writing to the Governors of Massachusetts and Rhode Island and now to Yourself. I end with humble cries to the Father of Mercies. . . ."

June 24, 1675, marked the beginning of what has come to be called King Philip's War, a war of utter devastation, as the Indians in league with each other (Wampanoags, Narragansets, Mohegans, and others) made one last desperate and bloody attempt to turn back the invasion of the English that had started more than a half century before. As leader of the military effort, Philip explained that land had steadily disappeared, year after year, into the hands of the English, adding, "I am determined not to live till I have no country." After one hundred Narraganset warriors marched against Warwick, Williams lost faith in his negotiating power and in tribal professions of loyalty to the English. Their words, he wrote, have become "falsehood and Treachery." And the Father of mercies seemed not to hear his or anyone else's humble cries.

For more than a year the war raged, with lives, houses, barns, crops, and cattle ruthlessly destroyed. New England had never suffered such a war, nor in terms of percentage of life and property lost has it suffered one of such severity since. Rhode Island was officially neutral in the war, but this did not help to spare its mainland. Though the Indians were outnumbered by about two to one, the battle was of such ferocity as to make those numbers mean little at first. Fifty-two of New England's ninety towns were attacked, with a dozen or more destroyed or critically damaged, including both Warwick and Providence. About six hundred English were slain, and of the Indians many more than that either killed or sold off into slavery at the war's end—men, women, and children. In August 1676 "King" Philip himself was killed, effectively bringing the war to an end. In all of New England, Indian power had forever been broken; English power would never again be challenged.

Over a thousand houses had been burned, Roger Williams' among them. As a precaution, he had sent his wife to the island of Aquidneck, where the English were less vulnerable to attack. Indeed, that island served as a kind of refuge center for displaced persons and as a hospital for wounded soldiers. When the bloodshed ended, it was time to restore Providence. Williams even presided over the sale of Indian slaves to raise funds to help citizens rebuild their homes. The events of 1675-1676 were enough to put one in mind, once again, of those leaves and flowers and smoke and dreams of earthly nothings. But by that time, Williams had fought yet other battles on the more familiar turf of religion.

THE AGED CONTENDER

The trouble with welcoming everyone to a haven of religious liberty was that, sooner or later, everyone came. Baptists arrived early, of course, and soon managed to divide themselves between Arminian or Six-Principle Baptists on the one hand and Calvinist or Particular Baptists on the other. Then they divided themselves between those who kept Sunday as the holy sabbath and those Seventh-day Baptists who thought that the Ten Commandments had never been repealed, including the one that said, "Remember the sabbath day, to keep it holy." When that commandment was delivered to Moses on Mt. Sinai, the sabbath was without question Saturday, the last day of creation, when God rested. Other Baptists, raising the familiar objection of Roger Williams, asked whether Christians followed Moses or Christ. But neither that question nor the question of the laying on of hands was answered to the satisfaction of all. Soon the church in Providence as well as the one in Newport found itself divided, and new churches formed.

Anglicans also arrived in Rhode Island in the seventeenth

century, though not in Roger Williams' lifetime. Though he strongly disagreed with and often denounced them, he would not have prevented their worship or excluded their missionaries. Congregationalists appeared at about the same time, too late to permit Williams the irony of a public welcome as opposed to a public trial. Jews emigrated while Williams was still alive, no doubt giving much satisfaction to one who had complained about the "incivilities and inhumanities" of England against them. In 1652 Williams declared that a proper civil magistrate—that is to say, one who understood his proper bounds—would "break down that superstitious wall of separation (as to Civil things) between us Gentiles and the Jews" so as to make way "for their free and peaceable Habitation amongst us." And many others came to Rhode Island seeking only to escape religion, not to embrace it, for here no one was required to attend or support or believe in any ecclesiastical institution whatsoever.

Liberty of conscience brought them all, but in largest numbers it brought the Quakers. The Society of Friends, to use the official title, did not even exist when Rhode Island was founded. A product of the religious ferment of the Cromwellian period, the Quakers were but one of dozens of new religious options bubbling forth in the 1650s. One stark fact separated them from all the others, however: they survived. Indeed, they not only survived but spread throughout northern England into Ireland and across the waters to America. Their missionaries, male and female, were visionary, ecstatic, single-minded, and, most of all, successful. As their numbers grew, fear and hostility correspondingly grew among their enemies, who were virtually everywhere. Quakers aroused such fear mainly because they spoke of an indwelling divine spirit, the Inner Light, that brooked interference from no one. God spoke directly; they responded immediately.

Two Quaker women arrived in Boston in 1656, a mere five years after George Fox brought the tiny group into being. The women were promptly arrested, stripped naked so that they could be examined for signs of witchcraft, then jailed, and finally exiled. Other Quakers arrived to take their place, however, and Massachusetts authorities quickly passed laws ensuring punishment of any such damnable heretics coming into their colony, of any ship's captain so benighted as to transport them across the ocean, and of any householder so deluded as to shelter them. In 1657 the Bay Colony decreed that any banished Quaker who returned would have his or her ear cropped; a second return would lead to the cropping of a second ear; a third return would bring a hot iron to the tongue until a hole had been burned clean through. But such threats did not prove sufficient to stem the flood. (What had Roger Williams told John Endecott about conscience?) Responding to the need for sterner measures, in 1658 Massachusetts imposed the penalty of death upon any who so stubbornly and so perversely came back into its jurisdiction. Four came back, and four were hanged, including Rhode Island's Mary Dyer in 1660. After the sentence of death had been passed against her, she appealed to the General Court to "be not found Fighters against God, but let my Counsel and Request be accepted with you, To Repeal all such Laws, that the Truth and Servants of the Lord may have free Passage among you, and you be kept from shedding Innocent Blood." Her counsel was not accepted.

Connecticut had similar laws against Quakers, though none met their death there. Rhode Island had no laws against Quakers nor anyone else "distressed for conscience." So Quakers flocked in large numbers to the small colony—in such numbers that by 1661 it was possible to hold a Yearly Meeting in Newport, the first large gathering of Quakers anywhere in America. (The founding of Pennsylvania was still two decades away.) Soon Quakers dominated the colony; one of their number was elected governor in 1672. In that same year, George Fox visited Newport, giving a further boost to Quaker increase and giving great anxiety to Roger Williams, who was firmly convinced that the Quakers were wrong.

Of course, they had a right to be wrong. But then he had a

right (did he not?) to try to convince them that they were wrong. Some historians have argued that because Williams "took on" the Quakers in a protracted debate and in an even more protracted book, his earnestness about liberty of conscience must have begun to fade. What nonsense. Williams believed deeply in liberty of conscience because he believed deeply in religion. Some modern defenders of liberty of conscience may take that position out of indifference to all religion, but nothing could be a greater distortion than to thrust that indifference back upon Roger Williams. He had his own convictions and he would defend them, but never by the sword. The Quakers had their religious convictions and he would attack them, but never by the sword. On grounds of religious conviction alone, no Quaker was ever jailed in Rhode Island, no Quaker was ever fined or whipped or burned or hanged. In choosing to challenge the Quaker missionaries to a debate in Newport in 1672, Williams neither compromised nor diluted his enduring commitment to liberty of conscience. Politeness and sweetness of temper may have been compromised, but that is a different matter altogether.

The arrival of George Fox himself along with some of his disciples ("G. Fox and his Fantastics," Williams later wrote) on May 30, 1672, soon attracted so much attention, made so much noise, that Williams felt he could not ignore the implied challenge. The vulgar, he said, looked upon this missionary team "as Paul and Barnabas, Mercury and Jupiter from Heaven." His hackles were even more aroused when William Harris cast his lot with the Quakers, though Williams regarded it as an altogether cynical political move, Harris caring "no more for the Quakers than the Baptists." On July 15, 1672, Williams wrote directly to Fox, challenging him to several days of debate, the time to be of Fox's own choosing, the place to be divided evenly between Newport and Providence. The debate, Williams suggested, should be orderly and without raucous interruptions and should take place from around nine in the morning to four in the afternoon. He even laid down the fourteen propositions that he regarded as central to his major differences with the Quakers. And once the debate was over, it would be "left to every Conscience to judge" which side, if either, was right.

Williams sent a copy of his letter to an old friend, John Throckmorton, another of those exiles who had sailed with him on the *Lyon* to New England. But now that old friend and "ancient neighbor" had been bitten by the "infectious Teeth" of Quakerism. Even though "newly bitten," Throckmorton responded angrily to Roger Williams' letter to Fox. "Thy Scurrilous Paper," Throckmorton spat out, "I advise thee to refrain from any further publishing thereof." Such advice was offered, he wrote, because that paper was "full fraught with impudent Lies and Slanders, with high flown airy imagination." And if Roger Williams lived to be as old as Methuselah, he could not duplicate the performance. Throckmorton urged Williams to forget the debate, but Williams replied, none too gently, that he would not "suddenly strike Sail" just because he heard "your simple and childish spirit Countermand me." Four more letters were quickly exchanged that warm July, but to no great purpose except to offer a kind of preview of what would soon be discussed in a more public forum.

The letter to Fox did not reach him in time; he left Newport on July 26, though Williams initially questioned whether the fox had thought it "best to run for it." In any case three missionaries (John Stubbs, John Burnyeat, and William Edmundson) were left behind to take up the challenge, if they so chose. They did so choose, and the debates took place in August: on the ninth, tenth, and twelfth in Newport, and on the seventeenth in Providence. The day before the first debate was to get underway, an aged Roger Williams rowed himself from Providence to Newport (about thirty miles), God "graciously" assisting him "in rowing all day with my old bones so that I got to Newport toward the Midnight before the morning appointed." But by nine the next morning, Williams was all set to go, no matter that it was three against one, no matter that it was really the Fox he had hoped to trap.

Williams thought well of two of his three adversaries: John Stubbs "was learned in the Hebrew and the Greek," and John Burnyeat was "of a moderate Spirit, and a very able Speaker." But William Edmundson was something else: a man ignorant of the Bible and of everything else, proud of his "loud and clamorous" voice, which he used to great excess. Each time Williams patiently waited until the long-winded adversary was at last done; then, he no sooner would begin his rebuttal than Edmundson "would stop my mouth with a very unhandsome Clout of a grievous interruption." In truth, said Williams, he was nothing "but a flash of wit, a Face of Brass, and a Tongue set on fire from the Hell of Lies and Fury." It promised to be a lively debate.

Four days had been set aside to debate Williams' fourteen propositions, an average of between three and four items per day. Day One did not manage to dispose of even the first. That proposition, that these Quakers were not real Quakers according to the Scriptures, allowed for many interpretations and endless biblical citations. What it did not allow for was any possibility of agreement or consensus. If Williams argued that trembling and quaking were only the devil's artful counterfeit of that godly fear and trembling of which the Bible spoke, his opponents responded that in their quaking it was God, not Satan, who was at work. Each side could advance its claims; neither side could offer proof for just what went on within the supernatural world.

What Williams pursued in this and all the propositions was his conviction that Quakers did not take seriously the "ancient pattern" set down in the New Testament. Rather, the Quakers experimented freely, rambled about wildly, held to no standard or authority, not even the Bible. As Williams later told the Commissioners of the United Colonies, he had spent his entire adult life seeking the restoration of "the Ordinances of Christ Jesus in purity," and he was not about to let the Quakers deflect him from that goal. Roman Catholicism had made the mistake of thinking that it could improve upon the New Testament with its papal teachings; now Quakers made the same mistake of "revising" the sacred words through their notion of an Inner Light. Both Catholics and Quakers claimed an infallibility, the first being papal, and the second being personal. Both pretended to honor the Scriptures, but both set themselves up as authorities superior to that historic foundation. There must, Williams argued, be a better way.

The substance of the debate had genuine merit, as Williams labored to save Christianity and his colony from what he perceived to be inevitable chaos—no authority but one's own private inspiration, no external standard by which either behavior or belief could be judged, no obedience to law (even civil law) unless such obedience was directed by the voice of God. Massachusetts felt the same way, of course, and could only be amused by the vision of that troublemaker Roger Williams valiantly defending law and order. Did he not know, the Puritans would say, that his Separatism led to the excesses of Quakerism? Of course, Anglicans might argue that Puritanism with equal inevitability led to those excesses, while Catholics might argue the very same about Protestantism in general. What was the logical result of Luther's "priesthood of the believer" if it was not to make every man a church unto himself?

So there was merit to the debate, though one could understandably lose sight of it. Williams' adversaries enjoyed referring to him as the "old man," or the "old bitter man," or the "old prejudiced man." Finally, one member of the audience stood up to object to this continued ad hominem slur. Williams for his part worried about those Quaker males who wore "extraordinary long hair"; he worried even more about those Quaker maidens who did not wear enough. Williams, who believed in civility, found something terribly uncivil and barbaric about the occasional practice of Quaker women making their witness by parading naked through the streets of Boston or Newport or wherever. Beyond being uncivil, however, it was decidedly unscriptural, there being "no shadow or color of Proof from the holy Scripture" that would justify such indecency. Williams was scandalized. Even the Indians, he said, "cover their Females from their birth." Only in drunkenness and madness did people ever behave this way, Williams concluded.

His adversaries seemed not too eager to discuss the matter, Williams reported, though John Stubbs did explain that Quakers believed in modesty and decency among their women as much as other Christians did. "But if God stirred them up and commanded them to this service to [reveal] the Nakedness of others, they could not but acknowledge God's hand, and submit to it." Such shedding of apparel was never done casually or flippantly, Stubbs added, but only under great conviction. Indeed, "it was a cruel Cross to a sober woman's spirit so to act, as well as an affliction and suffering to her body." Williams maintained that it was Satan, not God, who "stirred them up."

Such issues made that first day a very long one, only darkness breaking up the debate. That August 9 was also marked by an eclipse of the sun, which Williams promptly interpreted as the "Sun of Righteousness" hiding its face from all false Christs and false prophets. So long and grueling had the day been that when Roger Williams returned the next morning he had a hoarse voice and a severe headache, a "more than ordinary Weakness and moldering of my house of Clay." But he sought no mercy, nor gave any as "the Lord graciously carried me through the whole day with little hindrance in my self, and little disadvantage to the understanding of the Auditors." Those "auditors" included the Quaker governor, Nicholas Easton, and his wife, along with many of the magistrates and other prominent citizens of Newport. Occasionally, the debate aroused some of the listeners to such a point that they (even the governor and his wife) could not refrain from making contributions of their own. Nonetheless, the debaters managed sometime during the morning to pass on to the second proposition: namely, "That their Christ was not the true Lord Jesus Christ."

The scientific method was not very helpful on this point either. Williams, defending the orthodox position of Christ as both God and man joined in one person, argued that Quakers believed in only a spiritual or mystical Christ, showing no interest in the historical Jesus. "Their Christ was but half a Christ, a Light, an Image or Picture or Fancy," a product wholly of the Quaker imagination. Quakers, said Williams, may speak of a Christ born in Bethlehem and crucified in Jerusalem, but they "intend in truth and reality no other birth nor life nor death . . . but what may be extant and wrought in the heart of man." Quakers regarded the Christ within as something opposite or contrary to the "Christ without." The two were, in fact, complementary, each essential to the other. But Quakers concentrated so steadily on the light within that, said Williams, "they preached not Christ Jesus but Themselves."

George Fox was not present, of course, so Roger Williams tried him in absentia. He had read Fox's major work, *The Great Mystery of the Great Whore unfolded; and Anti-Christ's Kingdom revealed into Destruction,* published in London in 1659. Having read the book long before, Williams did not intend to let Fox's mere absence interfere with his plans. Often referring to that "book in Folio" along with many other Quaker pamphlets and tracts that he had read, Williams would read Fox's words, explain what they really meant, and then explain why that was wrong or just "impertinent and silly." His opponents complained that Fox was so clear that he needed no explication, certainly not from a hostile source such as Williams. Both sides, nonetheless, continued to bring Fox into the debate so that the leading Quaker could tell (when all this appeared in print) that he had not been forgotten. He could also tell that Williams had not taken kindly to his book, for the Rhode Islander proclaimed: "I observe his virulent and venomous Mind and Pen stabbing, damning, and reprobating all that truly believe in the true Lord Jesus"—that is, in the historical as well as risen Christ. Fox, on the other hand, believed that Christ was nowhere to be found except in the human heart, and "that is nowhere."

Progress was slow, the more so when William Edmundson could restrain himself no longer and began to preach a full-fledged sermon. Or, as Williams put it, "Upon a sudden, a violent, tumultuous disorderly Wind or Spirit filled all his Sails." On and on he went about how Roger Williams had "kept them long and . . . proved nothing." When he finally finished, Williams rose to reply, at which point John Stubbs stood up, "being moved (as he said) to Declare his mind and Thoughts to the people also." So Williams listened some more, "patiently," he reported, though that is harder to believe. When Stubbs finished, Williams began his reply to both. He had delivered only a single sentence when "that Pragmatical and Insulting Soul, W. Edmundson, stopped and Interrupted me." That was too much for Williams who, in the absence of a moderator, became one himself, complaining about the utterly improper procedures, in "no way befitting the Societies of Civil and Moral men." So they proceeded to debate the debate and each other's spirituality.

When Williams complained that Quakers diminished the sacraments or ordinances of the church (baptism was internal, not visible; the Lord's Supper was "nothing else than Spiritual joy"), his opponents thought they had him just where they wanted him. He complained about *their* interpretations of the ordinances, whereas he had abandoned the ordinances altogether! He associated himself with no visible church at all, joined in no Lord's Supper at all. Well, said Williams, that's different. It was one thing to be up "in Arms against the King of Kings and his visible Kingdom and Administration of it," quite "Another thing among so many pretenders to be the true Christian Army and Officer of Christ Jesus" to remain in some doubt as to which really was the true church of Christ. It is difficult to imagine that any not already firmly enlisted in Williams' army would have been convinced by this argument.

At last the second day ended, with only two propositions considered. Such a snail's pace would keep the debate going until fall, and the Quaker three insisted that they must quickly be about the Lord's business. Could something be done to speed the process up? Though he did not accept full blame for the creeping pace, Williams said that for the remaining five propositions (out of the seven they planned to cover the first day) he would pledge on the third day to spend no more than fifteen minutes per issue—an hour and one quarter for the whole package. Edmundson leaped at the offer with such swiftness that Williams was afraid he had gone too far. "I said they must not count me false & a Promise-breaker if I was not exact to a quarter of an hour." But Edmundson replied, "Nay, Roger, thou must be punctual if thou wilt be a Christian."

The next day was Sunday, which Williams thought presented no problem, since the Quakers worked on that day as on any other. But they decided (wisely, said Williams) to spend the day with their people shoring up the defenses that the Aged Contender believed he had torn down. So Newport's third day of debate was held on Monday, August 12, with many in attendance once more. The hottest procedural issue of the day was whether Roger would be permitted to read a letter from his brother Robert, then a schoolmaster in Newport. Having attended the first two days of debate, Robert wanted to pose some questions of his own to the Quakers. But the latter, having already accepted the elder brother's fourteen propositions, did not really feel that they needed still more. Thus, said Roger Williams, his brother's "poor letter" was "condemned unheard."

The debaters moved through the five propositions set for the third day, Williams trying—but failing—to keep within his self-imposed fifteen-minute limit. Williams also failed to keep his eye on the main themes, being diverted to discussions of many Quaker practices with which he disagreed: "dumb meetings," where they waited silently for a spirit that must be both "dumb and deaf"; their "brutish salutations"—their practice of greeting everyone as either "Friend" or "Foe"; their "brutish Irreverence to all their Superiors"; their objection to music as "a foolish and Devilish practice"; their "Crying out against Ornaments of Garments, and otherwise"; and their willingness to bless female ministers and female apostles. That last item Williams regarded as both unnatural and un-Christian, a practice that "all sober and modest Humanity abhor to think of." Some-

185

how, they managed to dispatch the five propositions on the third day, stopping in time for Williams to catch a boat that was "ready to set Sail for Providence." As he walked from the Quaker meeting house, his sister-in-law cried out that this "man hath discharged his Conscience . . . the words he has spoken shall Judge you at the last day."

From Tuesday through Friday, the principals rested, their theater of rhetoric and retort being dark. On Saturday, in Providence, the fourth and final day of debate was dedicated to the task of treating, or at least disposing of, the remaining seven propositions. Another attempt was made to introduce the letter of Robert Williams into the agenda, and again it was rejected. Other procedural issues were raised, but Williams decided not to push for any of them, for "I knew with whom I had to deal." In other words, let's get on with the propositions, for we have seven to cover in only one day, it having taken us three full days to deal with the first seven. For the desire to make haste, all could certainly be grateful.

For in arguing about the second seven, the contenders returned over and over to points made in connection with the first seven. Listeners and speakers alike must have had a growing sense that the same ground had been fought over so often that all traces of path or direction were now obscured. Williams attacked not only the doctrines of the Quakers (the "Foxians") but their character as well. All it took for a notorious sinner to believe himself sanctified was "to say, 'Thou' and 'Thee,' and think himself equal and above all his former Superiors." So swiftly was one made sinless and perfect, Williams unfairly charged. "Thus they pretend Repentance, Faith, and a change of heart because they changed their talk, their Garments, &c." It was too easy to become a Quaker, said Williams, and that explained their growth in Rhode Island and elsewhere.

Not so, said his opponents. Quakers were persecuted and endured suffering everywhere they went. How could one call it an "easy religion"? "For my part," William Edmundson noted, "I have not found it so. I have not found it easy to forsake all the

186

glory and honor and pleasures of this World, and to expose ourselves to hardships, to forsake Wives and Children, Friends and Relations, and to go about in strange Countries." Quakers, as Williams well knew, had even been put to death for their faith. They were holy martyrs. Williams knew of their deaths, of course, but he chose to distinguish carefully between the martyrs of that other Foxe (John), on the one hand, who were "slain for maintaining the Authority and Purity of the Holy Scriptures . . . against the Traditions and Inventions of men," and George Fox's martyrs on the other hand, who "have generally suffered for their Children's Baubles, fantastical Traditions and Inventions, for setting up a . . . Christ within all Mankind, above the holy Scriptures." With so great a gulf between them, the two sides were no more likely to find agreement on the fourth day than on the first.

After many more words and much more heat, the confrontation ended with none wiser and with the silver of Christian charity severely tarnished. "And thus it pleased the God and Father of Lights and Mercies to bring us to the end of the fourth day's Contest," Williams wrote, "and the end of the whole matter, in much Peace and Quietness." That was the major contribution of the debate: it ended. And the peace and quietness that followed must have been a welcome contrast to the noise and fury that preceded it. People in Providence as well as Newport could go about their daily business of raising their crops and their children, trusting that the four days of unseemly wrangling had done no permanent damage to either.

Trying to keep within those fifteen-minute limits (though he had to be called for time more than once) meant that Roger Williams left many things unsaid. He therefore resolved in the months following to put it all down in a big book, even adding a long appendix that would document Proposition #13: "That Quakers' Writings are Poor, Lame, and Naked (not able to defend themselves, nor comfort the Souls of others with any solidity)." Or, as he had put it in his earlier letter to George Fox, Quaker writings were "swelled up only with high Titles and

Words of boasting and Vapor." In a nineteenth-century reprinting of Williams' book it took one hundred and seventy pages to buttress that one proposition. Fortunately, not all required such sturdy support.

During the debates, Williams had often referred to George Fox's writings along with those of a prolific pamphleteer, Edward Burroughs. In naming them together, Fox and Burroughs, it sounded to his opponents as though he were trying to be funny. Williams denied it. Later, however, when he came to choose a title for his large book, the joke seemed too good to pass up, so his volume became *George Fox Digg'd out of his Burrowes.* As the manuscript neared completion in the spring of 1673, he wrote a Seventh-day Baptist friend that, having prepared "a large narrative of all those four days' agitation," he hoped to get it published in New England, but if not he might have to venture another long voyage to London. A sobering thought, that, for "Mine age, lameness, and many other weaknesses, and the dreadful hand of God at sea, call for deep consideration."

Boston, of course, had never been willing to allow any of Roger Williams' writings, long or short, onto their presses—understandably so, since Boston (and the surrounding territory) was either explicitly or implicitly generally under attack. But the matter of Quakers was different. Massachusetts felt even more threatened than Roger Williams did by the presence of "Fox and his Fantastics." So Boston at last agreed to publish a Williams book; more than that, Governor John Leverett offered to underwrite the costs of publication, this being no small matter, since the resources of Roger Williams were low. This volume, his last published work, thus appeared with a title page that included the words "Boston, Printed by John Foster, 1676."

PASSING OF A PATRIARCH

In the final decade of Williams' life, his privacy remained beloved but ever more painful. Health began to fail him, and fortune as well. In writing to Governor Leverett in January 1676, Williams closed his communication (which pertained, as so often, to Indian affairs) with this humiliating plea: "Sir, since I am oft occasioned to write upon the Public business, I shall be thankful for a little paper upon the Public account, being now near destitute." That request only made obvious what had long been implicit: Williams never feathered his own nest at the expense of the public he served. He never acquired great tracts of land even though, being first on the scene, a whole country lay before him. After coming to Rhode Island, he never received a salary, and after surrendering his trading post he never had a significant income. His wealth was in family and friends, in his sense of integrity and "sure calling" of God.

In his last years, Williams continued to offer help and counsel wherever he could. Even in the 1675 Indian War, he volunteered his services as a soldier to help defend the town of Providence. During that bloody strife, he ended a letter to Connecticut's Governor Winthrop (a letter that mostly contained bad news about loss of life) by asking, "Why is our Candle yet burning but to . . . [serve] God in serving the public in our generation?" In October of that dark year, he wrote to Massachusetts' Governor Leverett that while everyone was busy trying to keep their families from being murdered and their houses and barns from being burned, yet the principal task remained "to listen to what the Eternal Speaketh to the whole ship (the Country, Colonies, Towns, . . .) and each Private Cabin, family, person &c." Such spiritual reminders were regularly accompanied, however, by specific intelligence as to Indian forays and specific advice as to English responses.

The United Colonies took advantage of King Philip's War to reassert Connecticut's claims to Narraganset country. With troops in the field, it seemed like a good time to press the interests of Connecticut's charter over against those of Rhode Island. In October 1676 Williams wrote to the four governors (of Massachusetts, Plymouth, Connecticut, and New Haven) pleading once again that this whole matter be settled among themselves, that they not continue to fight about it or send off complaints to the king, a tactic that would inevitably lead to "unknown trouble." To that end, said Williams, "I humbly beg of God that a Committee from the four Colonies may (by way of prudent and godly wisdom) prevent many inconveniences and mischiefs." The letter included a postscript: "Excuse my Want of Paper."

One year later Williams was writing to a Special Court of Commissioners appointed to settle that other long-standing fight about land: Pawtuxet and William Harris. Williams apologized to the Court about the behavior of the latter, regretting that a "self-seeking Contentious Soul . . . should now (with his unreasonable and unjust Clamors) afflict our royal Sovereign," the very thing that Williams most wished to avoid. Though he held no political office at this time, he nonetheless knew more about the history of that whole controversy than anyone else. Consequently, he could not "be ungratefully and treacherously silent at such a time." And so Williams reviewed, one more time, the terms under which the original Indian grants had been made to him and the first settlers, how, out of their kindness, the Indians had permitted these first men to graze their cattle "upstream without limits," and how William Harris, out of his infinite greed, interpreted that as being the same as a title to all that land. What Williams hoped above all else was that this Court would settle this "Complaint and Clamor" in such a way as to make it unnecessary ever to bother the king or the king's council again. This should be done "for God's sake, for the King's sake, for the Country of New England's sake, for their own Souls' and Selves' and Posterity's sake." Would the clamor never end?

It would not, as Williams again and again recalled his own history and that of the earliest days, then stated his case, and pleaded for final arbitration. Arbitration, he told the Court in November 1677, "will be the only Medicine for this long and multiplied Disease now before you." And with utter weariness, he noted that it was "no new thing for me to bear all sorts of

Reproaches, Slanders, &c., from W. Harris about Forty Years together." To the dismay of Roger Williams, the Court found in Harris' favor. To the dismay of William Harris, the Court lacked the ability to enforce its verdict. Harris, in high dudgeon, sailed for London in 1679 to get the force of royal authority directly behind him, but even this did not work. Finding Rhode Islanders either recalcitrant or incompetent, Harris turned to Connecticut for its support. And on another voyage to London, his ship was captured by Algerian pirates and he was sold into slavery and held for ransom. Eventually ransomed, he died in London in 1681. But it would take more than his death to settle the matter: the wrangling persisted into the eighteenth century.

In 1679 Massachusetts ministers persuaded their General Court to call a "Reforming Synod" to address the general decline in religion as well as the awful judgment of God upon his people in the recent Indian war. "That God hath a Controversy with his New-England People is undeniable," the synod members observed, as they delineated the growing signs of "visible decay of the power of Godliness." Pride abounded, Sabbath breaking pervaded, "Sinful Heats and Hatreds" mounted, and "A public Spirit is greatly wanting in the most of men." Williams, though rarely in agreement with his Massachusetts brethren, would surely have given his fervent assent in this matter. Then in 1680 "Newton's Comet" flashed across the sky, interpreted by many as further evidence of divine displeasure and warning of chastisement to come. Williams' wife, Mary, had died several years before, and his daughter of the same name passed away in 1681. Such signs and omens offered little promise.

In January 1682 Roger Williams wrote once more to the town of Providence to see if their "heats and hatreds" might yet cool and heal. He made the case yet again that government had its proper function to fulfill and therefore needed to be obeyed. "There is not a Man in World," he sternly told them, "(except Robbers, Pirates, Rebels) but doth Submit to Government." Unless the citizens of Providence chose to place themselves in one of those three categories, it was time for them to behave as good citizens and good Christians ought. Williams was even willing to cite "that Ancient Maxim" that it was better to live under a tyrant in peace than under the sword where every man was a tyrant. The people of Providence must choose which of the two great laws of the world they wanted for their own: the one of judges and courts of peace, or the other of incessant warfare and blood. And one more time he reminded them that "Our Charter Excels all in New England or the World, as to the Souls of Men."

Williams signed most of his letters, "Your unworthy Servant." He signed this one, "Your old unworthy Servant." In May he wrote Massachusetts' Governor Simon Bradstreet to inquire whether he would help him pay for the printing of twenty-two sermons that he had delivered to the "scattered English" in Narraganset country; "there is no controversy in them," he assured Bradstreet. The sermons, never published, no longer survive. Williams also told the governor that he was "old and weak and bruised (with a Rupture and Colic) and lameness on both my feet." The next year he was dead, the exact date of his death like that of his birth being unknown. He was buried in the steep hillside behind his home, now burned to the ground. One witness later recalled that muskets were fired over his grave.

7 Exile No More

When the Massachusetts General Court took its historic action against Roger Williams in 1635, John Cotton remarked that Williams had not been banished so much as he had been "enlarged" to the whole country beyond. None would be more surprised than Cotton himself to learn that this indeed turned out to be the case. By assuming responsibilities for the colony of Rhode Island, Roger Williams was forced to wrestle continuously with the implications of liberty of conscience, with the heartaches as well as the opportunities such liberty brought. And by making his two charter-seeking trips to London, Williams forced many others in England to reflect on the possibility that liberty itself might be "enlarged."

The Rhode Island charter of 1663 acknowledged that the citizens of that small colony had it "much on their hearts (if they may be permitted), to hold forth a lively experiment." That experiment was to test the proposition that religious liberty could exist side by side with civil security and even prosperity. King Charles II and his royal advisers seemed ready in 1663 to place their bets on that possibility, blazing the way for freedom in religion in these words:

> That our royal will and pleasure is, that no person within the said colony, at any time hereafter, shall be any wise molested, punished, disquieted, or called in question, for difference in opinion in matters of religion, [that] do not actually disturb the civil peace of our said colony; but that all and every person and persons may, from time to time, and at all times hereafter, freely and fully have and enjoy his and their own judgments and consciences in matters of religious concernments.

The charter further specified that such freedom was not to be understood as a "liberty to licentiousness and profaneness," nor was the civil peace to be disturbed. Roger Williams praised this charter, finding the limitation wholly congenial to his own commitment to "civility" within the social order. More surprisingly, others well outside of Rhode Island found the charter praiseworthy as well.

In 1664 the "Lords Proprietors" of New Jersey, Lord John Berkeley and Sir George Carteret, offered a formal Concession and Agreement that promised settlers of this land, recently seized from the Dutch, the same liberty of conscience in the very same words. No person would be in any way "molested, punished, disquieted or called in question" for any difference in religious opinion or—the New Jersey document added—practice. But again, such liberty was no license for licentiousness or for disturbing the civil peace of the society.

The very next year Charles II granted a charter for the whole of Carolina that demonstrated that the words of the Rhode Island Charter had so soon acquired a special status of their own. Once more the proprietors were authorized to grant a liberty that assured that none would be in any way "molested, punished, disquieted, or called in question for any differences in opinion or practice in matters of religious concernments." "Practice" had by now become a standard partner to "opinion."

The usual proviso was added concerning licentiousness and civil peace; otherwise all persons might enjoy "freely and quietly" their "judgments and consciences in matters of religion." When later that year, the Lord Proprietors spelled out their agreement with potential settlers, in treating religion these titled gentlemen thought they could do no better than repeat the very same words.

The colony of New Jersey being divided into two halves in the seventeenth century, West New Jersey felt obliged to issue its own guarantee of liberty of conscience in 1677. Showing a little more originality in wording, this document went beyond "disquieted" and "molested" to declare that no person, on account of religion, would be "in the least punished or hurt, either in person, estate, or privilege." But then, originality exhausted, the statement followed the Rhode Island charter closely in affirming that all persons may "from time to time and at all times, freely and fully have and enjoy his and their judgments and *the exercise of their* consciences in matters of religious *worship*." The italicized words indicate West New Jersey's modifications, it being clear that "practice" or "exercise" needed to be explicitly included as an integral part of religious liberty. Religion was more than mere opinion; to allow persons to think freely but not act freely in religion made no sense to the libertarians of the seventeenth century nor to the libertarians who would follow.

Pennsylvania needed to follow no one else's handbook or model when it came to religious liberty. For that colony's founder, William Penn, had in 1670 published his own manifesto, *The Great Case of Liberty of Conscience*. There Penn made it clear that this liberty had to be more than a liberty of mind: it must include, he wrote, at a minimum the "exercise of ourselves in a visible way of worship." So when a dozen years later Penn's colony came into being, it is not surprising that guarantees to religious liberty were spelled out, and spelled out in quite modern-sounding terms, to both *him* and *her*. No person living "peaceably and quietly under the civil government, shall in any

195

case be molested or prejudiced for his or her conscientious persuasion or practice," this enactment being laid down in 1682. Penn also added that "he or she" would not be compelled at any time "to frequent or maintain any worship, place, or ministry whatever contrary to his or her mind."

John Milton and Roger Williams would both rejoice that the coerced tithe for the support of a hireling ministry was, at least in Rhode Island and Pennsylvania, a thing of the past. Anglicanism continued to enjoy tax moneys in Carolina and New Jersey—despite the assurances of religious liberty—until after the American Revolution. And in New England, of course, the legal tithe on behalf of Congregationalism continued well into the nineteenth century. Even in Pennsylvania religious liberty was assured only to those "who shall confess and acknowledge one almighty God to be the creator, upholder, and ruler of the world." The words of Rhode Island's charter were sometimes more faithfully copied than was the reality for which Roger Williams stood; nonetheless, the Western world was steadily moving further and further away from the bloody tenent.

John Locke gave that world (especially the English-speaking portion of it) a healthy nudge along its path toward freedom when in 1689, six years after Williams' death, he published his *Letter on Toleration.* Of course, that word *toleration* would have pleased Williams no more in 1689 than it did when Parliament had used it a generation or so before. Liberty was more than toleration, freedom more than a concession. Despite that unassailable fact, however, much of what Locke stated in his powerful Latin epistle would have greatly warmed the heart of the man who had said most of it a half century before. "I regard it as necessary above all to distinguish between the business of civil government and that of religion," Locke wrote, "and to mark the true bounds between the church and the commonwealth." This encapsulated much of what Williams had repeatedly declared, at far greater length, both in London and in Boston.

The civil magistrate, Locke continued, must concern himself only with civil goods, never with the salvation of souls. "It does not appear that God ever gave any such authority to one man over another as to compel other men to embrace his religion." The power of the magistrate lay in compulsion, while the power of religion lay in persuasion. Locke, who wrote persuasively himself about human understanding, added that "such is the nature of human understanding that it cannot be compelled by any outward force. Confiscate a man's goods, imprison or torture his body: such punishments will be in vain." (Williams could only have regretted that John Endecott, also in his grave, was not in a position to hear those words.) The whole of civil government, Locke concluded, "is confined to the care of the things of this world, and has nothing whatever to do with the world to come."

As for the church, Locke contended in words that would make every Separatist happy that it was strictly a "free and voluntary society." No one was born into it, no one could be compelled to it, no outside force could legislate for it. It is a union based on mutual consent, and one must have full freedom to join it as well as full freedom to depart from it. But someone will say, Locke wrote, that it is not a true church unless it has bishops and presbyters. Sounding much like Roger Williams, Locke stated that in quarrels of this sort we should look to the New Testament for an answer—and there we find the following: "Where two or three are gathered together in my name, there am I in the midst of them" (Matt. 18:20). The presence of Christ, not the dignity of church officers or the exact propriety of church ordinances, makes it a church. And where and how is Christ truly present? The answer to that question every voluntary association of worshipers has to determine for itself.

The church has the right of excommunication, Locke agreed, but excommunication means only that: placing one outside of a community of believers. Such a person, set out from one community, has a full right to join another; he should receive no "rough treatment," nor be injured in either body or estate. Christians should not mistreat each other on the grounds of religious errors, nor churches abuse each other—for who truly knows the error? Only the "Supreme Judge of all men, to whom also alone belongs the chastisement of the erroneous." Churches have no jurisdiction in earthly matters, Locke pointed out, "nor are fire and sword proper instruments for refuting errors or instructing and converting men's minds." Those tempted to think otherwise would do well to look to history, said Locke—as Williams had before him. Just consider "what limitless occasions for discords and wars, how powerful a provocation to rapines, slaughters, and endless hatreds" has the spirit of religious persecution brought down upon all humankind.

One need not look to antiquity or to medieval history to find these lessons sharply drawn. England offered all the examples necessary for Locke, as it had for Williams, of the bloodiness as well as the utter irrationality of state-coerced religion. We need only observe "how neatly and promptly under Henry, Edward, Mary, and Elizabeth the clergy changed their decrees, their articles of faith, their form of worship, everything, at a nod from the prince." Obviously, the rulers could not all have been right, and they may very well all have been wrong. But even assuming that any civil magistrate at any given time did chance to be correct, this altered the case against compulsion not one whit. "I may grow rich by an art that I dislike; I may be cured of a disease by remedies that I distrust; but I cannot be saved by a religion that I distrust or by a worship that I dislike." Religion and force can never be properly joined; they were and are in essence totally incompatible; in the end, a person "must be left to himself and his own conscience." Or, as they said in Pennsylvania, to his or her own conscience.

Locke, whose influential political treatises on government were published in this same year, exercised enormous influence in England and, later, in America. In justifying the Glorious Revolution of 1688 he helped his countrymen explain their deposing of King James II (who had succeeded his brother Charles II in 1685) and their choosing of William and Mary as their joint sovereigns. He also encouraged the passage of the Toleration Act of 1689, which ended the persecution of Protestant dissent, though it stopped well short of establishing a full freedom for all religious opinion and practice that did not disrupt the civil peace. The seventeenth century did not achieve a total liberty in religion, but by its final years the terrifying ideas that Roger Williams had described in 1644 had lost much of their terror.

THE EIGHTEENTH CENTURY

So far as the lasting reputation of Roger Williams went, the eighteenth century did not get off to a promising start. In 1702 Cotton Mather of Massachusetts published in London his *Magnalia Christi Americana; or, The Ecclesiastical History of New-England*. In that impressive historical work, Williams does not come off well. On the other hand, Mather's scorn of Williams was expressed with such verve and panache that no one, even now, can resist quoting him, the end result being that even modern students may learn of Rhode Island's maverick chiefly from that one source. Before Rhode Island, of course, Williams was a wild maverick in Massachusetts, and that seized most of Mather's attention. As historian and scholar, Mather would prefer "to leave a veil than a scar upon the memory of any person," but some people were too memorable to ignore. Mather's history would be but "an unfinished piece" were Roger Williams to be left out.

And so Mather began, very artfully, with an anecdote. In Holland, Mather had heard, a windmill in 1654 had been forced by extraordinarily high winds to turn faster and faster until the stone became so hot that it set the mill on fire, and then—those same high winds operating—the whole town was set ablaze. And so to the moral. "But I can tell my readers that, about twenty years before this, there was a whole country in America like to be set on fire by the rapid motion of a windmill in the head of one particular man." The "whole country" was Massachusetts, and the "particular man" was, to be sure, Roger Williams, and Cotton Mather was, to be equally sure, not one of his great admirers.

Williams had "less light than fire in him," Mather observed, that fire bringing him to the hot point of opposing the civil magistrate's enforcement of the First Table. That, said Mather, would have "opened up to a thousand profanities" and turned the Bay Colony into a "sink of abominations." Not content with that, however, "this hot-headed man publicly and furiously preached" against the Massachusetts charter "on an insignificant pretense of wrong thereby done unto the Indians." And, of course, he objected to a religious oath being administered to irreligious men. "These crimes," Mather noted with some relief, "at last procured a sentence of banishment upon him." Whereupon, Williams proceeded with others to the "gathering of a thing like a church" and the founding of a hodge-podge colony that contained "Antinomians, Familists, Anabaptists, Antisabbatarians, Arminians, Socinians, Quakers, Ranters—everything in the world but Roman Catholics and real Christians."

Cotton Mather did give Williams credit for his work with the Indians and his relationships with Massachusetts officialdom following his banishment. In fact, in several respects Williams "acquitted himself so laudably," Mather conceded, "that many judicious persons judged him to have had the 'root of the matter' in him, during the long winter of his retirement." Mather was particularly impressed, of course, by Williams' contesting against the Quakers, an effort in which "he maintained the main principles of the Protestant religion with much vigor." It was just too bad that this had not been his life's work, too bad that he had found it necessary, not to tilt at windmills, but to turn himself into an overheated one.

If Mather spoke for a great deal of Massachusetts in 1702, a Rhode Island clergyman and historian spoke for much of his colony a generation later in offering a rather different assessment of Williams. John Callender, graduate of Harvard (class of 1710), was ordained as a Baptist minister in 1718, one of the Congregational clergymen assisting in that ordination being none other than Cotton Mather. Accepting the invitation of the Baptist church in Newport (John Clarke's church) to become its pastor in 1731, Callender remained in that office until his death in 1748. In 1739 he wrote *An Historical Discourse, on the Civil and Religious Affairs of the Colony of Rhode-Island and Providence Plantations,* an invaluable account and the colony's only published history for a century after.

Callender praised not only Williams but the principles for which he fought. "I take it to have been no dishonor to the Colony," he wrote, "that Christians of every denomination were suffered to lead quiet and peaceable lives, without any fines or punishments for their speculative opinions, or for using those external forms of worship they believed God had appointed." Bigots, he added, may call this confusion and disorder, but Roger Williams knew what was truly the most "monstrous disorder"—namely, "trampling on the consciences" of humankind. Williams, said Callender, was "one of the most disinterested men that ever lived, a most pious and heavenly minded soul"—perhaps exactly what one would expect a Rhode Islander and Baptist to say.

But what about a Quaker in eighteenth-century Rhode Island? What kind of evaluation might Roger Williams expect from that source? Stephen Hopkins, many times governor of the colony between 1755 and 1768 and later signer of the Declaration of Independence, compiled materials for a history of Rhode Island that never was completed. In portions that he did publish in the 1760s, Quaker Hopkins acclaimed Roger Williams as deserving all honor for "having been the first legislator in the world . . . that fully and effectively provided for and established a free, full, and absolute liberty of conscience." Williams made that "beneficent principle" the "chief cornerstone of his infant colony," so much so that when Massachusetts asked Rhode Island in 1657 to cooperate in stamping out Quakerism, Williams' colony swiftly replied that it had "no law among us" that made any such religious persecution possible.

Hopkins was often enough governor himself, as Williams had been, that he clearly understood what havoc liberty of conscience could make for administrators. It even created problems for the economy and social order. Every "human felicity," Hopkins noted, "has some attendant misfortune." And of liberty of conscience this was conspicuously true, for it "hath ever been found to produce some disorders, factions, and parties." If one looked for a remedy for these "mischiefs," it could be found only in the "personal virtue and steady perseverance of the wise and good" among Rhode Island's citizens. Only this would ever be sufficient to "withstand the headlong passions of the giddy multitude." Roger Williams' task, said Hopkins, was on the one hand to "guard and maintain that sacred liberty and freedom they had established, and on the other, to prevent and suppress the licentiousness too naturally flowing from it." It was Hopkins' task as well, and perhaps the peculiar task and burden of democracy everywhere.

As Hopkins was publishing segments of his incomplete history in the pages of the *Providence Gazette*, another movement gave a greater reputation to the colony and ultimately to its founder. The College of Rhode Island, later Brown University, chartered in 1764, was to a considerable degree the creation of the Baptists, those in Rhode Island and far beyond. But it was never intended to be a narrowly sectarian institution, inhospitable to those of other denominations or of none. Indeed, in language as forceful as can readily be imagined, the charter specified that "into this liberal and catholic institution shall never be admitted any religious tests; but, on the contrary, all the members hereof shall forever enjoy full, free, absolute, and uninterrupted liberty of conscience." Not until nearly another century had passed did either Oxford or Cambridge admit dissenters into their midst. In the ringing affirmation of the Brown charter, the spirit of Roger Williams may be discerned, even as it may be discerned twelve years later when the colonies

Exile No More

agreed in July 1776 to declare their independence from England. Rhode Island had already issued its own declaration two months before.

In the period of the American Revolution, the historical reputation of Roger Williams received its greatest boost from a New England Congregationalist become Baptist: Isaac Backus. A native of Connecticut, Backus during the Great Awakening became a pro-revivalist New Light who separated from the official establishment of his home colony. Gradually he came to reject the notion of infant baptism, becoming by 1756 a Baptist pastor in Middleborough, Massachusetts, and remaining so to the end of his long life in 1806. In 1777 he published the first volume of his major work, *A History of New England with Particular Reference to the Denomination of Christians called Baptists.* Quite consciously, Backus sought to rescue Roger Williams from what he regarded as undue neglect, especially in the wider circles outside of Rhode Island. And writing at a time when the American Revolution was underway, Backus also thought that Williams' theme of liberty deserved every possible emphasis.

Gathering a great many documents himself, including twelve of Roger Williams' own letters, Backus was in a position to tell a far fuller story than anyone had before. Indeed, he wrote what almost amounted to a biography of Williams, though the data were immersed in a general historical development and in Backus' own theological commentary. Quoting extensively from manuscript sources, Backus helped to preserve some lost material and called attention to even more. He emphasized Williams' role in creating the country's first Baptist church in Providence, and he emphasized his total dedication to religious liberty. "The first founder and supporter of any truly civil government upon earth" was the encomium that Backus placed upon the head of Williams, adding that he knew of no other person coming to New England in the same period "who acted so consistently and steadily upon right principles about government and liberty as Mr. Williams did."

More than praising Roger Williams, Isaac Backus imitated

203

him in pleading for religious liberty as well as for profound personal piety in the late eighteenth century. When all America in 1774 was alarmed about a tax on tea, Backus thought that Massachusetts would do well to be equally alarmed about a tax on conscience—that is, the tithe collected by force to support the Congregational ministry, whether one attended that ministry or not. It was true, Backus acknowledged, that one could appeal to the state to receive a special exemption by proving that one supported some other church. But even that gave the state an authority over conscience that it did not deserve to have. The legislators of Massachusetts held that no violation of conscience was involved, for the tax was of a purely civil nature. Not so, replied Backus. If the state's clergy were truly "Christ's ministers, he has made laws enough to support them; if they are not" Christ's ministers, then what magistrate has the courage to point that out, while still collecting the taxes? We dissenters, we Baptists, Backus told the Massachusetts legislators face to face, ask only what is legitimately ours: "we claim charter rights, liberty of conscience." In 1779, Backus even suggested a bill of rights that Massachusetts might append to its constitution, a bill making it clear that "every person has an unalienable right to act in all religious affairs according to the full persuasion of his own mind, where others are not injured thereby."

So New England had a strong libertarian Baptist voice during the Revolution and after, as did the heavily populated state of Virginia. Following the religious excitement of mid-eighteenth century known as the Great Awakening, the number of Baptists grew rapidly; heretofore, they had been a small and not particularly aggressive body of believers. With a renewal of pietism and a removal of the Anglican establishment (notably in Virginia), Baptists flourished, and in their flourishing they waved the banners of religious liberty with vigor and effect. In the course of the American Revolution, Virginians moved early against continuing tax support for the Church of England. But in moving toward a full freedom in religion, the pace was slowed by those (for example, Patrick Henry) who thought that some connection between church and state needed to be retained. Thomas Jefferson and James Madison thought otherwise but needed popular support to carry the legislature along with them. Baptists led in that support, petitioning their representatives to defeat the Patrick Henry plan and support Jefferson's Bill for Establishing Religious Freedom.

Madison's justly famous *Memorial and Remonstrance*, presented to Virginia's House of Burgesses in 1785, helped turn the tide in favor of Jefferson and in favor of religious liberty. Madison (like Williams) argued that in matters of religious conscience citizens are accountable to God alone, not to man, and that the civil magistrate was no competent judge of religious truth, nor could he rightfully "employ Religion as an engine of Civil policy." Establishments of religion do far more harm than good to both the civil and ecclesiastical realms, Madison argued. They tend to erect either a spiritual or a political tyranny; "in no instances have they been seen the guardians of the liberties of the people." Should not all America (like Rhode Island) be an asylum "to the persecuted and oppressed of every Nation and Religion," or must we now after winning our own liberty erect "a Beacon on our Coast," warning all sufferers for conscience "to seek some other haven"? For Madison, that question had only one correct answer, and that answer came the next year in the form of Jefferson's long-delayed bill, at last passed in 1786.

Jeffersonian rhetoric required neither earlier documents nor earlier champions of religious liberty. Nevertheless, his statute did echo language of both Rhode Island's and Pennsylvania's charters as it provided that "no man shall be compelled to frequent or support any religious worship, place or ministry whatsoever, nor shall be enforced, restrained, molested, or burthened in his body or goods, nor shall otherwise suffer on account of his religious opinions or beliefs." Jefferson did not even worry about liberty as an excuse for licentiousness or profaneness or about threats to the civil peace. For him, as for Madison and Williams, the greatest threat to civil peace was not liberty of conscience but the farce of "fallible and uninspired men" setting themselves up as inspired and infallible judges of the consciences of others: war, rapine, ravishment, treachery, and torture—every student of recent history knew the bloody results.

So in 1786 Virginia had a Statute for Establishing Religious Freedom. In 1787 the new nation had a constitution to send out for ratification; here Rhode Island was not first, but last, this concern for too strong a central government also reflecting the spirit of Roger Williams and Rhode Island's "giddy multitude." That the Constitution would be ratified at all was far from clear in the early months of 1788, as many persons worried especially about the absence of any federal bill of rights. The Constitution expended too much time saying what government could do, not enough making clear what limits were being placed upon that government, especially with respect to human rights. Virginians, who had their own Declaration of Rights, were among those concerned that an even stronger government did not explicitly restrain itself. Madison, lobbying earnestly for ratification, soon discovered that Virginians in large numbers would vote against the Constitution unless it had a bill of rights.

He learned this in conversation with, among others, John Leland, a Baptist itinerant preacher of great force and great conviction with respect to the separation of church and state. Agreeing with Madison that church establishments had done far more harm than good, Leland declared that all persecution, inquisition, and martyrdom derived from one single "rotten nest-egg, which is always hatching vipers: I mean the principle of intruding the laws of men into the Kingdom of Christ." If one had to choose between persecution and state support, the former should instantly be chosen. "Persecution, like a lion, tears the saints to death," Leland observed, "but leaves Christianity pure; state establishment of religion, like a bear, hugs the saints but corrupts Christianity." Would the United States, like virtually all of Europe, have a national church and form a corrupting alliance with institutional religion? What guarantee did the Constitution provide that it would not?

This uneasiness led Madison to agree with Leland and other constituents that if the Constitution were ratified, Madison would personally pledge that the first order of business in the newly elected Congress would be the drawing up of a bill of rights. Virginia did ratify, though narrowly, and James Madison as a member of the House of Representatives did execute his pledge. In 1789 the first ten amendments to the Constitution were submitted to the people for their approval, the very first phrase of the very first amendment specifying that "Congress shall make no law respecting an establishment of religion, or prohibiting the free exercise thereof." By 1791 that amendment, along with all the others, had become fundamental law for the nation. Though it was a major milestone, neither Jefferson nor Madison nor others "distressed of conscience" would relax. "I have sworn upon the altar of god," Jefferson wrote in 1800, "eternal hostility against every form of tyranny over the mind of man." Jefferson believed that such tyranny had historically been exercised most often by religion. Roger Williams would only have wished to add that religious tyranny had been even bloodier with respect to the bodies of all humankind.

THE NINETEENTH CENTURY

The most famous wall in American history belongs to Jefferson, not to Williams. With similar but not identical concerns, both men wanted a clear division between the civil and ecclesiastical estates. Williams spoke of it as "the hedge or wall of separation between the garden of the church and the wilderness of the world." Jefferson spoke of it as "a wall of separation between church and state." No evidence demonstrates that the latter statement was dependent on the former, but the interests of both "parties"—pietist and deist—could on occasion happily coincide.

That coincidence led, in fact, to Jefferson's penning of the phrase. Baptists in Connecticut wrote to Jefferson to congratulate him on his election in 1800 to the presidency of the United States. As dissenters in New England, these pietists appreciated Jefferson's dedication to religious liberty in general and to their liberty against the Congregational establishment in particular. Jefferson, like Williams, distrusted religion wedded to power and despised those clergy who seemed more interested in wealth and position than in truth and humble service. Congregationalists, for their part, distrusted Jefferson, whom they saw as their enemy so far as the establishment of religion was concerned. In this, they were correct, for Jefferson eyed all official religion with keen suspicion, convinced that its practitioners looked for any way possible to circumvent or nullify the First Amendment.

Baptists, being powerless, aroused less suspicion, though Jefferson was surprised that in their letter they asked him to set aside a day of fasting so that the nation might heal its wounds from a bitterly divisive campaign between him and John Adams. Jefferson would declare no such day of fasting or feasting or anything else pertaining to religion, for to do so would be to add more fuel to the dangerous mixture of religion and politics. On the other hand, he did not want to ignore a letter from faithful supporters in Connecticut—where he had so few. Thus, he composed a careful reply, telling these pietists that he shared their view that religion was solely a matter between the believer and the Deity, with government standing quite aside. One owed to the state no account whatsoever concerning one's faith or worship, as the Constitution now made clear. "I contemplate with solemn reverence," Jefferson wrote, "that act of the whole American people"—that is, the First Amendment as ratified by the people. Then Jefferson gave his special spin to the amendment by describing its force as "thus building a wall of separation between church and state."

Jefferson, who had fought for so long in Virginia for religious freedom, would now fight for its preservation and fortification at the national level. Even with that precious amendment, religious liberty depended on an approving public, for public opinion, he argued, could itself become a kind of inquisition. During his eight years in the presidency as well as in many letters written in retirement at Monticello, Jefferson tried to remold people's minds to accept, perhaps even glory in, the possibility set forth in Rhode Island's 1663 charter: "to hold forth a lively experiment, that a most flourishing civil state may stand and best be maintained . . . with a full liberty in religious concernments." Jefferson devoutly wished to keep that Rhode Island experiment—now the American experiment—lively.

Jefferson was succeeded in the presidency by his colleague in the battle for religious freedom, James Madison. A scholarly and brilliant statesman and the most powerful mental force at the Constitutional Convention, Madison, when still in his early twenties, cried out against that "diabolical, hell-conceived principle of persecution" which he saw being practiced in his own Virginia neighborhood. In jailing some itinerant Baptist preachers, Anglicans unwittingly created a powerful enemy of all bloody swords wielded in the name of religion. His Memorial and Remonstrance, written when he was all of thirty-five years of age, made his position more explicit and firm. Then in his "generalship" of the First Amendment, Madison thought even more deeply about the questions of liberty of conscience, his own proposed draft including that favorite word of Roger Williams, *conscience*. Madison offered this initial version: "The Civil Rights of none shall be abridged on account of religious belief or worship, nor shall any national religion be established, nor shall the full and equal rights of conscience be in any manner, nor on any pretext infringed." Three months of discussion, debate, and modification would transpire before the much shorter form of the First Amendment's religion clauses emerged.

Thus eight years of a Madisonian presidency added to eight years of a Jeffersonian presidency worked to set the liberty of religion on as firm a foundation as possible. Not everyone was convinced. Indeed, counterpressures continued throughout the nineteenth century, including some persistent official establishments of religion. For the First Amendment specified only what Congress could or could not do, not what paths the individual states might follow. Connecticut, for example, continued its establishment until 1818, when it was overturned in a very close vote. This prompted Jefferson to rejoice (in a letter to John Adams—they now were friends again) that "this den of priesthood is at length broken up, and that a protestant popedom is no longer to disgrace American history and character." No longer in Connecticut, that is, for establishment continued for yet another fifteen years in Massachusetts. By the time it fell, neither Adams nor Jefferson could rejoice, for both had passed from the scene.

The deists did not speak for all the American people; in fact, they spoke for very few. The pietists, who came much closer to representing the broad public, made religious liberty real not so much by talking about it as by living it. In the westward expansion of the first half of the nineteenth century, along the ever-shifting frontier, religion moved with a freedom that belied all fear about how a nation could survive without a national church—or without at least some government protection of and support for the many churches. As it turned out, churches divorced from the state proved to be even more lively as they carried on the lively experiment; in the words of the Rhode Island charter, church members proceeded to "freely and fully have and enjoy his and their own judgments and consciences." To be sure, those judgments and consciences could be and often were wrong, conspicuously so in the case of the nineteenth-century alliances with nativism and defenses of slavery. In the long run, however, even so strong a defender of "official religion" as Lyman Beecher agreed that the voluntary system turned out to be far better for the whole country: it cut churches loose from the state and "threw them wholly on their own resources and on God." And that was where reliance needed to be, not upon heavy-handed civil magistrates who still had difficulty distinguishing between incivility on the one hand and impiety on the other.

In general, those denominations did best that loved the

state least. Baptists, Methodists, Disciples of Christ (a group of frontier origin in the 1830s) and others who had never known establishment and never cared for it took to this new freedom with alacrity and joy. It was as though they had suddenly broken free of all oppression, restraint, and political disfavor. The two major colonial establishments, Congregationalism and Anglicanism, on the other hand, reacted quite differently. Not suddenly unburdened, these two denominations felt suddenly heavy with the weight of fiscal responsibility. This was particularly true of the Anglicans, now Episcopalians, for whom disestablishment came abruptly, even harshly. In Virginia after the Revolution, Episcopalians bemoaned their dreary and outcast state: ministers unpaid, churches not maintained, "and there is no fund equal to the smallest want." For them, religious liberty was, at best, a mixed blessing.

The future, however, belonged to those who reveled in the freedom, splashed in it like adolescents at the swimming ponds. They would build their own churches without the help of anyone, they would ordain their own clergy without the authority of synod or benefit of university, they would arrive at their own creed innocent of most history and most theology. By the time Andrew Jackson became president in 1829, it had become the age of the people in politics no less than in religion. In a sense, the nation had decided between Roger Williams and John Cotton, and Cotton had lost.

Not everyone was happy with the way things had turned out. John Quincy Adams, for one, was certainly unhappy with how the election had turned out in 1828, for he was obliged to turn the presidency over to a rude westerner and Indian fighter. But this Adams was no happier about the way the contest between Cotton and Williams seemed to be turning out. When years later he had to prepare an address for the Massachusetts Historical Society, he discussed Roger Williams and the colony for which he was responsible and indicated that he did not care much for either. Williams, wrote Adams in 1843, came to Massachusetts "sharpened for controversy, a polemical porcupine from Oxford, an extreme puritan, quilled with all the quarrel-some metaphysical divinity of the age." *He* was the aggressor, Adams averred, not the Bay Colony, certainly not John Cotton, and "I cannot acquit him." Moreover, "his excommunications were all intolerant, his refusal to take the oath of allegiance was factious, his preaching against it seditious." Why at this time had the nose of John Quincy Adams been tweaked somewhat out of joint about Roger Williams?

The answer lay in a volume that had appeared a few years earlier. Written by a Massachusetts historian, it nonetheless seemed to take the part of the Narragansett colony against the Bay Colony. "It has in recent times," Adams wrote, "become a sort of literary fashion to extol the character of Roger Williams by disparaging" the character of Massachusetts. Though dead more than a century and a half, the "polemical porcupine" still had power in his quills. What had irritated Adams was the first volume of George Bancroft's monumental *History of the United States* which emerged in 1834, the whole ten volumes being completed some forty years later. A graduate of Harvard and a native son of Massachusetts, Bancroft alienated Adams by being both pro-Williams and pro-Jackson. In Bancroft's view, the age of the people had indeed arrived, automatically making heroes out of all those who had resisted entrenched privilege and aristocratic power.

Williams, more a political than a theological figure for Bancroft, emerged as "the first person in modern Christendom to establish civil government on the doctrine of liberty of con-science, the equality of opinions before the law." (Williams might have appreciated the compliment, but he would have despised the use of the term *Christendom*.) Williams, Bancroft added, "would permit persecution of no opinion, of no religion, leaving heresy unharmed by law, and orthodoxy unprotected by the terrors of penal statutes." Writing in the romantic mode, Bancroft went on at length about the virtues of Roger Williams, even of Rhode Island and "the excellency of the principles on which it rested its earliest institutions." Bancroft's credentials as

a Massachusetts man were certainly in danger of being challenged, especially as he launched into the following peroration:
"Let, then, the name of Roger Williams be preserved in universal
history as one who advanced moral and political science, and
made himself a benefactor of his race." It remained to be seen
whether Williams, who had endured countless persecutions,
would survive such ebullient praise.

More praise was on its way, for example, in the form of
biographies that began to appear, the first in 1834 (by James D.
Knowles), the second (by Romeo Elton) in 1853. In 1860 the
president of Brown University, Francis Wayland, joined in the
chorus by praising Williams' "stern love of individual liberty."
At this point Williams had not yet had any monuments erected
to him; there was not even a marker over his grave, its exact
location being uncertain. But, said Wayland, "there are some
men whose monuments are everywhere, who are known as
wide as civilization." The Pilgrims in America, Wayland added,
sought liberty for themselves; Roger Williams in America
sought "liberty for humanity."

If the first half of the nineteenth century brought both the
age of the people and the freedom of religion to full flower, the
second half of that century brought in a world to which Roger
Williams would have been a stranger: large cities, great facto-
ries, millions of immigrants, and a loss of cultural authority for
religion. As Americans advocated and exercised their liberty,
they gave little thought to the parable of the wheat and the tares
in determining the proper limits for either church or state.
Biblical arguments moved out of the public sphere into the
private domains of denominations and seminaries. So also arguments about the stature and significance of Roger Williams
tended to become the concern of the churches only.

On the whole, Congregationalists felt obliged to defend
the role of John Cotton and Massachusetts, while Baptists felt a
similar obligation to defend Roger Williams and Rhode Island.
In 1876 Congregationalist Henry Martyn Dexter published an

argumentative tract entitled *As to Roger Williams and His "Banishment" from the Massachusetts Plantation. With a few further words concerning the Baptists, the Quakers, and Religious Liberty.* To summarize the contents in fewer words than the title, Williams persecuted Massachusetts, not the other way around. A Baptist pastor in Providence, Henry Melville King, responded with an equally argumentative tract that defended the reputations of Roger Williams, John Clarke, and Obadiah Holmes while attacking the reputation of Massachusetts and the five-volume production of its current apologist historian, John Gorham Palfrey. At the end of the century, the denominational spat continued, with Congregationalist Leonard Bacon (*History of American Christianity*, 1897) squared off against Baptist Albert H. Newman (*A History of the Baptist Churches in the United States*, 1894).

Meanwhile, Roger Williams was being rescued by scholars in the academic world, and by one scholar in particular, Moses Coit Tyler. Despite his Congregational and Yale background, Tyler gave Williams very high marks. In 1878 he published his influential *History of American Literature during the Colonial Time*, a work that soon became the standard critical evaluation of the literary production for the years from 1607 to 1765. Tyler found Williams most refreshing, conceding that this might be because one became "rather fatigued by the monotony of so vast a throng of sages and saints, all quite immaculate, all equally prim and stiff." Williams, by contrast, moved with an easy swing, escaped "the paste-board proprieties," vented his impetuosity, and indulged his indiscretions. He was, in short, a man of "singular vitality." And by 1878, Tyler thought that Williams had in fact carried the day. "The world, having at last nearly caught up with him, seems ready to vote—though with a peculiarly respectable minority in opposition—that Roger Williams was after all a great man, one of the true heroes, seers, world-movers, of these latter ages." The "peculiarly respectable minority" did not disappear in the nineteenth nor in the twentieth century, but to the extent that Tyler's evaluation prevailed, the nineteenth century ended on a high note for the "polemical porcupine."

THE TWENTIETH CENTURY

Not to be outdone, the twentieth century likewise opened on a
high note. In 1902 Irving B. Richman published a two-volume
history entitled *Rhode Island: Its Making and Its Meaning*. Its
meaning, it turned out, derived directly if not solely from the
life and work of Roger Williams. Williams was, Richman wrote,
"by moral constitution a humanitarian, and by mental an ideal-
ist." Along with that, however, he was a "commonwealth-
builder, and his building was according to his qualities." Williams built Providence and made possible the colonization of
Aquidneck Island, Richman noted, and "his doctrine of Soul
Liberty" pervaded all. One year later another Brown University
president, W. H. P. Faunce, echoed Richman's sentiments but
added some of his own, as well as those of James Russell Lowell,
a poet and essayist of the previous generation. Lowell had
commented that seventeenth-century New England could boast
of only two great spirits: John Winthrop, Sr., and Roger Williams. Faunce agreed, adding that as Columbus gave substance
to the theories that the world was round, so Williams gave
substance to the theories that religious liberty was the friend
rather than the enemy of the civil state. In his battle with John
Endecott, Williams faced the sunrise and the future, Faunce
concluded, while Endecott faced "the sunset and the dark."

In the first third of the twentieth century, many thought
that the future did indeed lay with Roger Williams. Reform-
minded historians of the Progressive era lauded liberty and
promoted the cause of human dignity. In their reading of the
national past, the Puritans emerged as enemies to these causes;
indeed, Puritan-bashing became the fashion. As the historical
fortunes of Puritanism declined, those of Roger Williams rose.
Anyone that the Puritans criticized or banished must have done
or thought something right. So Williams came to be identified
with democratic reform and social progress.

In 1927 Vernon L. Parrington published the first of three
volumes under the general title of *Main Currents in American*

Thought. A student of both literature and history, Parrington— like Isaac Backus—sought to rescue the reputation of Williams, but not as a pietist or theologian so much as a democrat and political liberal. Roger Williams was, Parrington declared, "primarily a political philosopher rather than a theologian," and this he meant as high praise. Of an acute mind, Williams stood out as "the teacher of Vane and Cromwell and Milton, a forerunner of Locke and the natural-rights school, one of the notable democratic thinkers that the English race has produced." Determined to outmatch George Bancroft, Parrington expanded on the virtues of this seventeenth-century Separatist transformed into a twentieth-century democrat. "England gave her best," Parrington wrote, when she sent us Roger Williams. "A great thinker and a bold innovator, the repository of the generous liberalisms of a vigorous age, he brought with him the fine wheat of long years of English tillage to sow in the American wilderness." Parrington, who enjoyed his metaphors, pressed them for all they were worth, and sometimes beyond. But then he abandoned his agricultural allusions to state more directly, if extravagantly, that Williams was "certainly the most generous, most open-minded, most lovable of the Puritan emigrants—the truest Christian amongst many who sincerely desired to be Christian." After that eulogy, little remained to be said of John Cotton except that "his dreams and aspirations lie forgotten in the grave of lost causes and forsaken faiths."

While other Progressives were not so effusive, the votes— as Moses Coit Tyler would say—came in heavily on the side of Williams. In his massive *Colonial Period of American History* (1934), Charles M. Andrews even entered the denominational fray long enough to dismiss Henry Martyn Dexter as a biased witness when it came to Roger Williams, one whose historical judgments inspired no confidence in this area. Later in the 1930s, the concern for liberty took on a particular focus—namely, the suspicion of and antagonism toward the rising power of fascism and communism. Partisans for democratic liberty gathered in

216

all who might conceivably be enlisted on their side, and a major biography of Roger Williams appeared in 1940 under the title *The Irrepressible Democrat* (by Samuel H. Brockunier).

Following World War II intellectual history enjoyed a renaissance, with historians taking seriously the content of all ideas, even theological ones. Inspired by the labors of Harvard's Perry Miller, scholars gave up Puritan-bashing as a favorite indoor sport. But the fact that the Puritans received far more serious and sustained scholarly attention did not mean that Roger Williams' stock went down. The battle was no longer partisan. Now the key was whether theology ought once again to be read, weighed, and understood. With respect to Roger Williams, Miller took the lead here as well, publishing in 1953 a small but highly influential book entitled *Roger Williams: His Contribution to the American Tradition.* With some scorn, Miller dismissed the notion of Williams as "the precursor of Jefferson, of liberalism and of rationalism." Miller, who understood Williams as theologian first and political theorist second, changed the direction of scholarly studies. He influenced many, notably Ola E. Winslow, whose excellent biography of Williams appeared in 1957, and Edmund S. Morgan, whose first-rate extended essay was published a decade later.

In the broader culture, meanwhile, Roger Williams continued to attract attention. The U.S. Supreme Court even granted him a footnote as it decided in 1962 that a state-mandated prayer for New York's public schools was a violation of the First Amendment. (In the 1940s the Court made that Amendment applicable to the states, which is only one reason that religion cases now tumble over each other onto the judicial dockets.) Justice Hugo Black, speaking for the Court, noted that men and women had crossed the ocean to escape from "officially established state religions and religious persecution in Europe." They emigrated to America in order to be able to pray when and how they pleased, in terms of their own faith, not in terms of the faith of the civil magistrates. And that seemed the appropriate spot to nod in the direction of Roger Williams who (said Black in a footnote) was "perhaps the best example of the sort of man who came to this country for precisely this reason."

More than two decades later, the Court considered an Alabama law that authorized a moment of silence in the public schools for the purpose of "meditation or voluntary prayer." The Court decided in 1985 that this too was unconstitutional, although the opinion was not unanimous. Justice William Rehnquist vigorously dissented, rejecting not only this particular decision but also the tendency "for nearly forty years" to read the Constitution and its Bill of Rights as though Roger Williams, Thomas Jefferson, and James Madison were the primary authors of or authorities on it. The "wall of separation" was, Rehnquist argued, a misleading metaphor, and, having appeared in a private letter, it was totally without constitutional force. The First Amendment did not require the government to be strictly neutral with respect to religion, the justice stated; it only prohibited a national church or sectarian favoritism. Since the Alabama case dealt with prayer, Rehnquist thought it apropos to note that even George Washington proclaimed national days of thanksgiving and prayer. "History must judge," Rehnquist concluded, "whether it was the father of his country in 1789, or a majority of the Court today, which has strayed from the meaning of the Establishment Clause."

In 1985 Rehnquist was a dissenter and an associate justice. By 1990 he was less often a dissenter and served now as chief justice. In a case heard that year relating to religious free exercise, the justices pulled back from their jealous regard for the religious minority, the "distressed for conscience." In other words, they pulled back from Roger Williams, to say nothing of Jefferson and Madison. The case, which concerned the ritual use of peyote by two members of the Native American Church, resulted in a sharply narrowed understanding of just how free "free exercise" should be. Writing for the majority, Justice Anthony Scalia stated that government cannot afford the "luxury" of striking down laws just because they interfered with someone's religious practices. Religious practices "not widely engaged in" will inevitably suffer, Scalia conceded, but that must be preferred "to a system in which each conscience is law." John Cotton would have agreed. Others disagreed, including dissenter Justice Harry Blackmun, who firmly stated, "I do not believe the Founders thought their dearly bought freedom from religious persecution a 'luxury,' but an essential element of liberty." Though he probably did not have Roger Williams in mind as a founder, he nonetheless would have warmly embraced the Rhode Islander's remark that, "having bought truth dear, we must not sell it cheap, not the least grain of it for the whole world."

In the past half-century, American society has become noisily and notoriously pluralistic. This has made Roger Williams more relevant, for he had strong opinions about what government should do about religious pluralism: leave it alone. Turks, Jews, infidels, papists: leave them alone. By 1990 the list had grown much longer, but the principle remained the same. Religion has the power to persuade, never the power to compel. Government does have the power to compel, but that government is wisest and best which offers to liberty of conscience its widest possible range.

As to the year 2000 and beyond, one cannot anticipate what will happen to the reputation of Roger Williams, how praised or how damned, how distorted or how ignored he might be. For the sake of both the garden of the church and the wilderness of the world, however, the hope remains that he will not again become an exile.

A Note on the Sources

Neither the papers of Roger Williams nor those of early Rhode Island were carefully preserved. Williams wrote on the run, sometimes literally, in Boston and Plymouth, Salem and Providence, London and aboard ship. Sometimes he preserved copies of what he wrote, sometimes not. Sometime his correspondents kept his letters, sometimes not. In addition to the casual character of human nature, other dimensions of nature aggravated the problem. Williams' home was destroyed by fire in 1676. Great quantities of material collected by Stephen Hopkins for his projected history of Rhode Island were washed out to sea by a hurricane in 1815. If manuscript materials of Roger Williams were to be destroyed, it somehow seems more appropriate that they be destroyed by wind and fire rather than by mold and slow decay. In any event, historians of the colony—as of the man—have labored under severe handicaps in their efforts to tell a story without great gaps. While nature may abhor a vacuum, the historical record unfortunately has many of them.

The most ambitious collection of material pertinent to the

colony is that edited by John Russell Bartlett, *Records of the Colony of Rhode Island and Providence Plantations*, 10 vols. (Providence, 1856-1865). The most ambitious collection of Roger Williams' material appeared soon after, *The Publications of the Narragansett Club*, 6 vols. (1866-1874). The "club" in question consisted of a group of Providence men determined to rescue the obscure and rare books and tracts from total oblivion and to gather as many of Williams' widely scattered letters as they possibly could. Unfortunately, that edition itself was in danger of becoming rare and obscure when, in 1963, under the stimulus of Perry Miller's scholarship, those six volumes were reprinted (New York: Russell & Russell), along with a seventh volume of items that the Narragansett Club either did not know about or chose not to reprint. That seventh volume also includes a valuable interpretive essay by Perry Miller on Roger Williams. In addition, Miller provided a separate introduction for each of the five items appearing here for the first time since their original publication in the seventeenth century. This 1963 edition of *The Complete Writings of Roger Williams*, limited to only four hundred sets, has itself now gone out of print.

Williams has been made more accessible in bits and pieces through modern texts that avoid the illegibility of seventeenth-century printing. In 1951 Winthrop S. Hudson offered a fresh edition of Williams' *Experiments of Spiritual Life and Health* (Philadelphia: Westminster Press) that conformed "as nearly as possible to present-day usage," with modern spellings, corrected typographical errors, sensible paragraphing, and useful headings. All of this helps greatly. Two years later Perry Miller included generous excerpts of Williams' writing in his *Roger Williams: His Contribution to the American Tradition* (Indianapolis: Bobbs-Merrill, 1953; paperback edition, New York: Atheneum, 1962). Also offering a modern, "but definitely *not* a modernized text," Miller used no words but those of Williams, though he did omit numerous biblical references and the countless examples of "&c" that Williams added to so many of his sentences. Then in 1973 editors John J. Teunissen and Evelyn J. Hinz provided what they hoped would be the "definitive edition" of *A Key into the Language of America* (Detroit: Wayne State University Press). Seventeenth-century London printing being something less than a fine art, the editors corrected chapter numberings and page headings along with "the customary occurrence of repeated words, broken, turned, transposed, and omitted letters, mixed roman and italic fonts"—and so on, or in Williams' patois, &c.

By far the most significant recent contribution to Williams' scholarship has been a two-volume edition of his letters edited by Glenn W. LaFantasie (Hanover, N.H.: University Press of New England, 1988). This *Correspondence of Roger Williams* has all the editorial apparatus that one has come to expect in critical letter-press editions: extensive footnotes, helpful editorial notes, intriguing illustrations, useful maps, and a marvelously convenient index of nearly eighty pages. In addition to a fine introduction, the editor includes an essay on "Roger Williams and His Papers" that tells in illuminating if often depressing detail the fortune of his manuscripts, insofar as the story can now or ever be known.

With respect to the early history of Rhode Island, John Callender's 1739 *Historical Discourse* has enjoyed a modern reprinting (New York: Books for Libraries Press, 1971). Sydney V. James' *Colonial Rhode Island: A History* (New York: Scribner's, 1975) provides not only a reliable text but in addition an invaluable bibliography of about twenty-five pages in small print. The literature on Puritanism is too vast to name here, but regarding those who dissented against one or another aspect of that orthodoxy, two books deserve mention: William G. McLoughlin's *New England Dissent: The Baptists and the Separation of Church and State,* 2 vols. (Cambridge: Harvard University Press, 1971); and, Philip F. Gura's *Glimpse of Sion's Glory: Puritan Radicalism in New England, 1620-1660* (Middletown, Conn.: Wesleyan University Press, 1984). A more modest offering than either of those is Edwin S. Gaustad's *Baptist Piety: The Last Will and Testimony of Obadiah Holmes* (Grand Rapids: Eerdmans, 1978).

On Williams himself, two biographies of the last half century, both mentioned in Chapter 7, should be noted again here: Samuel H. Brockunier's *The Irrepressible Democrat: Roger Williams* (New York: Ronald Press, 1940) and Ola E. Winslow's *Master Roger Williams: A Biography* (New York: Macmillan, 1957). Brockunier pays too little attention to Williams' seventeenth-century milieu, while Winslow does more than anyone before or since with Williams' early years in London. A decade later Edmund S. Morgan wrote not a biography but an elegant and appreciative essay on the thought of this Separatist theologian, *Roger Williams: The Church and the State* (Harcourt, Brace & World, 1967). Also weighing in heavily on the theological side, W. Clark Gilpin wrote a perceptive volume entitled *The Millenarian Piety of Roger Williams* (Chicago: University of Chicago Press, 1979). Finally, in celebration of the bicentennial of Jefferson's Statute for Establishing Religious Freedom, William Lee Miller published *The First Liberty: Religion and the American Republic* (New York: Knopf, 1986). Though obviously treating both Jefferson and Madison, Miller also pays an unusual amount of attention to Roger Williams. He does so, moreover, in a rollicking fashion that Moses Coit Tyler (see Chap. 7) would have found "refreshing."

Wallace Coyle compiled a bibliographical guide that will greatly assist the student seeking further information on Williams or any aspect of his career: *Roger Williams: A Reference Guide* (Boston: G. K. Hall, 1977). Coyle's work offers detail on all writings about Williams from 1634 to 1974. He has helpfully included the many doctoral dissertations that have Williams as their principal subject, one of which has been published since Coyle's compilation: Hugh Spurgin, *Roger Williams and Puritan Radicalism in the English Separatist Tradition* (Lewiston, N.Y.: Edwin Mellen Press, 1989). Three indexes (author, subject, and title) enhance the utility of Coyle's small volume. For publications concerning Williams after 1977, the best single source for keeping up to date is *Rhode Island History,* a quarterly published by the Rhode Island Historical Society in Providence.

Index

INDEX

229